Prelude to Prosperity

Steve Owen

No part of this publication may be reproduced, stored in a retrieval system, or transmitted, in any form or by any means, electronic, mechanical, photocopying, recording, or otherwise, without the written permission of the author.

First published by Dog Ear Publishing
4010 W. 86th Street, Ste H
Indianapolis, IN 46268
www.dogearpublishing.net

ISBN: 978-1-4575-2714-2

This book is printed on acid-free paper.

Printed in the United States of America

CONTENTS

PRELUDE TO PROSPERITY

PREFACE

We the people of the United States, in order to form a
more perfect union, establish justice, insure domestic
tranquility, provide for the common defense, promote
the general welfare, and secure the blessing of liberty to
ourselves and our posterity, do ordain and establish this
Constitution for the United States of America.

That one sentence perfectly begins the Constitution of the United States, the document that created a government that is the most envied, the most unique, and the
most difficult to duplicate on planet earth. Many of us, especially elected government
officials, need to be reminded that our Constitution is what should control our lives in
America. Every citizen should be familiar with what rights and privileges the Constitution provides for us, that our politicians are bound by it, and that our courts are sworn
to uphold it. We need to be aware of the genius that went into its formation, and of
the challenging compromises necessary to settle issues between the populous and the
less populous states, between the slaveholders and the abolitionists, between those
favoring a powerful federal government and those wanting to retain supremacy of the
state governments, all of which were essential to its formation and ratification.

Many of the delegates to the Constitutional Convention, even though they were
wealthy **property-** and slave owners, were able to lay the foundation for a representative national government that defined and protected rights that are essential to all
of us. Slavery was a fact of life in 1787. The Southern states were not willing to immediately outlaw slavery, in spite of the arguments from those delegates who adamantly
opposed that atrocity, and this nation would not have survived without every state's
participation. Our Constitution temporarily permitted slavery but concurrently
encouraged its abolishment. Racial prejudices and ignorance of others' customs and
beliefs were a problem in 1787 and are still a problem today, perception being nurtured by viewpoint and agenda. The attitudes of the constitutional delegates regarding slavery were the result of many complex issues ranging from ignorance and greed
to convenience and heritage. Much has been written on the subject, and my intention
is not to lightly dismiss this issue but to encourage appreciation and respect for the
writers of the Constitution and to not condemn them because of their few shortcom-
ings.

Most of us hope for a comfortable and secure home, an opportunity to work and earn
money, and ample time to enjoy ourselves. Unfortunately, it is often easier to com-
plain about excessive government spending, a legal system that is sometimes more
concerned with fees than justice and that many times works harder at circumvention
than enforcement, and lengthy and ambiguous **laws** than to actively participate in the

legislative process that so directly affects our lives. Many of us studied history and government in school, found both subjects boring, and took solace knowing that graduation would rid us of them forever.

The Declaration of Independence, which officially declared our separation and independence from Britain and preceded the Constitution by eleven years, was able to **elucidate**, in just a few pages, all the specific colonial grievances that had accumulated during the 170 years of British domination and why Americans were willing to risk their lives and their property to obtain freedom from England. It is equally admirable that our Constitution, which established a new national government, was proposed, debated, agreed to, and written in only four months, in spite of complex issues such as slavery, states' rights, representation in the legislature, apportionment of taxes, power and limitations of the executive branch, and many diverse geographic and economic issues.

The beauty of the Constitution is that because it was to be ratified by the people, it was written so ordinary citizens could understand it. Don't be misled by those who profess that a scholarly review by legal authorities is prerequisite to understanding the Constitution. It is *our* document and was therefore written so *we*, with a little effort, can understand it.

Unlike many members of contemporary congressional committees, the recent US House **Impeachment** Committee being a typical example, many of the Constitutional Convention participants arrived with one opinion and left with another, the result of a delegation composed of people who came to listen as well as to speak. Notice that in nearly every interview of a member of our current Congress, or of the president, regarding why a compromise hasn't been reached, the interviewee's rhetoric is directed at those with different agendas and viewpoints, and never on specific proposals of how to solve the stalemate: "If only the Republicans would take yes for an answer." "I am not going to negotiate until the House members drop their demands for defunding of Obama Care." "The president is refusing to negotiate." "We have sent numerous proposals to the Senate, but they won't compromise." "The president is willing to negotiate as soon as the Republicans can come together on real issues." The people making these statements waste time blaming the other side and rarely propose specific solutions. Look at the discussions that took place during the Constitutional Convention: First, the delegates determined the issues that needed to be resolved; second, they listened to all the proposals for addressing those issues; third, they discussed the repercussions of each proposal; and finally, they decided by majority vote on the compromised solutions. They didn't have time to waste blaming each other for not negotiating, for not compromising, for why they failed. Failure was not an option. America couldn't pay its debts, the citizens had lost faith in their confederation, and chaos was on the horizon. Our future is resting on a very similar foundation right now, and our current Congress seems incapable of proposing workable solutions. Fortunately for the survival of the colonies, partisan politics did not overwhelm the governing process at the Constitutional Convention.

It is unfortunate that nearly every Republican member of Congress constantly complains that the president is refusing to negotiate. The president is not supposed to negotiate about pending legislation; his job is to execute our laws, not legislate. This behavior reminds me of young children who can't decide what clothes to wear to school without first talking to their mothers.

The recent events that are overwhelming our national government, such as the stalemate over deficit spending, the temporary shutdown, sequestration, the constant useless political bickering, gun control, and the continued hiring of private contractors (SEEDCO-Structured Employment Economic Development Corporation) that have been fined because of suspected fraudulent activities should prompt us to regain control over our elected officials. We can't continue to complacently sit by and allow our government to waste our money, to pass laws that erode our rights to privacy, hoping that natural evolution will guide and protect us. Our survival as a prosperous, secure nation can be achieved only if we take an active role in controlling our future, which control our Constitution has clearly granted to us through our right to vote and our right to amend the Constitution. It should be evident to nearly everyone that when choosing our president, our congressional members, and our state officials, we should be thoroughly aware of the duties, privileges, and powers of their offices; we should strive to elect persons (and perdaughters) who are motivated to unselfishly serve their constituents, pursuant to the authority and restraints unambiguously set forth in our Constitution.

When looking at the size of our federal government, it appears that in spite of the Founding Fathers' compromised intentions, the national government has indeed taken away power from the states and the people. Our Congress needs to be reminded of Article I, Section 8, when passing legislation that attempts to solve every need and want that can be thought of and supported by all the numerous special-interest groups. "Give an inch and they'll take a mile" indeed has in more than two hundred years created quite a long rope. We need to find solutions to our problems ourselves. We can't legislate away bullying, public shootings, rape, fraud, drunkenness, speeding, nonuse of seat belts, ignorance, selfishness, foreign terrorists, and every other dangerous or unpleasant action of every human being. There are solutions, but they can't all be implemented through legislation.

The best prevention of excessive governmental abuses and regulations is a thorough understanding and subsequent enforcement of our Constitution, by both those electing and those being elected. We need to use our voting power to elect officials who share our appreciation for freedom, agree with our agendas (or can convince us that theirs are better), possess administrative skills, have an unselfish desire to serve in the public arena, and possess the old-fashioned qualities of honesty, compassion, experience, and trustworthiness.

Our Constitution, the cumulative outcome of a convention attended by wonderfully talented, ambitious, and brave men who united during a time of immense crisis, has created a republican form of government that has outlasted any other. If we continue to reelect the same members of Congress, election after election, we may not last much longer, however. We have tried for years to reform federal campaign laws, attempting to limit both campaign contributions and spending, but without any success. Each new law gets more complicated and creates more ineffective governmental bureaucracy, and contributions and spending continue to skyrocket. Money, both freely given and extorted, controls Congress, and Congress controls us. I believe the first step toward reducing the costs to run our government, and the overwhelming intrusion into our lives by the federal government, is a constitutional amendment limiting all federal officials to one term in office and requiring all federal judicial appointments to terminate after four years, including those for Supreme Court justices. This will never be proposed by Congress, so we must attempt it at the state level, as is set forth in Article V of our Constitution. Sagacious old George Mason (constitutional delegate from Virginia) once said, "From the nature of man we may be sure, that those who have power in their hands will not give it up while they can retain it. On the contrary we know they will always when they can rather increase it."

Some consideration should also be given to a joint resolution that prohibits any and all government employees, officers, or elected officials, when being questioned by Congress concerning their job-related behavior, from refusing to answer fully and to the best of their ability all such questions. If they do refuse to answer any and all such questions, they will automatically be immediately terminated and will forfeit any and all emoluments, including retirement benefits, that would have been earned had they remained in office. This resolution does not, of course, preclude their refusal to answer questions regarding *criminal cases*, which is guaranteed by the Fifth Amendment. Additionally, this resolution should perhaps be included as part of their employment contracts and be retroactively applied to all existing employees. Remember, the Fifth Amendment reads in part "nor shall be compelled in *any criminal case* to be a witness against himself." I don't believe that all Congressional hearings can be classified as criminal cases.

Of course, my opinions have no **effect** on the consequences of either the decisions made by our Supreme Court or the laws passed by our legislatures; however, I believe it is important to care enough about who gets appointed to our courts, what potential laws are being discussed and proposed in both our state and federal legislatures, and which candidates really want to listen to their constituents instead of merely satisfying their **avarice** and narcissistic tendencies that we study and understand what is going on with our government. If we unite, educate ourselves about important issues, and choose our government representatives wisely by using our voting rights, we at least have a small chance to influence the future of our country and our world. Vote Smart (www.votesmart.org) is a great site where interested people can learn about pending legislation and about the educational history, vocational experience, voting records, and political tendencies of our legislators, judges, and other government officers. The internet is a tremendous resource where concerned citizens, liberal or conservative, can express their opinions, have discussions, review proposed legislation, and bombard their legislators with their mandates. Let's always remember the wise advice of Ben Franklin that "we are sent here to consult, not to contend, with each other; and declarations of fixed opinion, and of determined resolution never to change it, neither enlighten nor convince us."

This book also includes a brief synopsis of a few of the influential historical events preceding the Declaration of Independence (1776) and the Constitutional Convention (1787). It is important when attempting to understand the intentions and limitations of our Constitution that we be aware of the moods and needs of the colonies at the time our Constitution was formulated and ratified, as well as of the different cultures, religious backgrounds, and ambitions of the people of the various colonies. History had shown the necessities for unification and the difficulties of implementation.

Citizenship, as nurtured and protected by our Constitution, evokes not only privileges but also, concurrently, opportunities and responsibilities. Our country has for the most part sailed on smooth waters, but as Bob Dylan once said, "The times, they are a-changing." We old folks, in spite of Obamacare, are dying, and the stewardship of America is in the hands of our youth. The passage from child to adult, if fruitful, is arduous and not automatic. The Washingtons, the Lincolns, the Kings, we need you now.

The glossary herewith includes definitions taken from both the Universal Etymological English Dictionary by N. Bailey (published by Edward Harwood, D.D., on January 1, 1782) and more conventional sources, including Wikipedia and *Black's Law Dictionary*, for words that are displayed as boldface text.

CHAPTER I

HISTORY: COLONIZATION THROUGH CONSTITUTION

King James I (reigned 1603–1625) of England, House of Stuart, "too timid to be active, yet too vain to be indifferent" favored the design of enlarging his dominions. With this in mind, King James issued to Sir Ferdinand Gorges, Sir Thomas Gates, Sir George Somers, Richard Hakluyt, John Smith, Robert Hunt, Bartholomew Gosnold, Edward Maria Wingfield, and others a patent through the Virginia Company, a British joint stock company, "to deduce a Colony into Virginia." The control of the entire colonial system resided within a council in England, named by the king, although local management was assigned to those residing within each colony. Limited property ownership, restricted **liberty** of trade with other nations, and coinage of money, perhaps to facilitate **commerce** with the natives, was granted to the colonies, but all other rights were expressly reserved to the monarch.

> The charter, while it thus restricted the emigrants in the important article of internal regulations, secured to them and their descendants all the rights of **denizens**, in the same manner as if they had remained or had been born in England; and granted them the privilege of holding their lands in America by the freest and least burdensome tenure. The king permitted whatever was necessary for the sustenance or **commerce** of the new Colonies to be exported from England, during the space of seven years, without paying any **duty**; and, as a farther incitement to industry, he granted them liberty of trade with other nations; and appropriated the duty to be levied on foreign commodities, as a fund for the benefit of the Colonies, for the period of twenty-one years. He also granted them liberty of coining money, of repelling enemies, and of detaining ships trading there without their leave.
> *J. A. Spencer, *History of the United States, Vol. 1*, Johnson, Fry and Company, 1858, page 31

> The first written charter of a permanent American Colony, which was to be the chosen abode of liberty, gave to the mercantile corporation nothing but a desert territory, with the right of peopling and defending it, and reserved to the monarch absolute legislative authority, the control of all appointments, and a hope of an ultimate revenue. To the emigrants themselves it conceded not one elective franchise, not one of the rights of self-government. They were subjected to the ordinances of a commercial corporation, of which they could not be members; to the dominion of a domestic council, in appointing which they had no voice; to the control of a superior council in England, which had no sympathies with their

rights; and finally, to the arbitrary legislation of the sovereign. Yet, bad as was this system, the reservation of power to the king, a result of his vanity, rather than of his ambition, had at least the advantage of **mitigating** the action of the commercial corporation. The check would have been complete, had the powers of appointment and legislation been given to the people of Virginia.

—George Bancroft, *History of the Colonization of the United States,* Vol. I Charles C. Little and James Brown, 1850, p. 122

This first (1607) sustained English settlement in America, located in what is now Virginia, was named Jamestown, after King James I. It was not, however, the first European settlement in America. Since the Atlantic crossing by Columbus in 1492, many other explorers, such as the Italian Americus Vespucius sailing under the flag of Portugal; Spaniards Balboa, Cortes, Ponce de Leon, Hernando de Soto, and Coronado; Frenchmen Jacques Cartier and Samuel Champlain; Dutchmen de Vries; and Englishman Henry Hudson, sailing in the service of the Dutch, had also explored North America.

Jamestown initially consisted of about a hundred colonists from London. Most of the settlers came looking for wealth, adventure, and perhaps religious freedom but found instead angry Indians and a climate unfortunately not suited to growing food. Few of the men were laborers (four were carpenters) or merchants; the bulk were "gentlemen." It was evident that Jamestown was more of a commercial than a colonial establishment.

> The proud hopes which the beauty of the country had excited, soon vanished; and as the delusion passed away, they awoke and beheld that they were in the wilderness. Weak in numbers, and still weaker from want of habits of industry, they were surrounded by natives whose hostility and distrust had already been displayed; the summer heats were intolerable to their laborers; the moisture of the climate generated disease, and the fertility of the soil, covered with a rank luxuriance of forest, increased the toil of culture. Their scanty provisions had become spoiled on the long voyage. "Our drink," say they, "was unwholesome water; our lodgings, castles in the air: had we been as free from all sins as from gluttony and drunkenness, we might have been canonized for saints." Many times, three or four died in a night; in the morning, their bodies were trailed out of the cabins, like dogs, to be buried.

> Disunion completed the scene of misery. Ratcliffe [the captain of the Discovery, one of three ships that sailed from England on December 19, 1606, arriving May 13, 1607, founding Jamestown, Virginia], the new president, possessed neither judgment nor industry; so that the management of affairs fell into the hands of Smith, whose deliberate enterprise and cheerful courage alone diffused

light amidst the general gloom. He possessed by nature the buoy-
ant spirit of heroic daring.
—George Bancroft, *History of the Colonization of the United States,* Vol. I
Charles C. Little and James Brown, 1850, pages 126 and 127

Although John Smith was only twenty-seven years old when he landed on the Virginia shore, he was already a veteran in the service of humanity and Christendom. He had traveled through much of France, Hungary, and Italy, visited the shores of Egypt, and been a prisoner of war in Constantinople. All of these experiences helped assure his survival in Virginia.

The enthusiasm of the English for colonial expansion seemed to propagate even though the expected delivery of wealth never materialized. Unfortunately for the mis-placed colonial **inhabitants**, the newly revised Virginia charter of 1609 transferred the control of the settlement from the king into the hands of the corporate sponsors. The supreme council in England was now to be chosen by the stockholders; the powers of legislation were now totally independent of the monarch: "Thus the lives, liberty and fortune of the Colonists were placed at the arbitrary will of a governor who was to be appointed by a commercial corporation."*

Jamestown began to prosper in 1611 after the implementation of the right to private own-ership of property (denied, however, to the Indians and subsequently to the slaves). John Rolfe, the English husband of Pocahontas, began to raise tobacco and send it to England, where it brought a very high price. Potential for wealth attracted immigrants, and soon, Jamestown was so large that a representative government was needed to organize and control its inhabitants. In 1619, the colonists formed the first American legislature, the House of Burgesses. The initial meeting took place in the local church (our Supreme Court would certainly never have allowed that), and thus was born our system of government by the people, for in choosing the lawmakers, every freeman (excluding women, Indians, and slaves) had a vote. That same year, black slaves were brought to Jamestown by the Dutch to work the tobacco fields, and the evils of slavery began to ferment in America.

There had been quarrels between the local Indians and the English, but no wars. Powhatan, the dominant Indian leader, the father of Pocahontas, and the tolerant friend of the Jamestown colonists, died in 1618. His brother, not as tolerant of the for-eign settlers, inherited Powhatan's influence among the Indians. Concurrently, the colonial expansions were taking more and more land from the native Indians. On 22 March 1622, in an effort to "exterminate the English," the Indians attacked and killed approximately 350 settlers. Many of the fearful colonists returned to England, and in only one year, the population of Jamestown dropped from a little more than 4000 to less than 2500 European inhabitants. The perpetual territorial battles in America between the native inhabitants and the Europeans had officially begun.

---

*George Bancroft, *History of the Colonization of the United States,* Vol. I (Charles C. Little and James Brown, 1850, page 137)

In 1613, as a result of earlier exploration by the Englishman Henry Hudson, the Dutch began to settle the area of Manhattan Island and in 1626 established the town of New Amsterdam, later to be renamed New York. Because it had one of the finest harbors in the world and was an excellent trading station, New Amsterdam drew merchants from all parts of Europe and very soon became one of the busiest towns on the American coast.

Maryland, named after Queen Henrietta Maria, also had its independently patented beginnings at this time. In 1634, Leonard Calvert, who later became the first colonial governor of Maryland, with about two hundred colonists landed on the banks of the Potomac River and began the predominately Catholic settlement of St. Mary's. Catholics were unwelcome in Virginia, and Maryland became, although rarely without Protestant harassment, a haven for Catholicism in America.

Religious freedom was important to the people of both Maryland and Virginia, but as the boundaries between the two colonies began to overlap because of expansion, religious and monetary **factions** soon were at arms with each other, as well as with the local Indians.

The Pilgrims, most of whom were skilled in **husbandry**, settled the town of Plymouth, Massachusetts, in 1620. Although they had no official charter, they were nonetheless financially obligated to some members of the Virginia Company who sponsored their voyage.

> And, on the sixth day of September, 1620 thirteen years after the first colonization of Virginia, two months before the concession of the grand charter of Plymouth, without any warrant from the sovereign of England, without any useful charter from a corporate body, the passengers in the Mayflower set sail for a new world, where the past could offer no favorable **auguries**. The Pilgrims were Englishmen, Protestants, exiles for religion, men disciplined by misfortune, cultivated by opportunities of extensive observation, equal in rank as in rights, and bound by no code, but that of religion or the public will.*

"The leaders of the band were Brewster, the preacher, Bradford, the ruler, and Miles Standish, the fighter."** The landing was made in winter, and the sufferings of the Pilgrims were almost as terrible as were those of the original Jamestown colonists: "The bitterness of mortal disease was their welcome to the inhospitable shore."† When the Mayflower returned to England the following spring, however, all the Pilgrim colonists

---

*George Bancroft, *History of the Colonization of the United States,* Vol. I (Charles C. Little and James Brown, 1850, p. 308)
**S. E. Forman, *A History of the United States* (The Century Co., 1910, pp. 47–48)
†George Bancroft, *History of the Colonization of the United States,* Vol. I (Charles C. Little and James Brown, 1850, p. 310))

remained in America. Plymouth Colony was by charter of 1691 combined with Massachusetts.

Dover, New Hampshire, was settled in 1623, and Hartford, Connecticut, in 1636. Puritans occupied many of these territories, and early on, community leaders realized the problems with combining religious and state affairs.

England had stood idly by while the Dutch settlements in New York grew and prospered; however, in 1664, King Charles II of England decided he liked the look of the new Dutch colony and sent his fleet to replace the Dutch flag with that of England. The conquest of New Amsterdam secured for England control of the Atlantic coast from Nova Scotia to Florida. Although the Spaniard Ponce de Leon was probably the first European to explore Florida and the Spanish settled St. Augustine there in 1565, the British had always controlled the eastern coast of North America. Florida, although obtained by Britain through the Treaty of Paris of 1763 and returned to Spain under the terms of the Treaty of Paris of 1783, was finally acquired by the United States in 1819 by Secretary of State John Quincy Adams with the signing of the Florida Purchase Treaty.

Following are summaries of what are generally considered to be the important attempts at securing at least limited cooperation between the colonies, to present a common front against external aggression. The colonists at this time still felt united with Great Britain and opposed to their common enemy, the French.

NEW ENGLAND CONFEDERATION (1643), composed of Plymouth, Massachusetts Bay, New Haven, and Connecticut. Rhode Island was not invited because it would not consent to become a part of the jurisdiction of Plymouth. The purpose of the union was to protect the colonies from the French on the St. Lawrence, against the Dutch on the Hudson, against the ubiquitous Indians, and to preserve the liberties "of the gospel in purity and in peace."* Two commissioners represented each colony, and the union thus formed lasted until 1684. John Davenport, a preacher, and Theophilus Eaton, a merchant, led New Haven. They set up a Bible commonwealth, in which only church members could have a voice, and they made it very difficult for any outsiders to become church members. Charles II put an end to New Haven when, in 1662, he combined New Haven with Connecticut, still, however, allowing the united colony to govern itself.

> By the articles of confederation, these Colonies entered into a firm and perpetual bond of friendship and amity, for offence and defence, mutual advice and **succor**, upon all just occasions, both for preserving and propagating the truth and liberties of the Gospel, as they interpreted it, and for their own mutual safety and welfare.

---

*The Articles of Confederation of the United Colonies of New England, May 19, 1643 (http://avalon.law.yale.edu/17th_century/art1613.asp)

Each Colony was to retain its own jurisdiction and government; and no other plantation or Colony was to be received as a confederate, nor any of the two confederates to be united into one jurisdiction, without the consent of the rest. The affairs of the United Colonies were to be managed by a legislature, to consist of two persons, styled commissioners, chosen from each Colony. The commissioners were to meet annually in the Colonies, in succession, and when met, to choose a president, and the determination of any six was to be binding on all.
—J. A. Spencer, *History of the United States,* Vol. I
Johnson, Fry and Company, 1858, p. 94

It is certainly noteworthy that the ideas of preservation of individual colonial or state autonomy, return of runaway servants and fugitives, reimbursement of defense costs for invasion of individual colonies, etc. would be carried over into the Albany Plan of 1754, the Articles of Confederation of 1777, and the Constitution of 1787. The New England Confederacy continued essentially unchanged until the New England charters were revoked by King James II in the early 1680s.

King James II had succeeded Charles II in 1685.

Within narrow limits he reasoned correctly; but his vision did not extend far. Without sympathy for the people, he had no discernment of character, and was the easy victim of duplicity and **intrigue**. His loyalty was but devotion to the **prerogative** which he hoped to inherit. Brave in the face of expected dangers, an unforeseen emergency found him **pusillanimously** helpless. He kept his word sacredly, unless it involved complicated relations, which he could scarcely comprehend. As to religion, a service of forms alone suited his narrow understanding; to attend mass, to build chapels, to risk the kingdom for a rosary—all this was within his grasp. Freedom of conscience was, in that age, an idea yet standing on the threshold of the world, waiting to be ushered in; and none but exalted mind— Roger Williams and Penn, Vane, Fox, and Bunyan—went forth to welcome it; no glimpse of it reached James, whose selfish policy, unable to gain immediate dominion for his persecuted priests and his confessor, begged at least for toleration. Debauching a woman on promise of marriage, he next allowed her to be traduced, and then married her; he was conscientious, but his moral sense was as slow as his understanding. He was not bloodthirsty; but to a narrow mind fear seems the most powerful instrument of government, and he propped his throne on the block and the gallows. A libertine without love, a devotee without spirituality, an advocate of toleration without a sense of the natural right to freedom of conscience, he floated between the sensuality of indulgence and the sensuality of superstition, hazarding heaven for an ugly mistress, and, to the

great delight of abbots and nuns, winning it back again by pricking his flesh with sharp points of iron, and eating no meat on Saturdays. Of the two brothers, the duke of Buckingham said well, that Charles (II) would not and James (II) could not see.
—George Bancroft, *History of the United States of America*, Vol. I
D. Appleton and Company, 1892, pp. 575–576

KING PHILLIP'S WAR (1675–1676), also known as Metacom's Rebellion, marked the last major effort by the Indians of southern New England to drive out the English settlers. The war, led by Metacom, the Pokunoket chief called King Philip by the English, lasted fourteen months, destroyed at least twelve frontier towns, and resulted in the death of many colonists and Native Americans. The Indians' resentment of the colonists had been building since the 1660s; the Indians had become increasingly dependent on English goods, food, and weapons, and eventually, most of their lands had been confiscated by the colonists. Metacom and other Indian leaders finally decided to revolt instead of succeeding to English sovereignty. The war ended in August of 1676, shortly after Metacom was captured and beheaded.

In 1696, the English Board of Trade recommended the appointment of a captain-general of all the forces on the continent of North America. This was the first real step toward suppression of the colonial legislatures and the attempted consolidation of all the colonies under the rule of one English appointed governor. Again in 1721, to ensure the support of the colonies in England's dominance of France for North American territories, a similar plan provided for a captain-general to rule over all the colonies. The captain-general, in conjunction with a council composed of locally elected representatives from each colony, was to allot the quotas of men and money needed to fill the armies.

In 1700, the population of the colonies was approximately 250,000, most of whom were English immigrants. Beginning around 1700, however, people from all parts of Europe, although primarily from Germany and Ireland, began settling in America, the Germans choosing Pennsylvania and the Scotch-Irish (mostly Scottish Presbyterians living in Northern Ireland) inhabiting North Carolina. By 1740, the population of the colonies had increased to nearly one million, including African slaves and white servants.

THE ALBANY CONGRESS (1754), composed of a total of twenty-five members representing New Hampshire, Massachusetts, Connecticut, Rhode Island, New York, Pennsylvania, and Maryland. Ben Franklin drafted a plan again with the purpose of opposing the French, which called for a representative governing body, or grand council, to be chosen by the colonial legislatures. It could impose taxes, nominate civil executives, regulate Indian affairs, and take general charge of military concerns. A president-general with veto powers over the grand council, appointed and supported by the crown, would preside, and the acts of the congress would be honored throughout the colonies unless vetoed by the crown. It is interesting to note that this plan was to be presented to the king of England and enacted by Parliament. It was not endorsed by the colonies because of fear of loss of "states'" power and thus was never officially sent to England for approval. Men at that time referred to themselves as New Yorkers or Virginians, certainly not as Americans. Evidently, thoughts of separation from "the mother land" were still just incubating. Franklin's "Albany Plan" was, in the end, a stepping-stone to the founding of the American nation.

The 1754 Albany Plan of Union

It is proposed that humble application be made for an act of Parliament of Great Britain, by virtue of which one general government may be formed in America, including all the said Colonies, within and under which government each Colony may retain its present constitution, except in the particulars wherein a change may be directed by the said act, as hereafter follows.

That the said general government be administered by a President-General, to be appointed and supported by the crown; and a Grand Council, to be chosen by the representative of the people of the several Colonies met in their respective assemblies.

1. That within ____ months after the passing such act, the House of Representatives that happen to be sitting within that time, or that shall be especially for that purpose convened, may and shall choose members for the Grand Council, in the following proportion, that is to say:

2. – –- who shall meet for the first time at the city of Philadelphia, being called by the President-General as soon as conveniently may be after his appointment.

3. That there shall be a new election of the members of the Grand Council every three years; and, on the death or resignation of any member, his place should be supplied by a new choice at the next sitting of the Assembly of the Colony he represented.

4. That after the first three years, when the proportion of money arising out of each Colony to the general treasury can be known, the number of members to be chosen for each Colony shall, from time to time, in all ensuing elections, be regulated by that proportion, yet so as that the number to be chosen by any one Province be not more than seven, nor less than two. (It will be seen during the Constitutional Convention that representation or voting rights based on money would not be acceptable, that the rich states would

soon control legislation and self-aggrandizement would prevail.)

5.   That the Grand Council shall meet once in every year, and oftener if occasion require, at such time and place as they shall adjourn to at the last preceding meeting, or as they shall be called to meet at by the President-General on any emergency; he having first obtained in writing the consent of seven of the members to such call, and sent duly and timely notice to the whole.

6.   That the Grand Council have power to choose their speaker; and shall neither be dissolved, **prorogued**, nor continued sitting longer than six weeks at one time, without their own consent or the special command of the crown.

7.   That the members of the Grand Council shall be allowed for their service ten shillings sterling per diem, during their session and journey to and from the place of meeting; twenty miles to be reckoned a day's journey.

8.   That the **assent** of the President-General be **requisite** to all acts of the Grand Council, and that it be his office and duty to cause them to be carried into execution.

9.   That the President-General, with the advice of the Grand Council, hold or direct all Indian treaties, in which the general interest of the Colonies may be concerned; and make peace or declare war with Indian nations. That they make all purchases from Indians, for the crown, of lands not now within the bounds of particular Colonies, or that shall not be within their bounds when some of them are reduced to more convenient dimensions.

10.   That they make new settlements on such purchases, by granting lands in the King's name, reserving a **quitrent** to the crown for the use of the general treasury.

11.   That they make laws for regulating and governing such new settlements, till the crown shall think fit to form them into particular governments.

12.   That they raise and pay soldiers and build forts for the defence of any of the Colonies, and equip vessels of force to guard the coasts and protect the trade on the ocean, lakes, or great rivers; but they shall not

impress men in any Colony, without the consent of the Legislature.

13. That for these purposes they have power to make laws, and lay and levy such general duties, **imposts**, or taxes, as to them shall appear most equal and just (considering the ability and other circumstances of the inhabitants in the several Colonies), and such as may be collected with the least inconvenience to the people; rather discouraging luxury, than loading industry with unnecessary burdens.

14. That they may appoint a General Treasurer and Particular Treasurer in each government when necessary and, from time to time, may order the sums in the treasuries of each government into the general treasury or draw on them for special payments, as they find most convenient.

15. Yet no money to issue but by joint orders of the President-General and Grand Council; except where sums have been appropriated to particular purposes, and the President-General is previously empowered by an act to draw such sums.

16. That the general accounts shall be yearly settled and reported to the several Assemblies.

17. That a quorum of the Grand Council, empowered to act with the President-General, do consist of twenty-five members; among whom there shall be one or more from a majority of the Colonies.

18. That the laws made by them for the purposes aforesaid shall not be **repugnant**, but, as near as may be, agreeable to the laws of England, and shall be transmitted to the King in Council for **approbation**, as soon as may be after their passing; and if not disapproved with three years after presentation, to remain in force.

19. That, in case of the death of the President-General, the Speaker of the Grand Council for the time being shall succeed, and be **vested** with the same powers and authorities, to continue till the King's pleasure be known.

20. That all military commission officers, whether for land or sea service, to act under this general constitution, shall be nominated by the President-General; but the approbation of the Grand Council is to be obtained, before they receive their commissions. And all **civil officers** are to be nominated by the Grand

Council, and to receive the President-General's approbation before they officiate.

21. But, in case of vacancy by death or removal of any officer, civil or military, under this constitution, the Governor of the Province in which such vacancy happens may appoint, till the pleasure of the President-General and Grand Council can be known.

22. That the particular military as well as civil establishments in each Colony remain in their present state, the general constitution notwithstanding; and that on sudden emergencies any Colony may defend itself, and lay the accounts of expense thence arising before the President-General and General Council, who may allow and order payment of the same, as far as they judge such accounts just and reasonable."

THE FRENCH AND INDIAN WAR, also known as the Seven Years' War, began officially in 1756 and lasted until the Treaty of Paris of 1763. France and England had both staked claim to America, and this war was the decisive confrontation to settle their land-ownership disputes in North America. The first serious armed confrontation between France and England in America began in 1689 (King William's War) and was followed in 1702 by Queen Anne's War and in 1744 by King George's War. The only significant outcome of these wars was that Nova Scotia was granted to England by the Treaty of Utrecht in 1713.

Militarily, the war began with the defeat of British General Braddock, accompanied by Major George Washington, near Fort Duquesne, which later became Pittsburgh. This war was fought between France and her Indian allies, excluding the Iroquois (who sided with England because of their dislike of the Huron more than their fondness of the British), on one side and Britain on the other. The English government at the outset planned to gain control of the Atlantic seacoast by capturing Louisburg and seizing French forts in Nova Scotia and New Brunswick, therein controlling the St. Lawrence, by recapturing Fort Duquesne (Pittsburgh), by capturing Fort Niagara (northwestern New York state), and then to move northward into Canada, by way of Crown Point on Lake Champlain, and eventually capture Quebec. England eventually accomplished these goals, and with the Treaty of Paris (1763), France surrendered all her land, with the exception of two small territories in the Gulf of St. Lawrence. All the land east of the Mississippi went to England, and all that west went to Spain (subsequently purchased by the United States in 1803 during the presidency of Thomas Jefferson).

When the French and Indian War had ended, Britain resumed its monarchial prewar treatment of the colonies with renewed vigor. Since the Treaty of Utrecht in 1713, which ended Queen Ann's War (between England and France) and gave Nova Scotia to England, the population of the colonies had risen from about 250,000 to more than 1,500,000, bringing about corresponding increases in African slaves, foreign trade, and the size of major urban centers. All these factors contributed to making the colonies important sources of trade, both importing and exporting, and sources of potential tax revenue, for England. The war with France had been expensive, and now it was time for the colonies to pay their fair share for the protection England afforded them.

The revenue measures such as the Sugar Act (1764), the Stamp Act (1765), the Quartering Act (1765), and the Townshend Acts (1767) imposed upon the colonies by England subsequent to the Treaty of Paris of 1763 were to lay a foundation for the impending American Revolution.

THE STAMP ACT CONGRESS (1765) was composed of twenty-seven delegates representing Massachusetts, Rhode Island, Connecticut, New York, New Jersey, Pennsylvania, Delaware, Maryland, and South Carolina. The congress was called in response to the English Stamp Act, a law requiring that an English stamp be purchased and placed on all legal documents and publications circulated within the colonies. The colonists saw this as taxation without representation. At this time, England also issued **writs of assistance**, which were merely general search warrants enabling British officers to enter private houses and search for smuggled goods.

> But the most grievous Innovation of all, is the alarming Extension of the Power of Courts of Admiralty. In these Courts, one Judge presides alone! No Juries have any Concern there!—The Law, and the Fact, are both to be decided by the same single Judge, whose Commission is only during Pleasure, and with whom, as we are told, the most mischievous of all Customs has become established, that of taking Commissions on all Condemnations; so that he is under a **pecuniary** Temptation always against the Subject. Now, if the Wisdom of the Mother Country has thought the Independency of the Judges, so essential to an impartial Administration of Justice, as to render them independent of every Power on Earth, independent of the King, the Lords, the Commons, the People, nay independent, in Hope and Expectation, of the Heir apparent, by continuing their Commissions after a Demise of the Crown; What Justice and Impartiality are we, at 3000 Miles distance from the Fountain (**source**) to expect from such a Judge of Admiralty? We have all along thought the Acts of Trade in this Respect a Grievance; but the Stamp-Act has opened a vast Number of Sources of new **Crimes**, which may be committed by any Man, and cannot, but be committed by Multitudes, and prodigious Penalties are annexed, and all these are to be tried by such a Judge of such a Court!—What can be wanting, after this, but a weak or wicked Man for a Judge, to render Us the most **sordid** and forlorn of Slaves?"
> —John Adams, "Instructions of the Town of Braintree on the Stamp Act," October 1765
> http://en.wikipedia.org/wiki/Braintree_Instructions

The Stamp Act also caused Samuel Adams to resign as a Boston tax collector (subsequently elected to the Massachusetts House of Representatives) and prompted The Virginia House of Burgesses (Virginia legislature) to propose the Virginia **Resolutions** on May 29 1765, in which Patrick Henry declared that Virginians would not tolerate taxation without representation.

England, seeing the problem with enforcement of the Stamp Act, repealed it in 1766, but with the parliamentary declaration that England still had a perfect right to tax the colonies if she so desired, and did so the next year with the passage of the Townshend Acts (1767), thereby imposing taxes on glass, paper, lead, paints, and tea when these articles were brought into American ports.

> The Townshend Acts of 1767 consisted of a series of taxes on goods imported into the American Colonies, a reorganized Board of Customs Commissioners stationed in Boston to collect the taxes and enforce other revenue measures and the New York Restraining Act. Reasons for passing these measures included a symbolic gesture to show the Colonies that the mother country had the right to tax the Colonies, raise a revenue to support some governors and justices, and punish New York for refusing to abide by the Mutiny Act [also known as the Quartering Act].
> —Jack P. Greene and J. R. Pole, editors, *The Blackwell Encyclopedia of the American Revolution*
> Blackwell Publishers, 1994, p. 126

John Dickinson of Pennsylvania wrote a pamphlet, "Letters from a Farmer in Pennsylvania," which played a crucial role in uniting resistance to the Townshend Acts. Dickinson would also be a major contributor to and signer of the Articles of Confederation and, as a delegate from Delaware, a signer of the Constitution of the United States. Although the colonists did not object outright to paying taxes on imported goods, they did object to Parliament fixing the salaries of colonial officers and then levying taxes with which to pay these salaries. This act was amended on March 5, 1770, coinciding with the shooting of four colonists in Boston (the Boston Massacre), to exclude all articles from taxation, except tea. Although the new tea tax of only six cents per pound was quite low, the American Board of Customs (American in name only, as all its members were British) was still intact, along with the principle of having governors appointed by English Parliament and independent of the local governments. The precedent that Parliament still ruled the colonists was set and eventually resulted in the famous Boston Tea Party of 1773.

> Early the next morning [following the Boston Massacre], the people resolved to insist upon the immediate removal of the soldiers, and a committee was appointed, with Samuel Adams at their head, to wait upon the governor, and inform him and the royal commander, that the troops must leave Boston, or a fearful collision would be

certain to ensue. After much hesitation and unwillingness on the part of Hutchinson and Colonel Dalrymple, the soldiers retired to Castle William. The "Boston Massacre," as it was then termed, caused wide-spread excitement, and the funeral of those who had been killed was celebrated with great display. The anniversary of the event was also kept up for a long time afterwards, as marking the period when the first blood was shed in the dispute with England.

—J. A. Spencer, *History of the United States of America,* Vol. I
Johnson, Fry and Company, 1858, pp. 295–296

Although the Stamp Act is conventionally considered one of the primary events initiating the revolution, it was only one of several policy decisions of Prime Minister George Grenville that caused alarm among the colonists. Elected in April 1763, Grenville, serving alongside King George III, immediately began to increase the size of the already present British army in America. Although the real reason was to protect England's interest in the New World from France and, to a lesser extent, Spain and to remain in control of the 90,000 or so colonists in Canada, a major portion of the cost of maintaining the army was to be charged to the thirteen American colonies.

A major concern to Grenville was the American evasion of British trade laws. Unsuccessful attempts at enforcement led to passage by Parliament of the American Duties Act of 1764. The most famous provision of this measure is known as the Molasses or Sugar Act, initially a 100% tax on imported foreign rum later reduced to 33%, which became not only a source of revenue to England but also indirectly a method of trade regulation and was the first deliberate attempt to tax the colonies.

Another of Grenville's confrontational legislative directives was called the Quartering Acts of 1765. These acts, an extension of Britain's Mutiny Act, called for the **billeting** of British soldiers within the colonies. Although the soldiers were to be housed only in uninhabited buildings if no barracks were available, the colonists were required to supply the soldiers, at no cost, with light, heat, bedding, beer, and cooking utensils. Note that this practice was listed as a specific grievance in the Declaration of Independence—"For quartering large bodies of armed troops among us"—and was later prohibited by the Third Amendment of the Constitution.

Because of the varied geography of the colonies, most of these British tariffs and duties affected some of the states more than others. The need to solicit help from neighboring colonies to thwart the common enemy was gaining importance, and the "united" states were beginning to appear on the horizon.

The Boston Tea Party angered England more than anything the colonists had done yet. Parliament took quick action and passed what the colonists called the Intolerable Acts (1774), which in general forbade passage of any ship from Boston Harbor until the town paid for the tea; deprived Massachusetts of free government; provided that any royal officer indicted in Massachusetts for murder or other **capital** crime, for suppressing riots, or performing his duties as a **magistrate**, could be tried in another colony or in Great Britain; and finally, required that troops should be quartered in Boston. George Washington of Virginia is quoted as saying, "If need be, I will raise one thousand men, subsist them at my own expense, and march myself at their head for the relief of Boston." Although the exact wording may be distorted (sometimes the result of passionate storytelling), I believe the message reflected the moods of many colonists and the courage and commitment of George Washington.

The Continental Association
(Created by the First Continental Congress)
May 27, 1774

We, his majesty's most dutiful and loyal subjects, the late representatives of the good people of this country, having been deprived, by the sudden interposition of the executive part of this government, from giving our countrymen the advice we wished to convey to them, in a legislative capacity, find ourselves under the hard necessity of adopting this, the only method we have left, of pointing out to our countrymen such measures as, in our opinion, are best fitted to secure our dear rights and liberty from destruction, by the heavy hand of power now lifted against North America. With much grief we find, that our dutiful applications to Great Britain for the security of our just, ancient, and constitutional rights, have been not only disregarded, but that a determined system is formed and pressed, for reducing the inhabitants of British America to slavery, by subjecting them to the payment of taxes, imposed without the consent of the people or their representatives; and that, in pursuit of this system, we find an act of the British Parliament, lately passed, for stopping the harbor and commerce of the town of Boston, in our sister Colony of Massachusetts Bay, until the people there submit to the payment of such unconstitutional taxes; and which act most violently and arbitrarily deprives them of their property [see Amendment V of the United States Constitution], in **wharves** erected by private persons, at their own great and proper expense; which act is, in our opinion, a most dangerous attempt to destroy the constitutional liberty and rights of all North America. It is further our opinion that as tea, on its importation into America, is charged with a duty imposed by Parliament, for the purpose of raising a revenue without the consent of the people, it ought not to be used by any person who wishes well to the constitutional rights and liberties of British America. And whereas the **[East] India Company** have ungenerously attempted the ruin of America, by sending many ships loaded with tea into the Colonies, thereby intending to fix a precedent in favor of arbitrary taxation, we deem it highly proper, and do accordingly recommend it strongly to our countrymen, not to purchase or use any kind of East India commodity whatsoever, except saltpeter and spices, until the grievances of America are **redressed**. We are further clearly of opinion, that an attack made on one of our sister Colonies, to compel submission to arbitrary taxes, is an attack made on all British America, and threatens ruin to the rights of all, unless the united wisdom of the whole be applied. And for this purpose it is recommended to the Committee of Correspondence, that they communicate with their several corresponding committees, on the expediency of appointing deputies from the several Colonies of British America, to meet in general congress, at such place, annually, as shall be thought most convenient; there to deliberate on those general measures which the united interest of America may from time to time require. A tender regard for the interest of our fellow-subjects, the merchants and manufactures of Great Britain, prevents us from going further at this time; most earnestly hoping, that the unconstitutional principle of taxing the Colonies without their consent will not be persisted in, thereby to compel us, against our will, to avoid all commercial intercourse with Britain. Wishing them and our people free and happy, we are their affectionate friends, the late Representatives of Virginia.

Signed, Peyton Randolph, President
First Continental Congress

Fairfax (Virginia) County Resolves [18 July 1774]

At a general Meeting of the Freeholders and Inhabitants of the County of Fairfax on Monday the 18th day of July 1774, at the Court House, George Washington Esquire Chairman, and Robert Harrison Gent. Clerk of the said meeting—

1. *Resolved* that this Colony and Dominion of Virginia can not be considered as a conquered Country; and if it was, that the present Inhabitants are the Descendants not of the Conquered, but of the Conquerors.

That the same was not setled [sic] at the national Expence [British spelling] of England, but at the private Expence of the Adventurers, our Ancestors, by solemn Compact with, and under the Auspices and Protection of the British Crown; upon which we are in every Respect as dependant, as the People of Great Britain, and in the same Manner subject to all his Majesty's just, legal, and constitutional Prerogatives. That our Ancestors, when they left their native Land, and setled [sic] in America, brought with them (even if the same had not been confirmed by Charters) the Civil-Constitution and Form of Government of the Country they came from; and were by the Laws of Nature and Nations, entitiled [sic] to all it's [sic] Privileges, Immunities and Advantages; which have descended to us their Posterity, and ought of Right to be as fully enjoyed, as if we had still continued within the Realm of England.

2. *Resolved* that the most important and valuable Part of the British

Constitution, upon which it's [sic] very Existence depends, is the fundamental Principle of the People's being governed by no Laws, to which they have not given their Consent, by Representatives freely chosen by themselves; who are affected by the Laws they enact equally with their Constituents; to whom they are accountable, and whose **Burthens** they share; in which consists the Safety and Happiness of the Community: for if this Part of the Constitution was taken away, or materially altered, the Government must degenerate either into an absolute and despotic Monarchy, or a tyrannical Aristocracy, and the Freedom of the People be annihilated.

3. *Resolved* therefore, as the Inhabitants of the American Colonies are not, and from their Situation can not be represented in the British Parliament, that the legislative Power here can of Right be exercised only by (our) own Provincial Assemblys [sic] or Parliaments, subject to the Assent or Negative of the British Crown, to be declared within some proper limited Time. But as it was thought just and reasonable that the People of Great Britain shou'd reap Advantages from these Colonies adequate to the Protection they afforded them, the British Parliament have claimed and exercised the Power of regulating our Trade and Commerce, so as to restrain our importing from foreign Countrys, such Articles as they cou'd furnish us with, of their own Growth or Manufacture, or exporting to foreign Countrys such Articles and Portions of our Produce, as Great Britain stood in Need of, for her own Consumption or Manufactures. Such a Power directed with Wisdom and Moderation, seems necessary for the general Good of that great Body-politic of which we are a Part; altho' in some Degree repugnant to the Principles of the Constitution. Under this Idea our Ancestors submitted to it: the Experience of more than a Century, during the government of his Majesty's Royal Predecessors, hath proved it's Utility, and the reciprocal Benefits flowing from it produced mutual uninterrupted Harmony and Good-Will, between the Inhabitants of Great Britain and her Colonies; who during that long Period, always considered themselves as one and the same People: and tho' such a Power is capable of Abuse, and in some Instances hath been stretched beyond the original Design and Institution. Yet to avoid Strife and Contention with our fellow-Subjects, and strongly impressed with the Experience of mutual Benefits, we always Chearfully [sic] acquiesced in it, while the entire Regulation of our internal Policy, and giving and granting our own Money were preserved to our own provincial Legislatures.

17

4. *Resolved* that it is the Duty of these Colonies, on all Emergencies, to contribute, in Proportion to their Abilities, Situation and Circumstances, to the necessary Charge of supporting and defending the British Empire, of which they are Part; that while we are treated upon an equal Footing with our fellow Subjects, the Motives of Self-Interest and Preservation will be a sufficient Obligation; as was evident thro' the Course of the last War; and that no Argument can be fairly applyed [sic] to the British Parliament's taxing us, upon a Presumption that we shou'd refuse a just and reasonable Contribution, but will equally operate in Justification of the Executive-Power taxing the People of England, upon a Supposition of their Representatives refusing to grant the necessary Supplies.

5. *Resolved* that the Claim lately assumed and exercised by the British Parliament, of making all such Laws as they think fit, to govern the People of these Colonies, and to extort from us our Money with out our Consent, is not only diametrically contrary to the first Principles of the Constitution, and the original Compacts by which we are dependant [sic] upon the British Crown and Government; but is totally incompatible with the Privileges of a free People, and the natural Rights of Mankind; will render our own Legislatures merely nominal and nugatory, and is calculated to reduce us from a State of Freedom and Happiness to Slavery and Misery.

6. *Resolved* that Taxation and Representation are in their Nature inseperable [sic]; that the Right of withholding, or of giving and granting their own Money is the only effectual Security to a free People, against the Incroachments [sic] of Despotism and Tyranny; and that whenever they yield the One, they must quickly fall a Prey to the other.

7. *Resolved* that the Powers over the People of America now claimed by the British House of Commons, in whose Election we have no Share, on whose Determinations we can have no Influence, whose Information must be always defective and often false, who in many Instances may have a seperate [sic], and in some an opposite Interest to ours, and who are removed from those Impressions of tenderness and compassion arising from personal intercourse and Connections, which soften the Rigours of the most despotic Governments, must if continued, establish the most grievous and intollerable [sic] Species of Tyranny and Oppression, that ever was inflicted upon Mankind.

8. *Resolved* that it is our greatest Wish and Inclination, as well as Interest, to continue our Connection with, and Dependance upon the British Government; but tho' we are it's [sic] Subjects, we will use every Means which Heaven hath given us to prevent our becoming it's [sic] Slaves.

9. *Resolved* that there is a premeditated Design and System, formed and pursued by the British Ministry, to introduce an arbitrary Government into his Majesty's American Dominions; to which End they are artfully prejudicing our Sovereign, and inflaming the Minds of our fellow-Subjects in Great Britain, by propagating the most malevolent Falsehoods; particularly that there is an Intention in the American Colonies to set up for independant [sic] States; endeavouring at the same Time, by various Acts of Violence and Oppression, by sudden and repeated Dissolutions of our Assemblies, whenever they presume to examine the Illegality of ministerial Mandates, or deliberate on the violated Rights of their Constituents, and by breaking in upon the American Charters, to reduce us to a State of Desperation, and dissolve the original Compacts by which our Ancestors bound themselves and their Posterity to remain dependant [sic] upon the British Crown: which Measures, unless effectually counteracted, will end in the Ruin both of Great Britain and her Colonies.

10. *Resolved* that the several Acts of Parliament for raising a Revenue upon the People of America without their Consent, the creating new and dangerous Jurisdictions here, the taking away our Trials by Jurys [sic], the ordering Persons upon Criminal Accusations, to be tried in another Country than that in which the Fact is charged to have been committed, the Act inflicting ministerial Vengeance upon the Town of Boston, and the two **Bills** lately brought into Parliament for abrogating the Charter of the Province of Massachusetts Bay, and for the Protection and Encouragement of Murderers in the said Province, are Part of the above mentioned iniquitous System. That the Inhabitants of the Town of Boston are now suffering in the common Cause of all British America, and are justly entitled to it's [sic] Support and Assistance; and therefore that a Subscription ought imediatly [sic] to be opened, and proper Persons appointed, in every County of this Colony to purchase Provisions, and consign them to some Gentleman of Character in Boston, to be distributed among the poorer Sort of People there.

11. *Resolved* that we will cordially join with our Friends and Brethren of this and the other Colonies, in such Measures as shall be judged most effectual for procuring Redress of our Grievances,

and that upon obtaining such Redress if the Destruction of the Tea at Boston be regarded as an Invasion of private Property, we shall be willing to contribute towards paying the East India Company the Value: but as we consider the said Company as the Tools and Instrument of Oppression in the Hands of Government and the Cause of our present Distress, it is the Opinion of this Meeting that the People of these Colonies shou'd forbear all further Dealings with them, by refusing to purchase their Merchandize [sic], until that Peace Safety and Good-order, which they have disturbed, be perfectly restored. And that all Tea now in this Colony, or which shall be imported into it shiped [sic] before the first Day of September next, shou'd be deposited in some Storehouse to be appointed by the respective Committees of each County, until a sufficient Sum of Money be raised by Subscription to reimburse the Owners the Value, and then to be publickly [sic] burn'd and destroyed; and if the same is not paid for and destroyed as aforesaid, that it remain in the Custody of the said Committees, at the Risque [sic] of the Owners, until the Act of Parliament imposing a Duty upon Tea for raising a Revenue in America be repealed; and imediatly [sic] afterwards be delivered unto the several Proprietors thereof, their Agents or Attorneys.

12. *Resolved* that Nothing will so much contribute to defeat the pernicious Designs of the common Enemies of Great Britain and her Colonies as a firm Union of the latter; who ought to regard every Act of Violence or Oppression inflicted upon any one of them, as aimed at all; and to effect this desireable Purpose, that a Congress shou'd be appointed, to consist of Deputies from all the Colonies, to concert a general and uniform Plan for the Defence [British spelling} and Preservation of our common Rights, and continueing the Connection and Dependance of the said Colonies upon Great Britain under a just, lenient, permanent, and constitutional Form of Government.

13. *Resolved* that our most sincere and cordial Thanks be given to the Patrons and Friends of Liberty in Great Britain, for their spirited and patriotick [sic] Conduct in Support of our constitutional Rights and Privledges [sic], and their generous Efforts to prevent the present Distress and Calamity of America.

14. *Resolved* that every little jarring Interest and Dispute, which has ever happened between these Colonies, shou'd be buried in eternal Oblivion; that all Manner of Luxury and Extravagance ought imediatly [sic] to be laid aside, as totally inconsistent with the threatening and gloomy Prospect before us; that it is the indispensable Duty of all the Gentlemen and Men of Fortune to set

Examples of Temperance, Fortitude, Frugality and Industry; and give every Encouragement in their Power, particulary [sic] by Subscriptions and Premiums, to the Improvement of Arts and Manufactures in America; that great Care and Attention shou'd be had to the Cultivation of Flax, Cotton, and other Materials for Manufactures; and we recommend it to such of the Inhabitants who have large Stocks of Sheep, to sell to their Neighbors at a moderate Price, as the most certain Means of speedily increasing our Breed of Sheep, and Quantity of Wool.

15. *Resolved* that until American Grievances be redressed, by Restoration of our just Rights and Privileges, no Goods or Merchandize [sic] whatsoever ought to be imported into this Colony, which shall be shiped [sic] from Great Britain or Ireland after the first Day of September next, except Linnens [sic] not exceeding fifteen Pence [per] yard, (German Oznabrigs) coarse woolen Cloth, not exceeding two Shillings sterling [per] Yard, Nails Wire, and Wire-Cards, Needles & Pins, Paper, Salt Petre, and Medicines; which [three Articles only] may be imported until the first Day of September, one thousand seven hundred and seventy six; and if any Goods or Merchandize [sic], othe[r] than those hereby excepted, shou'd be ship'd from Great Britain, {or Ireland} after the time aforesaid, to this Colony, that the same, immediately upon their Arrival, shou'd either be sent back again, by the Owners their Agents or Attorn[ey]s, or stored and deposited in some Warehouse, to be appointed by the Committee for each respective County, and there kept, at the Risque [sic] and Charge of the Owners, to be delivered to them, when a free Importation of Goods hither shall again take Place. And that the Merchants and Venders of Goods and Merchandize [sic] within this Colony ought not to take Advantage of our present Distress b[u]t continue to sell the Goods and Merchandize [sic] which they now have, or which may be shiped [sic] to them before the first Day of September next, at the same Rates and Prices they have been accustomed to do, within one Year last past; and if any Person shall sell such Goods on any other Terms than above expressed, that no Inhabitant of this Colony shou'd at any time, for ever thereafter, deal with him, his Agent, Factor, or Store keepers for any Commodity whatsoever.

16. *Resolved* that it is the Opinion of this Meeting, that the Merchants and Venders of Goods and Merchandize [sic] within this Colony shou'd take an Oath, not to sell or dispose of any Goods or Merchandize [sic] whatsoever, which may be shiped [sic] from Great Britain {or Ireland} after the first Day of September next as afoes

21

[sic], except the (three) Articles before excepted, and that they will, upon Receipt of such prohibited Goods, either send the same back again by the first Opportunity, or deliver them to the Committees in the respective Countys [sic], to be deposited in some Warehouse, at the Risque [sic] and Charge of the Owners, until they, their Agents or Factors be permitted to take them away by the said Committees: the Names of those who refuse to take such Oath to be advertized [British spelling] by the respective Committees in the Countys [sic] wherein they reside. And to the End that the Inhabitants of this Colony may know what Merchants, and Venders of Goods and Merchandize [sic] have taken such Oath, that the respective Committees shou'd grant a Certificate thereof to every such Person who shall take the same.

17. *Resolved* that it is the Opinion of this Meeting, that during our present Difficulties and Distress, no Slaves ought to be imported into any of the British Colonies on this Continent; and we take this Opportunity of declaring our most earnest Wishes to see an entire Stop for ever put to such a wicked cruel and unnatural Trade.

18. *Resolved* that no kind of Lumber shou'd be exported from this Colony to the West Indies, until America be restored to her constitutional Rights and Liberties if the other Colonies will accede to a like Resolution; and that it be recommended to the general Congress to appoint as early a Day as possible for stopping such Export.

19. *Resolved* that it is the Opinion of this Meeting, if American Grievances be not redressed before the first Day of November one thousand seven hundred and seventy five, that all Exports of Produce from the several Colonies to Great Britain {or Ireland} shou'd cease; and to carry the said Resolution more effectually into Execution, that we will not plant or cultivate any Tobacco, after the Crop now growing; provided the same Measure shall be adopted by the other Colonies on this Continent, as well those who have heretofore made Tobacco, as those who have n[o]t. And it is our Opinion also, if the Congress of Deputies from the several Colonies shall adopt the Measure of Non-exportation to Great Britain, as the People will be thereby disabled from paying their Debts, that no Judgements shou'd be rendered by the Courts in the said Colonies for any Debt, after Information of the said Measure's [sic] being determined upon.

20. *Resolved* that it is the Opinion of this Meeting that a solemn Covenant and Association shou'd be entered into by the Inhabitants of all the Colonies upon Oath, that they will not, after the

Times which shall be respectively agreed on at the general Congress, export any Manner of Lumber to the West Indies, nor any of their Produce to Great Britain {or Ireland}, or sell or dispose of the same to any Person who shall not have entered into the said Covenant and Association; and also that they will no[t] import or receive any Goods or Merchandize [sic] which shall be ship'd from Great Britain {or Ireland} after the first Day of September next, other than the before enumerated Articles, nor buy or purchase any Goods, except as before excepted, of any Person whatsoever, who shall not have taken the Oath herein before recommended to be taken by the Merchants and Venders of Goods nor buy or purchase any Slaves hereafter imported into any Part of this Continent until a free Exportation and Importation be again resolved on by a Majority of the Representatives or Deputies of the Colonies. And that the respective Committees of the Countys [sic], in each Colony so soon as the Covenant and Association becomes general, publish by Advertisements in their several Counties {and Gazettes of their Colonies}, a List of the Names of those (if any such there be) who will not accede thereto; that such Traitors to their Country may be publickly [sic] known and detested.

21. *Resolved* that it is the Opinion of this Meeting, that this and the other associating Colonies shou'd break off all Trade, Intercourse, and Dealings, with that Colony Province or Town which shall decline or refuse to agree to the Plan which shall be adopted by the general Congress.

22. *Resolved* that shou'd the Town of Boston be forced to submit to the late cruel and oppressive Measures of Government, that we shall not hold the same to be binding upon us, but will, notwithstanding, religiously maintain, and inviolably adhere to such Measures as shall be concerted by the general Congress, for the preservation of our Lives, Liberties and Fortunes.

23. *Resolved* that it be recommended to the Deputies of the general Congress to draw up and transmit an humble and dutiful Petition and **Remonstrance** to his Majesty, asserting with decent Firmness our just and constitutional Rights and Privileg[es,] lamenting the fatal Necessity of being compelled to enter into Measur[es] disgusting to his Majesty and his Parliament, or injurious to our fellow Subjects in Great Britain; declaring, in the strongest Terms, ou[r] Duty and Affection to his Majesty's Person, Family [an]d Government, and our Desire to continue our Dependance upon Great Bri[tai]n; and most humbly conjuring and beseeching [sic] his Majesty, not to reduce his faithful Subjects of America to a State of desperation, and to reflect, that from

23

our Sovereign there can be but one Appeal. And it is the Opinion of this Meeting, that after such Petition and Remonstrance shall have been presented to his Majesty, the same shou'd be printed in the public Papers, in all the principal Towns in Great Britain.

24. *Resolved* that George Washington Esquire, and George Broadwater Gent. lately elected our Representatives to serve in the general Assembly, be appointed to attend the Convention at Williamsburg on the first Day of August next, and present these Resolves, as the Sense of the People of this County, upon the Measures proper to be taken in the present alarming and dangerous Situation of America.

THE FIRST CONTINENTAL CONGRESS (September 5, 1774) met in Philadelphia and was attended by delegates from all the thirteen colonies except Georgia. The universal feeling for a union of the colonies was gaining strength, although most still opposed independence from Britain. This congress met to respond to the appointment of an English officer, General Gage, as governor of Massachusetts and the blockade of Boston Harbor by British ships (because of the Intolerable Acts). The congress declared that no government had the right to deprive Americans of their life, liberty, or property and asserted that the colonists had every right that an Englishman had and "that this Congress approves the opposition of the inhabitants of Massachusetts to the execution of the late acts of Parliament, and if the same shall be attempted to be carried into execution by force, in such case all America ought to support them in their opposition." The United States herein served notice that if England didn't abandon her present course, war was imminent. Notice how united participation between the colonies grew steadily from four at the New England Confederation to seven at the Albany Congress, then nine at the Stamp Act Congress and twelve at the First Continental Congress. The seeds of revolution were beginning to sprout.

In an effort to attain their objectives, Congress endorsed a document known as the Continental Association. The document, written and signed by eighty-nine members of the House of Burgesses of Virginia on May 27, 1774, specifically listed the Acts, which Parliament was to repeal, and favored nonimportation of British goods. The association also laid the groundwork for a system of national government and encouraged the colonists to adapt an economically conservative lifestyle, in hopes of demonstrating to England their "willingness to sacrifice."

The First Continental Congress adopted a similar "Declaration and Resolves" on October 14, 1774, that specifically listed the more serious grievances of the colonists and put forth the first colonial "Bill of Rights."

And whereas, assemblies have been frequently dissolved, contrary to the will of the people, when they attempted to deliberate on grievances; and their dutiful, humble, loyal, and reasonable petitions to the crown for redress, have been

repeatedly treated with contempt, by his Majesty's ministers of state: ... That they are entitled to life, liberty and property: and have never ceded to any foreign power whatever, a right to dispose of either without their consent. ... But, from the necessity of the case, and regard to the mutual interest of both countries, we cheerfully consent to the operation of the acts of the British parliament, as are bon[a]fide, restrained to the regulation of our external commerce, for the purpose of securing the commercial advantages of the whole empire to the mother country, and the commercial benefits of its respective members; excluding every idea of taxation internal or external, for raising a revenue on the subjects, in America, without their consent. ... That they are entitled to the benefit of such of the statutes, as existed at the time of their colonization; and which they have, by experience, respectively found to be applicable to their several local and other circumstances. ... That the keeping of a standing army in these Colonies, in times of peace, without the consent of the legislature of that Colony, in which army is kept, is against law. ... It is indispensably necessary to good government, and rendered essential by the English constitution, that the constituent branches of the legislature be independent of each other; that, therefore, the exercise of legislative power in several Colonies, by a council appointed, during pleasure, by the crown, unconstitutional, dangerous and destructive to the freedom of America.
—Declaration and Resolves of the First Continental Congress, October 14, 1774

It is clear that even in late 1774, just twenty months before the Declaration of Independence, most of the colonists were still loyal to Great Britain and to parliamentary sanctions, with certain limitations. England, however, chose to ignore the pleas from the Continental Congress and remained committed to its unrestrained domination of the American colonies.

The country was not long in finding out that England intended to use force in dealing with the potential insurrections in Massachusetts. Before the beginning of 1775, British General Gage, the English appointed governor of Massachusetts, was erecting fortifications around Boston and British troops were appearing more frequently. The fall of 1775 found eastern Massachusetts filled with well-armed troops on both sides.

Samuel Adams and John Hancock, both of whom would later sign the Declaration of Independence, led the Americans in Massachusetts. Gage received orders that these two men should be arrested and sent to England for trial. On the evening of April 18, 1775, Gage left Boston for Lexington, Massachusetts, to arrest Adams and Hancock, with plans to continue to Concord to seize colonial ammunition that he thought was stored there. Adams and Hancock escaped because of the famous ride of Paul Revere. A subsequent armed confrontation between the colonists and British soldiers under Major Pitcairn led to the exchange of gunfire often referred to as the shot heard round the world. The battles continued with increased intensity at Concorde, and thus the American Revolution was underway. The British soldiers returned to Boston, many of their troops either killed or wounded during their retreat.

Benedict Arnold and Ethan Allen soon led an attack against Ft. Ticonderoga and accepted its surrender on May 10, 1775. The surrender by British forces at Fort Crown Point, also located in New York, quickly followed. Ft. Ticonderoga was recaptured by British General Burgoyne in July 1777 from American General Arthur St. Claire. Although St. Claire was exonerated on charges of desertion by court martial, he never again was given a field command.

THE SECOND CONTINENTAL CONGRESS (May 10, 1775) met in Philadelphia to deal with outbreak of war with Britain, which began the morning of April 19, 1775, with the killing of Americans by British Major Pitcairn at Lexington, Massachusetts. All the colonies this time sent delegates, including Samuel Adams, John Hancock, Robert Livingston, John Jay, Ben Franklin, George Washington, Patrick Henry, and Richard Henry Lee. The most noteworthy function of this initial meeting of the second congress was to appoint Washington as head of the colonial army, but subsequent meetings of this congress approved the Declaration of Independence, and in July of 1778, the Articles of Confederation (although not fully ratified until March 1781 by Maryland, being the last to do so).

> You may believe me, I should enjoy more real happiness in one month with you at home than I have the most distant prospect of finding abroad if my stay were to be seven times seven years. I have used every endeavor in my power to avoid this appointment, from a consciousness of its being a trust too great for my capacity, but, as a kind of destiny has thrown me upon this service, I shall hope that my undertaking it is designed to answer some good purpose. I shall rely confidently on that Providence which has hitherto preserved and been bountiful to me.
> —Letter from Washington to his wife, June 18, 1775
> http://avalon.law.yale.edu/18th_century/resolves.asp

On December 22, 1775, Parliament passed the Prohibitory Act, halting American commerce and giving the British Navy legal authority to seize any American vessels. This act seriously weakened the arguments in the Continental Congress for reconciliation.

George Washington immediately began to prepare for war and independence. He created a navy, insisted that captured Americans be treated as prisoners of war, decided to invade Canada, and specifically sought to define **treason** (see Article 3, Section 3.1 of the Constitution). Although many, probably a majority, in the congress continued to oppose independence and to hope for reconciliation, General Washington was clearly plotting a revolution.

Thomas Paine (January 29, 1737–June 8, 1809) deserves some mention at this point. He was born in England in 1737 but left for America in 1774 with a letter of introduction from Ben Franklin. Because he was editor of the *Pennsylvania Magazine*, his writings had become familiar to many leading activists, including George Clymer (Constitutional Convention delegate from Pennsylvania), Samuel Adams, and Benjamin Rush. In January of 1776, Thomas Paine published an essay that Rush titled *Common Sense*, which plainly exposed the "monarchial **tyranny**" of the English constitution and **evinced** the rights of the colonists to self-government and separation from British rule. Paine volunteered into the Continental Army, was an aide to General Greene, and became secretary of the Committee of Foreign Affairs in 1777. He moved to France in 1787, was imprisoned during the French Revolution (1787–1799), and returned to the United States in 1802. He never held public office under the United States federal government, dying in New York City a forgotten man. It is strange that a man so vocal in support of independence contributed nothing to help sustain it.

> There is something exceedingly ridiculous in the composition of monarchy, it first excludes a man from the means of information, yet empowers him to act in cases where the highest judgment is required. The state of a king shuts him from the world, yet the business of a king requires him to know it thoroughly; wherefore the different parts, unnaturally opposing and destroying each other, prove the whole character to be absurd and useless.

> The authority of Great-Britain over this continent, is a form of government, which sooner or later must have an end: And a serious mind can draw no true pleasure by looking forward, under the painful and positive conviction, that what he calls "the present constitution" is merely temporary. As parents, we can have no joy, knowing that this government is not sufficiently lasting to ensure anything which we may bequeath to **posterity**: And by a plain method of argument, as we are running the next generation into debt, we ought to do the work of it, otherwise we use them meanly and pitifully. In order to discover the line of our duty rightly, we should take our children in our hand, and fix our station a few years farther into life; that **eminence** will present a prospect, which a few present fears and prejudices conceal from our sight.

> Though I would carefully avoid giving unnecessary offence, yet I am inclined to believe, that all those who **espouse** the doctrine of reconciliation, may be included within the following descriptions. Interested men, who are not to be trusted; weak men who cannot see; prejudiced men who will not see; and a certain set of moderate men,

who think better of the European world than it deserves; and this last class by an ill-judged deliberation, will be the cause of more calamities to this continent than all the other three.
—Thomas Paine, *Common Sense*
Penguin Classics, 1986, pp. 69, 87–88

After many battles and much bloodshed, it became apparent, even to many of the heretofore steadfast Tories (men who did not want independence and who took sides with the king) that separation from England and from British rule was the only solution. With this end in mind, the Second Continental Congress issued on July 4, 1776, our Declaration of Independence. This not only was our official declaration of war but also notified the world that the colonies had separated from Britain and would henceforth accept alliances with any powers willing to support their cause. Fortunately for us, France disliked the British even more than the colonists did and soon joined the Americans in battle against England. By the Treaty of Amity and Commerce, signed on February 6, 1778, France recognized the United States as an independent new nation, naming ambassadors and promising no peace with Britain until she did the same.

As the war progressed, so did the need to unify the colonies. The delegates of the Second Continental Congress quickly realized they had no power over the colonies, and in November of 1777, they proposed for ratification by the states the Articles of Confederation; Virginia was the first to do so on December 16, 1777. In general, the articles authorized the new confederated government to assume the following powers and duties:

1. To determine questions of peace and war
2. To attend to foreign affairs of every kind
3. To manage Indian affairs
4. To call upon the states for their share of the expenses of the central government
5. To settle disputes between states concerning boundaries
6. To establish and regulate post offices
7. To regulate coinage

The states retained all their individual rights, except those specifically ceded to the confederated congress, each state having only a single vote, irrespective of the states' population. Although the Articles of Confederation began the discussion, at least, of viewing the colonies as the United States of America, they were ineffective in establishing a national entity that could either enforce the collection of revenues from the individual states or regulate commerce between the states or with foreign nations.

Madison summarized the difficulties in effecting a confederation between the states as the natural repugnance of the parties to a relinquishment of power, a natural jealousy of its abuse in other hands than their own, the rule of suffrage among parties unequal in size, but equal in sovereignty, the ratio of contributions in money and in troops among parties whose inequality in size did not correspond with that of their wealth, or of their military or free population, the selection and definition of the powers, at once necessary to the federal head, and safe to the several members.

Undefined but implied Federal ownership of "Crown Lands" [lands still owned by Britain and not yet granted to individuals or States at the time of the Declaration of Independence]. Dissatisfaction of some land-bound states being subject to indirect import and export taxation by neighboring states who geographically were blessed with sea ports.

But the radical infirmity of the "art of Confederation" was the dependence of Congress on the voluntary and simultaneous compliance with its Requisitions, by so many independent Communities, each consulting more or less its particular interests and convenience and distrusting the compliance of the others. Whilst the paper emissions of Congress continued to circulate they were employed as a sinew of war, like gold and silver. When that ceased to be the case, the fatal defect of the political System was felt in its alarming force. The war was merely kept alive and brought to a successful conclusion by such foreign aids and temporary **expedients** as could be applied; a hope prevailing with many, and a wish with all, that a state of peace, and the sources of prosperity opened by it, would give the Confederacy in practice, the efficiency which had been inferred from its theory.
—James Madison, *Notes of Debates in the Federal Convention of 1787* Ohio University Press, 1966, Preface, pp. 6–7

The individual states, still suffering from the recent **usurpations** by Great Britain, were reluctant to forfeit their individual sovereignty to a newly created national government. Although the creation of the federation pursuant to the Articles of Confederation was a step in the right direction, the articles were weak and quickly became ineffective in dealing with postwar America.

Even though we, with critical assistance from France, had won a military victory against Great Britain, the survival of the American colonies as a single nation was far from secure. George Washington, as head of the Continental Army, early on realized the need for a strong national government. In December of 1778, he wrote to George Mason "not to be satisfied with places in their own state while the common interests of America were mouldering [wasting away] and sinking into irretrievable ruin, but to attend to the momentous concerns of an empire. I lament the fatal policy of the states of employing their ablest men at home. How useless to put in fine order the smallest parts of a clock, unless the great spring which is to set the whole in motion is well attended to! Let this voice call forth you, Jefferson, and others to save their country." In a letter to James Duane, Mayor of New York City (1784–1789), member of the First and Second Continental Congresses and first federal judge of the district of New York, Washington wrote, "the liberty to reject or alter any act of congress which in a full representation of states has been solemnly debated and decided on should be **abrogated** or there was no hope of consolidating the union."

In a letter to his stepson, John Parke Custis, Washington wrote, "The fear of giving sufficient powers to congress is futile. Under its [the United States in Congress Assembled] present constitution, each assembly will be annihilated, and we must once more return to the government of Great Britain, and be made to kiss the rod preparing for our correction. A nominal head, which at present is but another name for congress, will no longer do." In another letter to his friend, Joseph Jones, he wrote, "Without a controlling power in congress it will be impossible to carry on the war; and we shall speedily be thirteen distinct states, each pursuing its local interests, till they are annihilated in a general crash. The fable of the bunch of sticks may well be applied to us."

Washington, the retiring commander in chief, realized the absolute necessity of a uniform organization of the militia throughout the continent and a much stronger national government than currently existed.

> The citizens of America, the sole lords and proprietors of a vast tract of continent, are now acknowledged to be possessed of absolute freedom and independency. Here Heaven has crowned all its other blessings, by giving a fairer opportunity for political happiness than any other nation has ever been favored with. The rights of mankind are better understood and more clearly defined than at any former period. The collected wisdom acquired through a long succession of years is laid open for our use in the establishment of our forms of government. The free cultivation of letters (freedom of speech and freedom of the press) the unbounded extension of commerce, the progressive refinement of manners, the growing liberality of sentiment, and, above all, the pure and benign light of revelation, have had a **meliorating** influence on mankind. At this auspicious period, the United States came into existence as a nation.

> Happiness is ours, if we seize the occasion and make it our own. This is the moment to give such a tone to our federal government as will enable it to answer the ends of its institution. According to the system of policy the states shall adopt at this moment, it is to be decided whether the revolution must ultimately be considered as a blessing or a curse, not to the present age alone, for with our fate will the destiny of unborn millions be involved.

Essential to the existence of the United States is the friendly disposition which will forget local prejudices and policies, make mutual concessions to the general prosperity, and, in some instances, sacrifice individual advantages to the interest of the community. Liberty is the basis of the glorious fabric of our independency and national character, and whoever would dare to sap the foundation, or overturn the structure, under whatever **specious** pretext he may attempt it, will merit the bitterest **execration** and the severest punishment which can be inflicted by his injured country.

It is indispensable to the happiness of the individual states that there should be lodged somewhere a supreme power to regulate and govern the general concerns of the confederated republic, without which the union cannot be of long duration, and everything must very rapidly tend to **anarchy** and confusion. Whatever measures have a tendency to dissolve the union, or to violate or lessen the sovereign authority, ought to be considered as hostile to the liberty and independence of America. It is only in our united character that we are known as an empire, that our independence is acknowledged, that our power can be regarded, or our credit supported among foreign nations. The treaties of the European powers with the United States of America will have no validity on a dissolution of the union. We shall be left nearly in a state of nature; or we may find by our own unhappy experience that there is a natural and necessary progression from the extreme of anarchy to the extreme of tyranny, and that arbitrary power is most easily established on the ruins of liberty abused to **licentiousness**.
—Circular letter from George Washington to the governors of the states, June 1783
George Bancroft, *History of the Constitution of the United States,* Vol. I
D. Appleton and Company, 1882, pp. 112–113

James Madison reported additional weaknesses of the Articles of Confederation to Congress during March of 1781: "The Articles of Confederation, which declare that every state shall abide by the determinations of Congress, imply a general power vested in Congress to enforce them and carry them into effect. The United States in congress assembled, being desirous as far as possible to cement and invigorate the federal union, recommend to the legislature of every state to give authority to employ the force of the United States as well by sea as by land to compel the states to fulfill their federal engagements." Although during the Constitutional Convention, Madison abandoned this remedy, he always supported a stronger national government than existed under the Articles of Confederation.

Alexander Hamilton, although only twenty-five at the time, published in August 1781 a series of papers called *The Continentalist,* in which he stated

There is hardly a man who will not acknowledge the confederation unequal to a vigorous prosecution of the war, or to the preservation of the union in peace. The federal government, too weak at first, will continually grow weaker. Already some of the states have evaded or refused the demands of congress; the currency is depreciated; public credit is at the lowest ebb; our army deficient in numbers and unprovided with everything; the enemy making an alarming progress in the southern states; Cornwallis still **formidable** to Virginia. As in explanation of our embarrassments nothing can be alleged to the disaffection of the people, we must have recourse to impolicy and mismanagement in their rulers. We ought therefore not only to strain every nerve to render the present campaign as decisive as possible, but we ought without delay to enlarge the powers of congress. Every plan of which this is not the foundation will be illusory. The separate exertions of the states will never suffice. Nothing but a well-proportioned exertion of the resources for the whole, under the direction of a common council with power sufficient to give **efficacy** to their resolutions, can preserve us from being a conquered people now, or can make us a happy one hereafter. I wish to see a convention of all the states, with full power to alter and amend, finally and irrevocably, the present futile and senseless confederation."

In February of 1781, Congress proposed to the states that as an indispensable necessity, the United States in Congress assembled should be granted the power to levy a duty of five per cent ad valorem on most imports. This request was agreed to by all the states except Rhode Island, which on November 1, 1782, unanimously rejected the measure because the impost would bear hardest on the most commercial states, particularly upon Rhode Island, and congress would not be accountable to the states from which the revenue was obtained. The Articles of Confederation requiring approval of all thirteen states to effect amendments, the motion was defeated and America continued to languish.

After many battles, loss of life (8000 Americans and 9000 British), suffering, and steadfast commitment to freedom by the colonists, the war officially ended on September 3, 1783, with the signing of the Treaty of Peace (1783) in Paris.

THE TREATY OF PARIS (1783), negotiated by Benjamin Franklin, John Jay, and John Adams, first and foremost affirmed the independence of the United States and officially ended the war with Great Britain. In addition, it attempted to established the boundaries of our new nation (southern: Florida, northern: Canada, western: the Mississippi River, eastern: the Atlantic Ocean); gave Americans the right to fish on the coast of Newfoundland and the British rights to navigate the Mississippi River; and decreed that creditors on either side should "meet with no lawful impediment" to the recovery of prewar debts, that hostilities would cease between America and Britain, that British land and sea forces be evacuated "with all convenient speed," and that Congress should "earnestly recommend" to the several states restoration of all **Tory** property, although these earnest recommendations fell mostly on deaf ears. Attempts were made by Franklin, Jay, and Adams to abolish the **Navigation Acts** and to set up free trade between England and the United States. Because of the ambiguities of the treaty, the deep-seated hatred between England and America, and the vast wealth at stake, the hostilities were to quickly resume. Although withdrawal was required by the terms of the treaty, England not only failed to withdraw troops from her western and northwestern interior posts but continued policies of restricted commerce with the United States. England continued to regard the colonies as separate nations and to believe, as British Minister Fox stated, that "a definitive treaty with the United States was perfectly superfluous," which is understandable, because until June 21, 1788 (date of ratification of the United States Constitution by New Hampshire), there was no united authority within the colonies with which to effect the treaty.

The Articles of Confederation, still the controlling contract between the states at the time of the Treaty of Peace, was ineffective in enforcing our obligations created under the treaty. The new union of states was soon in total disarray. The United States could not keep peace between the states, could not honor its treaties with foreign countries, and could not raise money or pay its debts. Congress lost the respect of the country, and statesmen did not even care to attend the meetings of Congress. Edmund Randolph, Constitutional Convention delegate from Virginia, outlined the following weaknesses of the Articles of Confederation during the first week of the convention:

> That the confederation produced no security against foreign invasion; congress not being permitted to prevent a war nor to support it by their own authority; that particular states might by their conduct provoke war without controul [sic]; the federal government could not check the quarrels between states, nor a rebellion in any [as **Shay's Rebellion** in Massachusetts], not having constitutional power nor means to interpose according to the **exigency;** could not initiate productive imposts which might counteract the commercial regulations of other nations, and could not defend itself against the encroachments from the states.
> —James Madison, *Notes of Debates in the Federal Convention of 1787*
> Ohio University Press, 1966, p. 29

Within the separate states, there were disorders and violence. People were heavily in debt, and enforcement of court-ordered property confiscations caused riots and vigilante justice, the most noteworthy being Shays' Rebellion (August–February 1786), wherein a group of approximately 1200 Massachusetts citizens rebelled against the state legislature for adjourning without the legislature heeding their petitions for debt relief. Ultimately, all were pardoned, and future legislatures agreed to avoid direct taxation, to exempt such items as household goods and workmen's tools from debt recovery, and to lower court fees. This rebellion, along with angry unpaid soldiers, high debt, and disorder and violence within the states, was instrumental in necessitating the proposal to assemble the Constitutional Convention in 1787.

George Washington's efforts in preventing an insurrection of the colonial militia over unpaid war salaries cannot be overlooked. Without his individual efforts, the survival of the confederation would have been extremely difficult, if not impossible.

It must also be remembered that in 1787, prior to the Constitutional Convention, most people living in the United States were still fearful of Britain and realized that a more powerful union of the individual states than existed under the Articles of Confederation would be necessary for their survival. Also, the states did not wish to lose through disunion their property interest in the great Northwest Territory, a region that included what are now Ohio, Indiana, Illinois, Michigan, Wisconsin, and parts of Minnesota. The weaknesses of the Articles of Confederation had surfaced during attempts by Congress to deal with the issues confronting the colonies now that the war with England had temporarily ended. It was time for a new national government, one with more central power and control over the individual states. With this in mind, a special Congressional Congress was convened in Philadelphia on May 14, 1787.

In spite of the difficult issues facing the colonies subsequent to the Treaty of Peace of 1783, we should not overlook the masterful negotiations done by Jay, Franklin, and Adams on behalf of the colonies. Many of the terms favoring America were so distasteful to England that support for the treaty was strongly opposed in Parliament by Lord North (prime minister, 1770–1782) and Charles James Fox (the "Honourable", prominent House of Commons statesman) and delayed the signing by Britain until September of 1783.

THE CONSTITUTIONAL CONVENTION OF 1787 (May 14–September 17) met in Philadelphia, some delegates wanting to merely revise the Articles of Confederation, but many wanting to form an entirely new national government. All the states except Rhode Island sent representatives. George Washington presided. Fifty-five delegates attended, including Ben Franklin, Robert Morris, James Wilson, Gouverneur Morris, George Mason, Edmund Randolph, James Madison, George Wythe, Elbridge Gerry, Rufus King, Oliver Ellsworth, Roger Sherman, Charles Pinckney, Charles Cotesworth Pinckney, William Paterson, Alexander Hamilton, and John Dickinson (who had refused to sign the Declaration of Independence). Thomas Jefferson and John Adams were both in Europe and did not attend the Constitutional Convention.

After establishing the rules of protocol, the main topic of debate centered around the Randolph (or Virginia) Plan, proposing a two-branch national legislature and a national executive, the first branch to be elected by the people of the various states and the second branch elected by the first branch, in which representation would be based on state wealth and population (thus favoring the large and prosperous states) and the power to "negative" all laws passed by the several states, abolishing the Articles of Confederation and replacing them with a new Constitution; and the **New Jersey**

34

(Paterson) Plan, retaining and merely amending the Articles of Confederation to include a national executive (being comprised of a committee instead of a single magistrate) and a national judiciary, and retaining equal state representation.

Most of the small-state delegates initially were opposed, and in the case of Delaware even prohibited by their state legislature, to a plan abolishing equal voting rights among the states, and Delaware's George Read, on just the sixth day of the convention threatened to "retire from the Convention." A motion to postpone discussions related to suffrage at least stalled this threat.

The discussions and debates continued until September 17, at which time our formal Constitution was signed by thirty-nine of the forty-two delegates still present and was submitted to the states for ratification. George Mason and Edmund Randolph from Virginia and Elbridge Gerry from Massachusetts refused to sign the Constitution primarily because it gave too much power to the president, didn't contain a bill of rights, and didn't allow any amendments prior to ratification by the states. The Constitution was adopted by the ninth state (New Hampshire) on June 21, 1788, and we officially became the United States of America. The last of the thirteen states, Rhode Island (which, remember, didn't even send delegates to the Constitutional Convention), finally ratified the Constitution on May 29, 1790, by the close vote of 34-32.

Now that we have briefly reviewed the history preceding the writing and signing of the United States Constitution, let's analyze our Constitution paragraph-by-paragraph, line by line, and word by word, keeping in mind the history preceding it, the issues with Britain proclaimed in the Declaration of Independence, the strengths and weaknesses of the Articles of Confederation, and the goals and desires of the men who wrote it. Only two of our Founding Fathers (Roger Sherman and Robert Morris) signed all three documents (Declaration of Indepenence, Articles of Confederation, and U.S. Constitution), and many others were at least present during all or part of the Continental Congresses and Constitutional Convention. Thanks to James Madison, who took notes during the Constitutional Convention, we can gain valuable insight into the development of the Constitution by reviewing his diary from the convention.

The Federalist Papers—written primarily by Alexander Hamilton (delegate to the Confederation Congress and Constitutional Convention, first secretary of the Treasury), John Jay (delegate to the Second Continental Congress, signer of the Treaty of Peace, first chief justice, and signer of Jay's Treaty with England), and James Madison (delegate to the Constitutional Convention, secretary of state under Jefferson, and fourth president of the United States)—were published in support of, and the Anti-Federalist Papers opposed to, ratification of the Constitution. These publications are good references related to understanding the Constitution, but care must be taken to remember they were written as much for purpose (ratification) as for insight.

We have left the foxes to guard the hen house, and we don't even bother to stop by and see how things are going. The one critical step ensuring the survival of our constitutional rights is to *vote*, but because of the economic comforts existing in our country today, and the complacency that always follows peace and security, many of us don't even bother to do that. The main advantage we have in America, the thing that has separated us from the rest of the world, is the legislative encouragement of our public and private business climate, the judicial enforcement of our individual rights, and the protection supplied by our armed forces, all provided for and secured by our Constitution. Our Founding Fathers were men of vision who wrote a document that has allowed us to become the premier nation on Earth.

CHAPTER II

THE DECLARATION OF INDEPENDENCE: JULY 4, 1776

When, in the course of human events, it becomes necessary for one people to dissolve the political bands which have connected them with another, and to assume, among the powers of the earth, the separate and equal station to which the laws of nature and of nature's God entitle them, a decent respect to the opinions of mankind requires that they should declare the causes which impel them to the separation.

We hold these truths to be self-evident: that all men are created equal; that they are endowed by their Creator with certain **unalienable** rights; that among these are life, liberty, and the pursuit of happiness. That to secure these rights, governments are instituted among men, deriving their just powers from the consent of the governed; that, whenever any form of government becomes destructive of these ends, it is the right of the people to alter or abolish it, and to institute new government, laying its foundation on such principles, and organizing its powers in such form, as to them shall seem most likely to effect their safety and happiness. **Prudence**, indeed, will dictate that governments long established, should not be changed for light and transient causes; and, accordingly, all experience hath shown, that mankind are more disposed to suffer, while evils are sufferable, than to right themselves by abolishing the forms to which they are accustomed. But, when a long train of abuses and usurpations, pursuing invariably the same object, evinces a design to reduce them under absolute **despotism**, it is their right, it is their duty, to throw off such government, and to provide new guards for their future security. Such has been the patient sufferance of these Colonies; and such is now the necessity which **constrains** them to alter their former systems of government.

"That they [the people] are entitled to life, liberty and property: and have never ceded to any foreign power whatever, a right to dispose of either without their consent."*

The history of the present king of Great Britain is a history of repeated injuries and usurpations, all having in direct

*Declaration and Resolves of the First Continental Congress, N.C.D.1, October 14, 1774

object the establishment of an absolute tyranny over these States. To prove this, let facts be submitted to a candid world.

He has refused his assent to laws, the most wholesome and necessary for the public good.

He has forbidden his governors to pass laws of immediate and pressing importance, unless suspended in their operation till his assent should be obtained; and, when so suspended, he has utterly neglected to attend to them.

"That our ancestors, who first settled these Colonies, at the time of their emigration from the mother country, entitled to all the rights, liberties, and immunities of free and natural-born subjects, within the realm of England..."*

He has refused to pass other laws for the accommodation of large districts of people, unless those people would relinquish the right of representation in the legislature, a right **inestimable** to them [the people] and formidable to tyrants only.

Up to this point, the Declaration of Independence has done no more than set forth general reasons, almost like an opening statement in a court proceeding, why the colonists have the right to object to their treatment by England and, in general terms, what those objectionable treatments are. From here on, the objections get more specific, and I will point out clauses in the Constitution that were to prevent our new US government from committing these same offences.

He has called together legislative bodies at places unusual, uncomfortable, and distant from the depository of their public records, for the sole purpose of fatiguing them into compliance with his measures.

Article I, Section 8.17 of the US Constitution establishes the method of selecting the specific location for the official "seat of the government." Article I, Section 4.1 requires the state legislatures to set aside a time and place for election of the US Congress. Article I, Sections 4 and 5 establish rules for assembly and adjournment, independent of the executive branch.

He has dissolved representative houses repeatedly, for opposing, with manly firmness, his invasions on the rights of the people.

---

*Declaration and Resolves of the First Continental Congress, N.C.D.2, October 14, 1774

Article I, Section 5.4 of the US Constitution prevents either house from adjourning "without the consent of the other, nor to any other place than that in which the two Houses shall be sitting."

"And whereas, assemblies have been frequently dissolved, contrary to the (wishes) of the people..."*

> He has refused, for a long time after such dissolutions, to cause others to be elected; whereby the legislative powers, incapable of annihilation, have returned to the people at large for their exercise; the State remaining, in the meantime, exposed to all the dangers of invasion from without, and **convulsions** within.

Article I, Sections 2.4 and 3.2 of the US Constitution both stipulate the method of replacing the representatives. Article II, Section 2.3 gives the president authority to temporarily replace all vacancies that may happen during the recess of the Senate.

> He has endeavored to prevent the population of these States; for that purpose obstructing the laws for naturalization of foreigners; refusing to pass others to encourage their migration hither, and raising the conditions of new appropriations of land.

Article I, Section 8.4 of the Constitution gives Congress power to establish uniform rules of naturalization.

> He has obstructed the administration of justice, by refusing his assent to laws for establishing judiciary powers.

Article III of the Constitution establishes the judicial branch of the US government and gives Congress the power to establish most judicial guidelines, and Article I, Section 7.2 prevents the president from obstructing legislation by stating, "If any bill shall not be returned by the President within ten days (Sundays excepted) after it shall have been presented to him, the same shall be a law."

> He has made judges dependent on his will alone for the tenure of their offices, and the amount and payment of their salaries.

---

*Declaration and Resolves of the First Continental Congress, October 14, 1774

Article III, Section 1 of the Constitution: "...shall hold their Offices during good Behavior." I think now we see perhaps too much of the other extreme, that of judges outliving their usefulness.

> He has erected a multitude of new offices, and sent hither swarms of officers to harass our people, and eat out their substance.

Article II of the Constitution, which deals with the executive branch, severely limits the powers of the president by establishing his salary, establishing him or her as commander in chief of the army and navy of the United States, and securing the power to grant reprieves and pardons and to temporarily fill vacancies. Most other duties are done with the advice and consent of the legislature.

> He has kept among us in times of peace, standing armies, without the consent of our legislature.

Article I, Section 8.12 of the Constitution, and the Third Amendment, regulate this potential infringement. Many of the state constitutions specifically prohibited "standing armies during times of peace." The Massachusetts Constitution of 1780, Article XVII of its Bill of Rights, said, "The people have a right to keep and to bear arms for the common defence. And as in time of peace armies are dangerous to liberty, they ought not to be maintained without the consent of the legislature; and the military power shall always be held in an exact subordination to the civil authority, and be governed by it."

> He has affected to render the military independent of, and superior to, the **civil power**.

Article II, Section 2.1 of the Constitution puts the military under the command of the president, but only after their use is authorized by Congress, pursuant to Article I, Sections 8.11, 8.12, 8.15, and 8.16.

> He has combined, with others, to subject us to a jurisdiction foreign to our constitution, and unacknowledged by our laws; giving his assent to their acts of pretended legislation.

> For quartering large bodies of armed troops among us:

Specifically prohibited by the Third Amendment of the US Constitution and many of the state constitutions.

"That the keeping a standing army in these Colonies, in times of peace, without the consent of the legislature of that Colony, in which army is kept, is against law."*

Indirectly, Amendments VI and VII of the US Constitution deal with this potential problem.

For cutting off our trade with all parts of the world:

Article I, Section 8.3 of the Constitution gives this power to the legislative branch.

For imposing taxes on us without our consent:

Article I, Section 7.1 of the Constitution specifically delegates this power to the House of Representatives, originally the only branch of Congress elected directly by the people. The Seventeenth Amendment, by empowering the people to directly elect the Senate, significantly reduces the importance of requiring all money bills to originate in the House.

For depriving us, in many cases, of the benefits of trial by jury:

This threat is significantly reduced by the Sixth and Seventh Amendments of the Constitution.

For transporting us beyond seas to be tried for pretended offenses:

Amendment VI of the US Constitution says, "In all **criminal prosecutions**, the accused shall enjoy the right to a speedy and public trial, by an impartial jury of the State and district wherein the crime shall have been committed."

For abolishing the free system of English laws in neighboring provinces, establishing therein an arbitrary government and enlarging its boundaries, so as to render it at once an example and fit instrument for introducing the same absolute rule into these Colonies:

For taking away our charters, abolishing our most valuable laws, and altering, fundamentally, the forms our governments: [Specifically the colonial charters and states' constitutions and legislation]

---

*Declaration and Resolves of the First Continental Congress, N.C.D.9, October 14, 1774

For suspending our own legislatures [those already established within the individual States], and declaring themselves invested with power to legislate for us in all cases whatsoever.

He [the king] has **abdicated** government here by declaring us out of his protection, and waging war against us.

He has plundered our seas, ravaged our coasts, burnt our towns, and destroyed the lives of our people.

He is, at this time, transporting large armies of foreign mercenaries to complete the works of death, desolation, and tyranny, already begun with circumstances of cruelty and **perfidy** scarcely paralleled in the most barbarous ages, and totally unworthy the head of a civilized nation.

He has constrained our fellow citizens, taken captive on the high seas, to bear arms against their country, to become the executioners of their friends and brethren, or to fall themselves by their hands.

He has **excited** domestic insurrections amongst us and has endeavored to bring on the inhabitants of our frontiers, the merciless Indian savages, whose known rule of warfare is an undistinguished destruction of all ages, sexes, and conditions.

In every stage of these oppressions, we have petitioned for redress in the most humble terms: our repeated petitions have been answered only by repeated injury. A prince, whose character is thus marked by every act, which may define a tyrant, is unfit to be the ruler of a free people.

Nor have we been wanting in attention to our British brethren. We have warned them, from time to time, of attempts by their legislature to extend an unwarrantable jurisdiction over us. We have reminded them of the circumstances of our emigration and settlement here. We have appealed to their native justice and **magnanimity**, and we have **conjured** them, by the ties of our common kindred, to disavow these usurpations, which would inevitably interrupt our connections and correspondence. They too have been deaf to the voice of justice and **consanguinity**. We must, therefore, **acquiesce** in the necessity which denounces our separation, and hold them, as we hold the rest of mankind, enemies in war, in peace friends.

We, therefore, the representatives of the United States of America, in general Congress assembled, appealing to the Supreme Judge of the world for the rectitude of our intentions, do, in the name, and by authority of the good people of these Colonies, solemnly publish and declare, That these United Colonies are, and of right ought to be, free and independent States; that they are absolved from all allegiance to the British crown, and that all political connection between them and the state of Great Britain is, and ought to be, totally dissolved; and that, as free and independent States, they have full power to levy war, conclude peace, contract alliances, establish commerce, and to do all other acts and things which independent States may of right do. And for the support of this declaration, with a firm reliance on the protection of Divine Providence, we mutually pledge to each other our lives, our fortunes, and our sacred honor.

JOHN HANCOCK, President _**New Hampshire**_**:** Josiah Bartlett, Wm. Whipple, Matthew Thornton
**New Jersey****:** Richd. Stockton, Jno. Witherspoon, Fras. Hopkinson, John Hart, Abra. Clark
**Massachusetts Bay****:** Saml. Adams, John Adams, Robt. Treat Paine, Elbridge Gerry
**Rhode Island****:** Step. Hopkins, William Ellery
**Connecticut****:** Roger Sherman, Sam'el Huntington, Wm. Williams, Oliver Wolcot
**New York****:** Wm. Floyd, Phil. Livingston. Frans. Lewis, Lewis Morris
**Pennsylvania****:** Robt. Morris, Banjamin Rush, Benja. Franklin, John Morton, Geo. Clymer, Jas. Smith, Geo. Taylor, James Wilson, Geo. Ross
**Delaware****:** Caesar Rodney, Geo. Read, Tho. M'Kean
**Maryland****:** Samuel Chase, Wm. Paca, Thos. Stone, <u>Charles Carrol of Carrollton</u>
**Virginia:** George Wythe, Richard Henry Lee, Th Jefferson. Banja. Harrison, Thos. Nelson Jr., Francis Lightfoot Lee, Carter Braxton
**North Carolina:** Wm. Hooper, Joseph Hewes, John Penn

South Carolina: Edward Rutledge, Thos. Heyward, Junr., Thomas Lynch, Junr., Arthur Middleton

Georgia: Button Gwinnett, Lyman Hall, Geo. Walton

The union of the colonies into the United States of America is hereby decreed and war against Great Britain is formally declared. The colonies will soon learn that they will not survive as independent states, and the necessity for a government of united states will soon come to fruition.

This formal declaration of war against Britain came after the Boston Massacre of 1770, the blockade of Boston Harbor by the British Navy in 1774, the battles of Lexington and Concorde in early 1775, and the capture of Ft. Ticonderoga by forces under the command of Etahn Allen and Benedict Arnold.

The Declaration of Independence, although written primarily by Thomas Jefferson, was the joint effort of the Second Continental Congress. The motion for independence was first brought directly before Congress by Richard Henry Lee, delegate from Virginia and future president of the Continental Congress in 1784, on June 7, 1776, when he submitted a resolution "that the United Colonies are and ought to be free and independent States; that they are absolved from all allegiance to the British crown; and that all political connection between them and the state of Great Britain is, and ought to be, totally dissolved."

"Mr. Lee, the mover, and Mr. John Adams, were particularly distinguished in supporting, and Mr. John Dickinson, in opposing the resolution. On the 10th [June] it was adopted in Committee, by a bare majority of the Colonies. The delegates from Pennsylvania and Maryland, were instructed to oppose it; and the delegates from some of the other Colonies, were without special instructions on the subject. To give time for greater unanimity, the resolution was postponed in the House, until the 1st of July. In the mean time, a Committee, consisting of Mr. Jefferson, John Adams, Dr. Franklin, Mr. Sherman, and R.R. Livingston, was appointed to prepare a Declaration of Independence. During this interval, measures were taken to procure the assent of all the Colonies."*

> American independence was ratified not by congress only, but by the nation. The unselfish enthusiasm of the people was its support; the boundlessness of the country formed its natural defence; and the self-asserting individuality of every state and of every citizen, though it delayed the organization of an efficient government with executive unity, imposed on Britain the impossible task of conquering them one by one.
> —George Bancroft, _History of the United States of America_, Vol. V
> D. Appleton and Company, 1895, p. 16

---

*J. A. Spencer, History of the United States, Vol. I Johnson, Fry and Company, 1858, p. 404

The Declaration of Independence was submitted to Congress as written by Thomas Jefferson, and subsequently discussed, amended, and officially adopted by Congress on July 4, 1776. John Dickinson and Robert Livingston were the only members present who did not sign the Declaration of Independence; Dickinson did, however, represent Delaware at the Constitutional Convention and become a signer of the Constitution.

CHAPTER III

ARTICLES OF CONFEDERATION
AND PERPETUAL UNION
Ratified March 1, 1781
(Perpetual here meaning at least six years)

Articles of Confederation and Perpetual Union between the states of New Hampshire, Massachusetts-Bay, Rhode Island and Providence Plantations, Connecticut, New York, New Jersey, Pennsylvania, Delaware, Maryland, Virginia, North Carolina, South Carolina, and Georgia.

I.   The stile of this Confederacy shall be "The United States of America".

II.   Each state retains its sovereignty, freedom, and independence, and every power, jurisdiction, and right, which is not by this Confederation expressly delegated to the United States in Congress Assembled.

III.   The said states hereby severally enter into a firm league of friendship with each other, for their common defence, the security of their liberties, and their mutual and general welfare, binding themselves to assist each other, against all force offered to, or attacks made upon them, or any of them, on account of religion, sovereignty, trade, or any other pretence whatever.

IV.   The better to secure and perpetuate mutual friendship and intercourse among the people of the different states in this union, the free inhabitants [which did not include slaves] of each of these states, paupers, vagabonds, and fugitives from justice excepted, shall be entitled to all privileges and immunities of free citizens in the several states; and the people of each state shall have free ingress and regress to and from any other state, and shall enjoy therein all the privileges of trade and commerce, subject to the same duties, impositions and restrictions as the inhabitants thereof respectively, provided that such restriction shall not extend so far as to prevent the removal of *property* [emphasis added] imported into any state, to any other state, of which the owner is an inhabitant; provided also that no imposition,

> duties or restriction shall be laid by any state, on the property of the United States, or either of them [meaning any of the states].

The above paragraph was written to promote commerce between the states and the inhabitants of the states. The attempt was powerless, however, without corresponding punishments for violations.

For some reason, probably related to arguments during a lawsuit, the meaning of "property" has become very complicated and restrictive. In discussing the Constitution, I have heard the argument that "property" as used therein refers only to land. However, the meaning of "property" in the Articles of Confederation is certainly not restricted to land. The legal profession has divided up property into many specific types of property, such as absolute property, common property, general property, intangible property, mislaid property, literary property, movable property, personal property, private property, public property, qualified property, real property, separate property, special property, state property, tangible property, unclaimed property (one often used by governments in place of legally confiscated property), and chattel.

> If any person guilty of, or charged with treason, felony, or other **high misdemeanor** in any state, shall flee from justice, and be found in any of the United States, he shall, upon demand of the Governor or executive power of the state from which he fled, be delivered up and removed [returned] to the state having jurisdiction of his offense.

This sentence is of particular importance because, in my opinion, it somewhat refutes those who claim that "high crimes and misdemeanors" refers to offenses by persons in high office, rather than that "high" simply describes the type of crime itself. "Any person," as used herein, is certainly not limited to persons in high office. The same men who wrote the US Constitution also wrote or were certainly intimately familiar with the Articles of Confederation. Article I, Sections 2.5 and 3.6, of the US Constitution, which set forth the impeachment process, contain the words "high crimes and misdemeanors," which, in reality, can be interpreted by the House of Representatives to include any actions they deem unbecoming by a civil officer. The required two-thirds vote in the Senate to convict on impeachment charges will almost always prevent superfluous convictions, in spite of party loyalties.

> Full faith and credit shall be given in each of these states to the records, acts and judicial proceedings of the courts and magistrates of every other state [meaning they will be relied upon as truthful and factual].

Article IV, Section 1, of the US Constitution contains almost identical wording; the Constitution adds another sentence that somewhat restricts the state's power and extends the federal power.

> V.   For the most convenient management of the general interests of the United States, delegates shall be annually appointed in such manner as the legislature of each state shall direct, to meet in Congress on the first Monday in November, in every year, with a power reserved to each state to recall its delegates, or any of them, at any time within the year, and to send others in their **stead** for the remainder of the year.

> No state shall be represented in Congress by less than two, nor by more than seven members; and no person shall be capable of being a delegate for more than three years in any term of six years; nor shall any person, being a delegate, be capable of holding any office under the United States, for which he, or another for his benefit receives any salary, fees or emolument of any kind.

Similar restrictions can also be found in the US Constitution in Article I, Section 6.2, which applies both to senators and representatives.

> Each state shall maintain its own delegates in a meeting of the states, and while they act as members of the committee of the states.

> In determining questions in the United States in Congress assembled, each state shall have one vote.

> Freedom of speech and debate in Congress shall not be impeached [hindered] or questioned in any court or place out of Congress, and the members of Congress shall be protected in their persons from arrest and imprisonments, during the time of their going to and from, and attendance on Congress, except for treason, felony, or breach of the peace.

Article I, Section 6.1 of the Constitution provides an almost identical privilege to Congress.

> VI.   No state, without the consent of the United States in Congress assembled, shall send any embassy to, or receive any embassy from, or enter into any conference, agreement,

alliance or treaty with any king, prince or state; nor shall any person holding any office of profit or trust under the United States, or any of them, accept of any present, emolument, office or title of any kind whatever from any king, prince or foreign state; nor shall the United States in Congress assembled, or any of them, grant any title of nobility.

See Article I, Section 9.8 of the US Constitution.

No two or more states shall enter into any treaty, confederation or alliance whatever between them [between the states], without the consent of the United States in Congress assembled, specifying accurately the purposes for which the same is to be entered into, and how long it shall continue.

No state shall lay any imposts or duties, which may interfere with any stipulations in treaties, entered into by the United States in Congress assembled, with any king, prince or state, in **pursuance** of any treaties already proposed by Congress, to the courts of France and Spain.

This clause was to prevent passage of duties and imposts that might provoke either France or Spain into supporting England against the United States. The support of France was critical to our victory in the Revolutionary War. We had already signed the Treaty of Amity and Commerce with France on February 6, 1778.

No vessels of war shall be kept up in time of peace by any state, except such number only, as shall be deemed necessary by the United States in Congress assembled, for the defence of such state, or its trade; nor shall any body of forces be kept up by any state in time of peace, except such number only, as in the judgment of the United States in Congress assembled, shall be deemed requisite to garrison the forts necessary for the defence of such state; but every state shall always keep up a well regulated and disciplined militia, sufficiently armed and **accoutred**, and shall provide and constantly have ready for use, in public stores, a due number of field pieces and tents, and a proper quantity of arms, ammunition, and camp equipage.

No state shall engage in any war without the consent of the United States in Congress assembled, unless such state be actually invaded by enemies, or shall have received certain advice of a resolution being formed by some nation of Indians to invade such state, and the danger is so imminent as not to admit of a delay till the United States in Congress assembled can be consulted: nor shall any state grant commissions to any ships or vessels of war, nor **letters of marque or reprisal,** except it be after a declaration of war by the United States in Congress assembled, and then only against the kingdom or state and the subjects thereof, against which war has been so declared, and under such regulations as shall be established by the United States in Congress assembled, unless such state be infested by pirates, in which case vessels of war may be fitted out for that occasion, and kept so long as the danger shall continue, or until the United States in Congress assembled, shall determine otherwise.

Article 1, Sections 10.1, 10.2, and 10.3 of the Constitution similarly restricts the states.

VII.   When land-forces are raised by any state for the common defence, all officers of or under the rank of colonel, shall be appointed by the legislature of each state respectively, by whom such forces shall be raised, or in such manner as such state shall direct, and all vacancies shall be filled up by the state which first made the appointment.

VIII.   All charges [expenses] of war, and all other expenses that shall be incurred for the common defence or general welfare, and allowed by the United States in Congress assembled, shall be defrayed out of a common treasury, which shall be supplied by the several states in proportion to the value of all land within each state, granted to or surveyed for any person, as such land and the buildings and improvements thereon shall be estimated according to such mode as the United States in Congress assembled, shall from time to time direct and appoint.

The taxes for paying that proportion shall be laid and levied by the authority and direction of the legislatures of the several states within the time agreed upon by the United States in Congress assembled.

Article I, Section 2.3 of the US Constitution calls for these direct taxes to be paid in proportion to the number of inhabitants of each state as opposed to in proportion to land values.

IX. The United States in Congress assembled, shall have the sole and exclusive right and power of determining on peace and war, except in the cases mentioned in the sixth article [actual invasion by enemies] of sending and receiving ambassadors—entering into treaties and alliances, provided that no treaty of commerce shall be made [by the United States in Congress assembled] whereby the legislative power of the respective states shall be restrained from imposing such imposts and duties on foreigners, as their own people [the inhabitants of the respective states] are subjected to, or from prohibiting the exportation or importation of any species of good or commodities whatsoever—of establishing rules for deciding in all cases, what captures on land or water shall be legal, and in what manner prizes taken by land or naval forces in the service of the United States shall be divided or appropriated--of granting letters of marque and reprisal in times of peace—appointing courts for the trial of piracies and felonies committed on the high seas and establishing courts for receiving and determining final appeals in all cases of captures, provided that no member of Congress shall be appointed a judge of any of the said courts.

Similar language is found in Article I, Section 8.11of the US Constitution.

The United States in Congress assembled shall also be the last resort on appeal in all disputes and differences now subsisting or that hereafter may arise between two or more states concerning boundary, jurisdiction or any other causes whatever; which authority shall always be exercised in the manner following. Whenever the legislative or executive authority or lawful agent of any state in controversy with another shall present a petition to Congress stating the matter in question and praying for a hearing, notice thereof shall be given by order of Congress to the legislative or executive authority of the other state in controversy, and a day assigned for the appearance of the parties by their lawful agents, who shall then be directed to appoint by joint consent, commissioners or judges to constitute a court for hearing and determining the matter in question: but if they cannot agree, Congress shall name three persons out of each of the United States, and from the list of such persons each party shall alternately strike out one, the petitioners beginning, until the number shall be reduced to thirteen; and from that number not less than seven, nor more than nine names as Congress shall direct, shall in the presence of Congress be drawn out by lot, and the persons whose names shall be so drawn or any five of them, shall be commissioners or judges, to hear and finally determine the controversy, so always as a major part of the judges who shall hear the cause shall agree in the determination: and if either party shall neglect to attend at the day appointed, without showing reasons, which Congress shall judge sufficient, or being present shall refuse to strike, the Congress shall proceed to nominate three persons out of each state, and the secretary of Congress shall strike in behalf of such party absent or refusing: and the judgement and sentence of the court to be appointed, in the manner before prescribed, shall be final and conclusive; and if any of the parties shall refuse to submit to the authority of such court, or to appear or defend their claim or cause, the court shall nevertheless proceed to pronounce sentence, or judgment, which shall in like manner be final and decisive, the judgment or sentence and other proceedings being in either case transmitted to Congress, and lodged among the acts of Congress for the security of the parties concerned: provided that every commissioner, before he sits in judgment, shall take an oath to be administered by one of the judges of the supreme or superior court of the state, where the cause shall be tried, "well and truly to hear and determine the matter in question, according to the best of his judgment, without favour, affection or hope of reward": provided also, that no state shall be deprived of territory for the benefit of the United States.

The US Constitution, pursuant to Article III, Section 2, establishes the national judicial power to extend to, among other things, "Controversies between two or more States; between a State and Citizens of another State; between Citizens of different States, between Citizens of the same State claiming lands under Grants of different States."

All controversies concerning the private right of soil [ownership by individual citizens] claimed under different grants of two or more states, whose jurisdictions as they may respect such lands, and the states which passed such grants are adjusted, the said grants or either of them being at the same time claimed to have originated **antecedent** to such settlement of jurisdiction, shall on the petition of either party to the Congress of the United States, be finally determined as near as may be in the same manner as is before prescribed for deciding disputes respecting territorial jurisdiction between different states.

The United States in Congress assembled shall also have the sole and exclusive right and power of regulating the alloy and value of coin struck by their own authority, or by that of the respective states — fixing the standard of weights and measures throughout the Unites States [See Article I, Section 8.5 of the US Constitution] — regulating the trade and managing all affairs with the Indians, not members of any of the states, provided that the legislative right of any state within its own limits be not **infringed** or violated — establishing or regulating post-offices from one state to another, throughout all the United States [See Article I, Section 8.7 of the Constitution], and exacting such postage on the papers passing through the same as may be requisite to defray the expenses of the said office — appointing all officers of the land forces, in the service of the United States, excepting regimental officers [Regimental officers were to be appointed by the state legislatures as outlined below.] appointing all the officers of the naval forces, and commissioning all officers whatever in the service of the United States — making rules for the government and regulation of the said land and naval forces, and directing their operations.

No Executive branch was established under the Articles of Confederation, and so many of the powers given to the executive branch in the US Constitution were assumed by "the United States in Congress Assembled" under the Articles of Confederation.

The United States in Congress assembled shall have authority to appoint a committee, to sit in the recess of Congress, to be denominated "A Committee of the States", and to consist of one delegate from each state; and to appoint such other committees and civil officers as may be necessary for managing the general affairs of the United States under their direction — to appoint one of their number to preside, provided that no person be allowed to serve in the office of president more than one year in any term of three years; to ascertain the necessary sums of money to be raised for the service of the United States, and to appropriate and apply the same for defraying the public expense — to borrow money, or emit bills on the credit of the United States [See Article I, Section 8.2 of the US Constitution.] transmitting every half-year to the respective states an account of the sums of money so borrowed or emitted — to build and equip a navy — to agree upon the number of land forces, and to make requisitions from each state for its quota, in proportion to the number of white inhabitants [no mention of slaves in determining these requisitions (taxes)] in such state; which requisition shall be binding, and thereupon the legislature of each state shall appoint the regimental officers, raise the men and cloath [sic], arm and equip them in a solid-like manner, at the expense of the United States; and the officers and men so cloathed [sic], armed, and equipped shall march to the place appointed, and within the time agreed on by the United States in Congress assembled. But if the United States in Congress assembled shall, on consideration of circumstances judge proper that any state should not raise men, or should raise a smaller number than its quota, and that any other state should raise a greater number of men than the quota thereof, such extra number shall be raised, officered, cloathed [sic], armed, and equipped in the same manner as the quota of such state, unless the legislature of such state shall judge that such extra number cannot be safely spared out of the same, in which case they shall raise, officer, cloath [sic], arm, and equip as many of such extra number as they judge can be safely spared. And the officers and men so cloathed [sic], armed, and equipped, shall march to the place appointed, and within the time agreed on by the United States in Congress assembled.

The United States in Congress assembled shall never engage in a war, nor grant letters of marque and reprisal in time of peace [although retaining that power during times of war], nor enter into any treaties or alliances, nor coin money, nor regulate the value thereof, nor ascertain the sums and expenses necessary for the defence and welfare of the United States, or any of them, nor emit bills, nor borrow money on the credit of the United States, nor appropriate money, nor agree upon the number of vessels of war, to be built or purchased, or the number of land or sea forces to be raised, nor appoint a commander in chief of the army or navy, unless nine states [the same number of states later required for ratification of the Constitution] assent to the same: nor shall a question on any other point, except for adjourning from day to day be determined, unless by the votes of a majority of the United States in Congress assembled.

The US Constitution unconditionally assigns to Congress, under Article I, Section 8, many powers enumerated above that required states' approval under the Articles of Confederation.

The Congress of the United States shall have power to adjourn to any time within the year, and to any place within the United States, so that no period of adjournment be for a longer duration than the space of six months, and shall publish the journal of their proceedings monthly, except such parts thereof relating to treaties, alliances or military operations, as in their judgment require secrecy; and the yeas and nays of the delegates of each state on any question shall be entered on the journal, when it is desired by any delegate; and delegates of a state, or any of them, at his or their request shall be furnished with a transcript of the said journal, except such parts as are above excepted, to lay before the legislatures of the several states.

What we see repeatedly throughout these articles is a desire not to infringe upon states' rights, to keep the power of the confederation dependent upon the legislatures of the individual states. This issue will continue to be important throughout the upcoming Constitution Convention debates.

X.   The Committee of the States, or any nine of them, Shall be authorized to execute, in the recess of Congress, such of the powers of Congress as the United States in Congress assembled, by the consent of nine states, shall from time to time think expedient to vest them with; provided that no power be delegated to the said Committee, for the exercise of which, by the Articles of Confederation, the voice of nine states in the Congress of the United States assembled is requisite.

This simply means that no Committees, appointed pursuant to Section IV above, shall ever assume any powers of Congress without the consent of at least nine of the States.

XI.   Canada **acceding** to this confederation, and joining in the measures of the United States, shall be admitted into, and entitled to all the advantages of this union; but no other Colony shall be admitted into the same, unless such admission be agreed to by nine states.

XII.   All **bills of credit** emitted [issued], monies borrowed, and debts contracted by, or under the authority of Congress, before the assembling of the United States, in pursuance of the present confederation, shall be deemed and considered as a charge against the United States, for payment and satisfaction whereof the said United States, and the public faith are hereby solemnly pledged.

XIII. Every state shall abide by the determinations of the United States in Congress assembled, on all questions which by this confederation are submitted to them. And the Articles of this Confederation shall be inviolably observed by every state, and the union shall be perpetual; nor shall any alteration at any time hereafter be made in any of them; unless such alteration be agreed to in a Congress of the United States, and be afterwards confirmed by the legislatures of every state.

The Articles of Confederation required ratification by all thirteen states, whereas the United States Constitution required ratification by only nine states. Amending the Articles of Confederation also required assent by all thirteen states; the procedures to amend the US Constitution require ratification by three-fourths of the several states.

And Whereas it hath pleased the Great Governor of the World [I assume this means with God's blessings.] to incline the hearts of the legislatures we respectively represent in Congress, to approve of, and to authorize us to ratify the said articles of confederation and perpetual union. Know Ye that we the undersigned delegates, by virtue of the power and authority to us given for that purpose, do by these presents, in the name and in behalf of our respective constituents, fully and entirely ratify and confirm each and every of the said articles of confederation and perpetual union, and all and singular the matters and things therein contained: And we do further solemnly plight and engage the faith of our respective constituents, that they shall abide by the determinations of the United States in Congress assembled, on all questions, which by the said confederation are submitted to them. And that the articles thereof shall be inviolably observed by the states we respectively represent, and that the union shall be perpetual. In Witness whereof, we have hereunto set our hands in Congress.

NEW HAMPSHIRE (August 8, 1778)
    Josiah Bartlett
    John Wentworth, junr

MASSACHUSETTS BAY
    John Hancock
    Samuel Adams
    Elbridge Gerry
    Francis Dana
    James Lovell
    Samuel Holten

STATE OF RHODE-ISLAND AND PROVIDENCE PLANTA-
TIONS
        William Ellery
        Henry Marchant
        John Collins

CONNECTICUT
        Roger Sherman
        Samuel Huntington
        Oliver Wolcott
        Titus Hosmer
        Andrew Adams

NEW YORK
        Jas Duane
        Fra: Lewis
        Wm Duer
        Gouvr Morris

NEW JERSEY (November 26, 1778)
        Jno Witherspoon
        Nathl Scudder

PENNSYLVANIA (July 22, 1778)
        Robert Morris
        Daniel Roberdeau
        Jon. Bayard Smith
        William Clingar
        Joseph Reed

DELAWARE (February 22, 1779)
        Thos Mckean
        John Dickinson
        Nicholas Van Dyke

MARYLAND (March 1, 1781)
        John Hanson
        Daniel Carroll, do

VIRGINIA (December 16, 1777)
        Richard Henry Lee,
        John Banister,
        Thomas Adams,
        Jno Harvie,
        Francis Lightfoot Lee

NORTH CAROLINA (July 21, 1778)
John Penn,
Corns Harnett,
Jno Williams

SOUTH CAROLINA (February 5, 1778)
Henry Laurens,
William Henry Drayton,
Jno Mathews,
Richd Hutson,
Thos Heyward, junr.

GEORGIA (July 24, 1778)
Jno Walton,
Edwd Telfair,
Edwd Langworthy

Although the Articles were finished in November 1777, they were not ratified until March of 1781. Ben Franklin had presented the first proposal for confederation of the colonies to the Continental Congress in 1775. Many delegates had still been hopeful of reconciliation with England, however, and because they feared that a confederation would lead to a declaration of independence, Franklin's plan had foundered, unapproved. In June of 1776, a subsequent draft was written by John Dickinson just thirty days later, and Dickinson's draft became the model for the final version of the Articles of Confederation. Dickinson declined to sign the Declaration of Independence, believing the states should first complete the Articles of Confederation and secure a foreign alliance.

> The main hindrance to the establishment of a strong, overruling central force was an unwillingness of the separate states to give up power, and reluctance to establish it in hands other than their own. There was not at that time one civilian who fully comprehended the need of the country, or was fit to be the architect of a permanent national constitution; and zeal to guard against the predominance of the central power heightened the imperfections which had their deep root in the history of the states.

> Every English administration had aimed at acquiring the disposal of the military resources and revenues of the Colonies, while every American legislature had constantly resisted encroachments. This resistance, developed and confirmed by successive generations, had become the instinct and habit of the people.

> In raising a revenue, the Colonies had acknowledged in the king no function whatever except that of addressing to them severally

requisitions which they, after deliberation and consent, were to collect by their own separate power. The confederacy now stood in the place of the crown as the central authority; and to that federal union the Colonies, by general concurrence, proposed to confide only the same limited right of making requisitions.
—George Bancroft, *History of the United States of America,* Vol. V
D. Appleton and Company, 1895, p. 10

Representation in the Congress was a major issue between the small and large states during the debates regarding the Articles of Confederation, and it would continue to be during the Constitutional Convention; the small states wanted equal representation, and the large states wanted representation proportional to population.

The northern states wanted to count slaves in determining taxes, and the southern states did not. "Our slaves are our property; if that is debated, there is an end of confederation. Being our property, why should they be taxed more than sheep?" said Lynch of South Carolina. Replied Franklin: "There is a difference; sheep will never make insurrections."

"To exempt slaves from taxation," said Wilson of Pennsylvania, "will be the greatest encouragement to slave-keeping and the importation of slaves, on which it is our duty to lay every discouragement. Slaves increase profits, which the southern states take to themselves; they increase the burden of defence, which must fall so much the more heavily on the northern. Slaves prevent freemen from cultivating a country. Dismiss your slaves, and freemen will take their places."

Another point of major disagreement was the conflict of claims to the ungranted territories that before the Declaration of Independence belonged to the King of England: "The king had possessed all land not alienated by royal grants. On the declaration of independence, the royal quitrents ceased to be paid; and each state assumed the ownership of the royal domain within its limits. The validity of the act of parliament which transferred the region north-west of the Ohio to the province of Quebec was denied by all; but the states which by their charters extended indefinitely west, or west and north-west, refused to accept the United States as the umpire to settle their boundaries, except with regard to each other."*

The weaknesses of the Articles of Confederation have already been discussed in Chapter I. It must be remembered, however, that at the time the articles were written, the colonies had just begun a war with England over mistreatment by a central power, and transferring that same power to another central government was unacceptable.

---

*George Bancroft, *History of the United States of America,* Vol. V (D. Appleton and Company, 1895, pp. 203–204)

Yet the young republic failed in its first effort at forming a general union. The smoke in the flame overpowered the light. The articles of confederation endeavored to reconcile a partial sovereignty in the union with complete sovereignty in the states, to subvert a mathematical axiom by taking away a part and letting the whole remain. The polity then formed could hardly be called an organization, so little did the parts mutually correspond and concur to the same final actions. The system was imperfect, and was acknowledged to be imperfect. A better one could not then have been accepted; but with all its faults it contained the elements for the evolution of a more perfect union. The sentiment of nationality was forming. The framers of the confederacy would not admit into that instrument the name of the people of the United States, and described the states as so many sovereign and independent communities; yet already in the circular letter of November 1777 to the states, asking their several subscriptions to the plan of confederacy, they avowed the purpose to secure to the inhabitants of all the states an "existence as a free people." The child that was then born was cradled between opposing powers of evil; if it will live, its infant strength must strangle the twin serpents of separatism and central despotism.

—George Bancroft, *History of the United States of America,* Vol. V
D. Appleton and Company, 1895, p. 208

CHAPTER IV

THE CONSTITUTION OF THE UNITED STATES

We the people of the United States [This term had been used in the Declaration of Independence and the Articles of Confederation.], in order to form a more perfect union [than existed under the Articles of Confederation], establish justice, insure domestic tranquility, provide for the common defense, promote the general welfare, and secure the blessings of liberty to ourselves and our posterity, do ordain and establish this Constitution for [Care was taken to use "for" instead of "of."] the United States of America.

"Establish justice, insure domestic tranquility, provide for the common defense, promote the general welfare," are merely generalized goals; the specific remedies and powers given to and limitations placed upon our national government are outlined in great detail in the specific articles of our Constitution that follow.

It is important to remember that when the Constitutional Convention convened, many of the delegates intended to merely modify the Articles of Confederation, not discard them entirely and replace them with a national constitution. After it became apparent that the Articles of Confederation were to be discarded and replaced with a new federal constitution, the Founding Fathers realized that maintaining some similarity between the existing Articles of Confederation and the new constitution would help assure approval by the majority of the delegates; therefore, we see many phrases in the Constitution that are nearly identical to those in the Articles of Confederation. These similarities will be cross-referenced as we proceed with the detailed review of the Constitution.

The Constitution purposely begins with "We the people" to emphasize that the citizens of America were to be united in a government that represented them more as citizens of the United States than as citizens of individual states.

James Madison, when comparing the Articles of Confederation with the Constitution, stated "The difference between a system founded on the [state] legislatures only [the Articles of Confederation] and one founded on the people is the difference between a treaty and a constitution. A law violating a treaty, ratified by a pre-existing law, might be respected by the judges; a law violating a constitution established by the people themselves would be considered by the judges as null and void [right of judicial review]. A breach of any one article of a treaty by any one of the parties frees the other parties from their engagements; a union of the people, under one constitution, by its nature excludes such an interpretation."

ARTICLE I

Section 1   All legislative powers herein granted shall be vested in a Congress of the United States, which shall consist of a Senate and House of Representatives.

More than half of the state constitutions that existed at the time of the Constitutional Convention had created two-branch state legislatures. What was unique and a very important compromise negotiated during the convention, however, was the equal state representation in the Senate and the representation in the House based on individual states' populations.

The federal congress that existed prior to ratification of this Constitution was composed of delegates appointed by the individual states' legislatures, and each state was given equal representation, regardless of its population or wealth. Many of the delegates to the Constitutional Convention believed it their mission to merely amend the Articles of Confederation; some believed it proper to do whatever necessary to save the union as already existed; and others (those from Delaware) felt prevented by their commissions (to attend the Constitutional Convention) from significantly changing the Articles of Confederation and even threatened to "retire from the Convention if forced to assent to any change of the rule of suffrage." The five delegates from Delaware remained at the convention, however, and unanimously signed the Constitution. Rhode Island, however, did not send any delegates to the Convention because of fear that the Articles of Confederation may be entirely revoked and also because they, being a major issuer of paper money, feared monetary reform (Article I, Section 10.1).

Edmund Randolph, on May 29, presented a plan, later to be known as the Randolph or Virginia Plan, proposing a national legislature, composed of two branches, one elected by the people of the several states, and the other branch chosen by the members of the first branch. The populations of the individual states, however, would determine the number of members in both branches. The delegates from the large states, of course, favored the Virginia Plan.

Although proposals were made for both a one- and a two-branch legislature, James Wilson from Pennsylvania probably showed the most insight when he said, "If the Legislative authority be not restrained, there can be neither liberty nor stability; and it can only be restrained by dividing it within itself, into distinct and independent branches. In a single House there is no check, but the inadequate one, of the virtue and good sense of those who compose it." Mr. Wilson certainly recognized the dangers of intrigue.

John Dickinson, then representing Delaware, was the first to propose equal state representation in one branch and proportional representation in the other. On June 2, he proposed "that each State would retain an equal voice at least in one branch of the National Legislature, and supposed the sums paid within each State would form a better ration for the other branch than either the number of inhabitants or the quantum of property." His proposal for representation based on "sums paid" would, however, be replaced with "according to their respective numbers."

James Madison on June 13 summarized what he felt to be the most serious short-comings of the Articles of Confederation and gave his reasons why the Randolph Plan (Virginia Plan) offered the more effective cures. First, treaties enacted with foreign nations under the Articles of Confederation were unenforceable: "The files of Congress contain complaints already, from almost every nation with which treaties have been formed. This can not be the permanent disposition of foreign nations. A rupture with other powers is among the greatest of national calamities." Second, it did nothing to prevent "encroachments on the federal authority." Individual states had already entered into treaties with various Indian nations, entered into compacts between themselves, and raised state militias. Mr. Madison supported the Virginia, or Randolph, Plan, and his persuasiveness was instrumental in dooming the Paterson Plan (New Jersey Plan).

> Section 2.1 [Article I] The House of Representatives shall be composed of members chosen every second year [chosen every year under the Articles of Confederation] by the people of the several States, and the electors in each State shall have the qualifications requisite for electors of the most numerous branch of the State legislature.

In North Carolina, as per Article VII and VIII of the North Carolina State Constitution (December 18, 1776), the electors were required to have paid public taxes to vote for representatives and be landowners to vote for the senate. Other states had their own voting restrictions and requirements; subsequent constitutional amendments have placed the voters in all states on more equal footing. Leaving the voting requirements to the individual states was a concession to retention of some states' rights.

The method of choosing the national legislature was often debated during the Constitutional Convention. Roger Sherman of Connecticut opposed election by the people, insisting that it "ought to be" by the state legislatures: "The people immediately should have as little to do as may be about the Government." Mr. George Mason of Virginia argued strongly for an election of the larger branch of the national legislature by the people: "It ought to be the grand depository of the democratic principle of the Government." James Wilson of Pennsylvania contended strenuously "for drawing the most numerous branch of the Legislature immediately from the people." Elbridge Gerry of Massachusetts did not like the idea of election by the people: "The evils we experience flow from the excess of democracy. The people do not want [lack] virtue, but are the dupes of pretended patriots. Experience had shown that the State legislatures drawn immediately from the people did not always possess their confidence." James Madison of Virginia felt the election by the people of one branch of the national legislature essential to every plan of free government:

"In some of the States one branch of the Legislature was composed of men already removed from the people by an intervening body of electors. That if the first branch of the general legislature should be elected by the State Legislatures, the second branch elected by the first—the Executive by the second together with the first; and other appointments again made for subordinate purposes by the Executive, the people would be lost sight of altogether; and the necessary sympathy between them and their rulers and officers, too little felt." James Wilson of Pennsylvania argued, "On examination it would be found that the opposition of States to federal measures had proceeded much more from the officers of the States, than from the people at large. No government could long subsist without the confidence of the people. There is no danger of improper elections if made by large districts. Bad elections proceed from the smallness of the districts which give an opportunity to bad men to intrigue [to plot] themselves into office." It was decided by majority vote on May 31 to suspend this discussion until a later date. The election by the people of the most numerous branch (House of Representatives) of the national legislature would ultimately prevail, however.

Biennial elections for the House were quickly agreed to after proposals were heard for elections ranging from one year to three years.

The issue of who would choose the members of the first branch [House of Representatives] was again taken up on June 6. Mr. Cotesworth Pinckney moved "that the first branch of the National Legislature be elected by the State Legislatures, and not by the people." Mr. Sherman thought if the new national government was to replace entirely the existing state governments, elections should be by the people, otherwise, "in order to preserve harmony between the National and State Government that the elections to the National should be made by the States." He thought the right of the people to participate in the national government would be ensured by their election of the state legislatures.

William Pierce from Virginia favored "an election by the people as to the first branch and by the States as to the second branch; by which means the Citizens of the States would be represented both individually and collectively."

During the first two weeks of the convention, the legislative branch was the main topic of debate. It was agreed upon early that the national legislature would consist of two branches, but how each branch would be elected and how representation would be weighted among the states was a more difficult proposition. We have seen that some of the delegates favored election by the state legislatures and some favored election by the people. Mr. Pierce's proposal that one branch be elected by the people and the other by the state legislatures planted the seed of compromise that would mold itself into the final draft of the Constitution.

As the debates over the legislative branch continued, it became apparent that the people would elect the House members and that the election of the senators would be made by the state legislatures. This would help ease friction between the states and the national government and would secure the support of the citizens with their direct involvement in national elections. Mr. King still favored election of both branches by the people (finally realized by passage of the Seventeenth Amendment on April 8, 1913): "If one branch of it should be chosen by the Legislatures, and the other by the people, the two branches will rest on different foundations, and dissensions will naturally arise between them." The strength of contemporary political parties has by itself created significant and constant dissensions.

Mr. Read of Delaware made his second motion of the convention when, on June 7, he proposed that "the Senate should be appointed by the Executive Magistrate out of a proper number of persons to be nominated by the individual legislatures." This motion, as with his first motion proposing that the national government should swallow up the state legislatures, found very little support.

Although he was unsure how many members would be most beneficial in each branch, Mr. Dickinson was in favor of the members of the most numerous branch being elected by the people and the members of the less numerous branch appointed by the state legislatures.

On June 12, before the final format for determining representation quotas among the various states had been agreed to, the motion was brought up for discussion regarding term lengths in the house branch of the legislature. As usual, there were numerous suggestions from the various delegates. Mr. Daniel Jenifer from Maryland favored "every three years," observing that too great frequency of elections "rendered the people indifferent to them, and made the best men unwilling to engage in so precarious a service." James Madison seconded the motion for three years, stating, "Instability is one of the great vices of our republic, to be remedied. Three years will be necessary, in a Government so extensive, for members to form any knowledge of the various interests of the States to which they do not belong, and of which they can know but little from the situation and affairs of their own."

Mr. Gerry, contemplating that the people of New England "will never give up the point of annual elections, they know of the transition made in England from triennial to septennial elections, and will consider such an innovation here as the prelude to a like usurpation," considered annual elections as "the only defence of the people against tyranny." Mr. Madison responded that because it would be difficult to know what the opinions of the people were, "we ought to consider what was right and necessary in itself for the attainment of a proper Government—the respectability of this convention will give weight to their recommendation of it." The motion for a triennial election of the first branch passed 7-3.

On June 16, Pennsylvania's James Wilson summed up for the delegates the main differences between the Randolph Plan and the Paterson Plan. After hearing Mr. John Lansing support the Paterson Plan because "we lack the power to discuss and propose the Randolph Plan" and "the improbability of its being adopted," Mr. Wilson considered himself "authorized to conclude nothing, but to be at liberty to propose anything"; with regard to the sentiments of the people, he "conceived it difficult to know precisely what they are." Most of the representatives attending the convention agreed with Mr. Randolph that the Articles of Confederation had not been successful and that "a National Government alone, properly constituted, will answer the purpose; and it should be considered that the present is the last moment for establishing one. After this select experiment, the people will yield to despair."

Alexander Hamilton spoke for the first time on June 18. He had remained silent up till now "partly from respect to others whose superior abilities, age, and experience rendered him unwilling to bring forward ideas dissimilar to theirs." Although he certainly favored the Randolph Plan to the Paterson Plan, Hamilton desired a stronger national government than either proposed. Hamilton wanted the "supreme Executive to be chosen by electors appointed by the people from designated election districts and to serve during good behavior." He proposed that the supreme legislature be composed of two branches: the Assembly, elected by the people every three years, and the Senate, elected by the same electors who chose the executive, and that the Senate also serve during times of good behavior. The executive was to have veto power over all legislation and to be responsible for the execution of all laws passed, to "have the direction of war when authorized or begun; to have with the advice and approbation of the Senate the power of making all treaties, to appoint, with Senate approval, the heads of Finance, War, and Foreign Affairs, and to have the power of pardoning all offences except Treason; which he shall not pardon without the approbation of the Senate." Hamilton's plan also called for the sole power of declaring war and for advising the executive and approving treaties to be placed in the hands of the Senate. His plan also was the first to suggest that the national judiciary should have original jurisdiction in some areas and **appellate** in others. Although Hamilton's plan, which took five hours to present, intended to create a stronger national government than most delegates preferred, many of his ideas were incorporated into the final draft of our Constitution.

> Section 2.2   [Article I] No person shall be a representative who shall not have attained to the age of twenty-five years, and been seven years a citizen of the United States, and who shall not, when elected, be an inhabitant [Many of the states required at least one year of prior residence.] of that State in which he shall be chosen.

Virginia's George Mason moved to include "twenty-five years of age as a qualification for the members of the 1st branch" because "he would if interrogated be obliged to declare that his political opinions at the age of 21 were too crude and erroneous to merit an influence on public measures."

Colonel Mason also proposed that the time of citizenship be increased from three, as originally proposed, to seven years. Gouverneur Morris seconded the motion, and it passed in the affirmative by all states except Connecticut.

Discussions followed suggesting that a period of residency within the particular state be required, but Mr. Read reminded the delegates that they were attempting to form a national government and such a regulation "would correspond little with the idea that we were one people." The more I think about Mr. Read's reasoning, the wiser I believe it to be.

Roger Sherman moved to replace the word "resident" with "inhabitant," which was seconded by Madison. The discussions that followed seem to imply more permanency with the word "inhabitant" than "resident," which was why "inhabitant" was ultimately chosen. In either case, there was no gender restriction.

> Section 2.3 [Article I] Representatives and **direct taxes** shall be **apportioned** among the several States which may be included within this Union, according to their respective numbers [population], which shall be determined by adding to the whole number of free persons, including those bound to service for a term of years, and excluding Indians not taxed, three fifths of all other persons. ["All other persons" were slaves; the "three-fifths" provision has, however, been effactually nullified by the Thirteenth and Fourteenth Amendments.] The actual enumeration shall be made within three years after the first meeting of the Congress of the United States, and within every subsequent term of ten years, in such manner as they shall by law direct. The number of representatives shall not exceed [it can, however, be less than and because of population increases, now stands at approximately one representative for every 550,000 persons] one for every thirty thousand, but each State shall have at least one representative; and until such enumeration shall be made, the State of New Hampshire shall be entitled to choose three, Massachusetts eight, Rhode Island and Providence Plantations one, Connecticut five, New York six, New Jersey four, Pennsylvania eight, Delaware one, Maryland six, Virginia ten, North Carolina five, South Carolina five, and Georgia three.

Article I, Section 2.3, dealing primarily with how to allocate representation to each state, contains three words ("and direct taxes") that have caused more debate, disagreement, and litigation than all the rest of this section combined. As early as 1794, during only the Third Federal Congress, legislation "laying duties upon carriages for the conveyance of persons" was passed by vote of 49-22, even though objected to by

James Madison (representative from Virginia) on the grounds that he believed the tax to be unconstitutional. The legality of this tax was eventually argued before the Supreme Court (*Hylton v. United States;* the Supreme Court failing to amend the ruling by the circuit court that the law was constitutional due to it not being a direct tax) in 1796. The problem was first to determine the intended meaning of "direct tax" and then to decide if this "carriage tax" was indeed a direct tax and, ultimately if it was a direct tax, had it been apportioned as required by the constitutional guidelines. (Hylton was misspelled; the defendant in this case was Daniel Hilton.)

It is quite evident to me that direct taxes were to be imposed upon the states, not upon the individual citizens. To imply that this carriage tax was to be collected directly from every person in the United States, when the source of the payment would include slaves (to be counted as three-fifths in the apportionment) who had no means to pay taxes, and collected from those people who did not own any carriages is absurd. Direct taxes were clearly to be assessed against each state according to the census that was demanded "within three years after the first meeting of the Congress" to be taken. The power to determine how to pay these "direct taxes" resides within each state, not within the federal government. It is also quite clear, considering that land or property has no common value and the "average" earning power of individual citizens is meaningless, that a fair "direct tax" is probably impossible to achieve.

The passage of the Sixteenth Amendment (giving Congress the authority to enact almost any type of tax legislation imaginable) in effect voided the restriction dealing with apportionment of direct taxes to the states.

> I am inclined to think, but of this I do not give a judicial opinion, that the direct taxes contemplated by the constitution, are only two, to wit, a **capitation** or **poll** tax, simply, without regard to property, profession or any other circumstance; and a tax on land. I doubt, whether a tax, by a general assessment of personal property, within the United States, is included within the term direct tax."
> —Justice Chase (*Hylton v. United States*), *The Founders' Constitution,* Vol. 3
> University of Chicago Press, 1987, pp. 358–359

> It was, however, obviously the intention of the framers of the constitution, that congress should possess full power over every species of taxable property, except exports [Article I, Section 9.5]. The term taxes, is generical, and was made use of, to vest in congress **plenary** authority in all cases of taxation. The general division of taxes is into direct and indirect; although the latter term is not to be found in the constitution, yet the former necessarily implies it; indirect stands

opposed to direct. There may, perhaps, be an indirect tax on a particular article that cannot be comprehended within the description of duties, or imposts or **excises**; in such case, it will be comprised under the general denomination of taxes. For the term tax is the genus, and includes: 1. Direct taxes. 2. Duties, imposts and excises. 3. All other classes of an indirect kind, and not within any of the classifications enumerated under the preceding heads.
—Justice Paterson (Constitutional Convention delegate from New Jersey), *The Founders' Constitution*, Vol. 3
University of Chicago Press, 1987, p. 359

Primarily as a result of the 1895 Supreme Court decision in *Pollack v. Farmers' Loan & Trust Co*, which struck down the Income Tax Act of 1894, the Sixteenth Amendment (granting power to the national government to directly tax individuals' personal income) was passed in 1913. Originally, our national government was to be financed by the state treasuries plus indirect national taxes as enumerated in Article I, Section 8.1.

I see an extremely dangerous precedent being set with the ruling that the Affordable Health Care Act is constitutional. Many members of Congress and citizens thought the act was unconstitutional, because providing federal health care is clearly not set forth as one of the obligations or privileges of the government of the United States pursuant to Article I, Sections 8.1–8.18, and because the Tenth Amendment, which was adopted on December 15, 1791, as part of the original Bill of Rights, clearly states, "The powers not delegated to the United States by the Constitution, nor prohibited by it to the States, are reserved to the States respectively, or to the people." However, and here is the scary part, the Affordable Health Care Act was ruled constitutional because of the interpretation that the Health Care Act falls under Congress's power to tax. Because of the Sixteenth Amendment, which gives the federal government the right to "lay and collect taxes on incomes from whatever source derived, without apportionment among the several States, and without regard to any census or enumeration," I foresee the federal government assuming the right to impose upon the citizens unlimited laws and regulations, proclaiming that because those programs are to be funded by the citizens, they are really just another form of taxation. We cannot continue to be complacent about who is running our government and why so much money is spent to get elected.

Representation in the House had been set at one per forty thousand until September 17, the last day of the convention, when Massachusetts's National Gorham suggested "to strike out forty thousand, and insert thirty thousand. This would not establish that as an absolute rule, but only give Congress a greater latitude which could not be thought unreasonable." George Washington, speaking for the first time except for when he had voted as a Virginia representative, stated, "The smallness of the proportion of Representatives had been considered by many members of the Convention an insufficient security for the rights and interests of the People, and had always appeared to me among the exceptionable parts of the plan; I think this of so much consequence that it would give me much satisfaction to see it adopted." This change was agreed to unanimously.

The idea of including slaves as three-fifths of the number of freemen when setting states' tax obligations proportional to states' populations in lieu of "property values" was first proposed by James Madison in 1783 as an amendment to the Articles of Confederation. This compromise was hoped to appease the rift between opposing northern and southern states' demands. The Continental Congress was desperately trying to find acceptable funding methods to pay the Revolutionary War soldiers. The Continental Army had effectually gone unpaid since the beginning of the war. Without an emotional appeal to General Gates and a group of officers by Washington himself it is quite likely that many of the army soldiers would have mutinied and the country fallen prey to Britain. This meeting took place at Newburg, New York. The proposed amendment was not ratified, and the United States continued to flounder.

On July 5, a committee composed of one delegate from each state proposed that "in the 1st branch of the Legislature each of the States now in the Union shall be allowed 1 member for every 40,000 inhabitants." Objections were voiced from almost every direction. Mr. Gouverneur Morris objected "to the scale of apportionment." He thought property ought to be taken into the estimate as well as the number of inhabitants, and stated, "Slavery [is] a **nefarious** institution. It [is] the curse of heaven on the States where it prevail[s]. Upon what principle is it that the slaves shall be computed in the representation? Are they men? Then make them Citizens and let them vote. Are they property? Why then is no other property included?" South Carolina's John Rutledge expressed his own belief that "the suffrages of the several States be regulated and proportioned according to the sums to be paid towards the general revenue by the inhabitants of each State respectively." As more delegates put forth their opinions, compromise seemed to be slipping away.

Charles Pinckney of South Carolina may have restored some singularity to the discussion when (July 6) he reminded the other delegates that "the value of land [the cornerstone for taxation under the Articles of Confederation] had been found on full investigation to be an impracticable rule. The contributions of revenue including imports and exports must be too changeable in their amount; too difficult to be adjusted and too injurious to the non-commercial States." The number of inhabitants, including three-fifths of "blacks" appeared to him the only "just and practicable rule."

Mr. Rufus King of Massachusetts, on July 9, stated that he had "always expected that as the Southern States are the richest, they would not league themselves with the North unless some respect were paid to their superior wealth. If the Northern States expect those preferential distinctions in Commerce and other advantages which they will derive from the connection, they must not expect to receive them without allowing some advantages in return. Eleven out of the thirteen States had agreed to consider slaves in the apportionment of taxation; and taxation and Representation ought to go together." Survival of our new nation depended upon unification of the north and south. The climatic conditions that united the accumulation of wealth with slavery in the south and precluded their connection in the north would continue to be a source of discontentment between their respective citizens and would ultimately lead to the Civil War.

The specific number of representatives set forth in Article I, Section 3.3 above was first put before the convention on July 10. The numbers were considered too high by some and too low by others. The southern states wanted more weight given to their wealth and their slaves. James Madison moved "that the number allowed to each State be doubled," whereas Mr. Ellsworth urged "the greater the number, the greater the expense and the slower the business would proceed." Many of the delegates felt obligated to **expound** their personal opinions, but in the end, because of the urgency of their common cause, compromise won the day.

Delaware's Jacob Broom may have planted the seed for approval of equal representation in the Senate when he gave notice to the convention, after voting in favor of the proposed representation in the House, that "he had concurred with a reserve to himself of an intention to claim for his State an equal voice in the 2nd branch, which he thought could not be denied after this concession of the small States as to the first branch."

There was also much discussion about crediting the southern states for only three-fifths of their slaves when determining representation in the national legislature. Mr. King (Thursday, July 12), representing the northern state of Massachusetts, thought "the admission of them [slaves] along with Whites at all, would excite great discontents among the States having no slaves." James Wilson "did not well see on what principle the admission of blacks in the proportion of three fifths could be explained. Are they admitted as Citizens then why are they not admitted on equality with White Citizens? Are they admitted as property, then why is not other property admitted into the computation?" Gouverneur Morris (Pennsylvania) declared himself "reduced to the dilemma of doing injustice to the Southern States or to human nature." He could never agree "to give such encouragement to the slave trade as would be given by allowing them a representation for their Negroes," and he did not believe "those States would ever confederate on terms that would deprive them of that trade." Gouverneur Morris also proposed that whatever formula be decided upon to determine representation, taxation "shall be in proportion to Representation." He later amended his proposal to include only "direct taxation," which excluded taxes on imports, exports, and consumption.

North Carolina's William Davie, rarely speaking at the convention, said, "I see it is meant by some gentlemen to deprive the Southern States of any share of Representation for their blacks. North Carolina will never confederate on any terms that did not rate them at least as three-fifths. If the Eastern States meant therefore to exclude them altogether the business is at an end." Edmund Randolph on July 12 "lamented that such a species of property existed. But as it did exist, the holders of it would require this security."

General Pinckney approved of Mr. Morris's plan and foresaw "that if the revision of the census was left to the discretion of the Legislature, it would never be carried into execution. The rule must be fixed, and the execution of it enforced by the Constitution."

On July 12, after numerous delegates expounded on why each proposal benefited their particular states, the basic terms of Article I, Section 2.3 were agreed to.

I find it somewhat strange that neither age nor gender were ever discussed when determining who were to be included as "free men."

> Section 2.4   [Article I] When vacancies happen in the representation from any State, the executive authority thereof [the state's governor] shall issue writs of election to fill such vacancies.

> Section 2.5   [Article I] The House of Representatives shall choose their speaker and other officers, and shall have the sole power of impeachment.

Only two presidents have been impeached: Andrew Johnson in 1868 and Bill Clinton in 1999; both were found not guilty by the Senate. Richard Nixon would probably have been impeached had he not resigned, and, if found guilty, could not have been pardoned (Article II, Section 2.1 of US Constitution) as he ultimately was by Gerald Ford.

> Section 3.1   [Article I] The Senate of the United States shall be composed of two Senators from each State [Congress, composed of only one branch, created under the Articles of Confederation, gave each state, large or small, one vote], chosen by the legislature thereof [of individual states] for six years [altered by the Seventeenth Amendment in 1913 to be elected by the people thereof]; and each senator shall have one vote.

Our two-branch legislature, comprised of the Senate, having equal representation from each state, and the House, having representation based upon state population, was the major compromise between the delegates.

George Mason, a constant proponent for the rights of the people, was of course in favor of the election of both houses of Congress by the citizens. "Under the existing confederacy," said Mason, "congress represents the states, and not the people of the states; their acts operate on the states, not on the individuals. In the new plan of government the people will be represented; they ought, therefore, to choose the representatives."

"If it is in view," said Sherman, "to abolish the state governments, the elections ought to be by the people. If they are to be continued, the elections to the national government should be made by them. I am for giving the general government power to legislate and execute within a defined providence. The objects of the union are few: defence against foreign danger, internal disputes, and a resort to force; treaties with foreign nations; the regulation of foreign commerce and drawing revenue from it. These, and perhaps a few lesser objects, alone render a confederation of the States necessary. All other matters, civil and criminal, will be much better left in the hands of the states." I think even men who shared Sherman's views could not have imagined a federal government as large and intrusive as ours.

James Madison considered "an election of one branch at least of the Legislature by the people immediately, as a clear principle of free Government." He agreed with Mr. Sherman that the obligations of the national government that Mr. had Sherman just presented were

> certainly important and necessary objects; but he combined with them the necessity of providing more effectually for the security of private rights, and the steady dispensation of Justice. Interferences with these [lack of security of private rights and unsteady dispensation of Justice] were evils which had more perhaps than any thing else, produced this convention. All civilized Societies would be divided into different Sects, Factions, and interests, as they happened to consist of rich & poor, debtors and creditors, the landed, the manufacturing, the commercial interests, the inhabitants of this district or that district, the followers of this political leader or that political leader, the disciples of this religious Sect or that religious Sect. In all cases where a majority are united by a common interest or passion, the rights of the minority are in danger. What motives are to restrain them? A prudent regard to the **maxim** that honesty is the best policy is found by experience to be as little regarded by bodies of men as by individuals. Respect for character is always diminished in proportion to the number among whom the blame or praise is to be divided. Conscience, the only remaining tie, is known to be inadequate in individuals: In large numbers, little is to be expected from it. Besides, Religion itself may become a motive to persecution and oppression. We have seen the mere distinction of colour made in the most enlightened period of time, a ground of the most oppressive dominion ever exercised by man over man. The only remedy is to enlarge the sphere, and thereby divide the community into so great a number of interests and parties, that in the

first place a majority will not be likely at the same moment to have a common interest separate from that of the whole or of the minority; and in the second place, that in case they should have such an interest, they may not be apt to unite in the pursuit of it. It was incumbent on us then to try this remedy, and with that view to frame a republican system on such a scale and in such a form as will controul [sic] all the evils which have been experienced."

I think Mr. Madison strayed a little from the issue of election methodology, but I find his words very prophetic and certainly worth repeating.

No topic invoked more debates than that which affected the legislative branch. In discussing Article I, Section 2.1, we have reviewed the speeches of many of the delegates relating to the House (the "first" or "most numerous" branch) and the Senate (the "second" branch). Almost all conceivable options, from equal representation in both branches and election by the people to representation based on state populations and election by the state legislatures, had been proposed and debated. During the first few weeks, the idea of one branch elected by the people and the other branch being elected by the state legislatures seemed to gain support. The matter of the size of each branch and the method of apportionment remained unsolved, however. The large states of course favored representation based on population, and the smaller states favored equal representation. James Madison favored the Senate to be smaller than the House. He reasoned, "Enlarge their number and you communicate to them the vices which they are meant to correct." He differed from Mr. Dickinson, who thought that the large number in the Senate would give additional weight to the body. "On the contrary," Madison said, "their weight would be in an inverse ratio to their number." He went on to give an example of how the Roman tribunes lost their influence and power in proportion as "their number was augmented."

Elbridge Gerry offered his reasons for desiring that the people should not elect the Senate: "The people have two great interests [comprise two predominant types of people], the landed interest [the farmers and ranchers], and the commercial including the stockholders [the merchants and business owners], the people being chiefly composed of the landed interest [being more populous than the commercial], and erroneously supposing, that the other interests are adverse to it." Mr. Gerry feared that to let the "landed interest" elect both branches of the national legislature would be unfair to the "commercial including the stockholders." The election of the Senate by the state legislatures eventually prevailed because of the desire of most of the delegates to retain as many "states' rights" as possible. We now know the Seventeenth Amendment placed the choosing of both branches in the hands of the people. Our country was much more diversified in 1913 (the date of ratification of the Seventeenth Amendment) than in 1787, and I suspect the fears expressed by Mr. Gerry either no longer existed or were considered unimportant. Influence of the national legislature by the state governments (because of the Seventeenth Amendment) has been significantly reduced, however. This notion of not having both Houses elected directly by the people was one of the few of the entire convention that passed unanimously.

> As such, the core of the problem with state's rights issues lies in the passage of the 17th Amendment in 1913, which abrogated the state legislatures' right to appoint United States Senators in favor of popular election of those officials. This amendment created a fundamental structural problem which, irrespective of the political party in office, or the laws in effect at any one time, will result, over time, in expanding federal control in every area.
>
> The 17th Amendment caused a failure in the federalist structure, federal deficit spending, inappropriate federal mandates, and federal control over a number of state institutions.
>
> The amendment has also caused a fundamental breakdown in campaign finance issues with respect to United States Senators. As to United States Senators, campaign finance reform, a hot topic in Congress now, can be best achieved by repealing the 17th Amendment to the United States Constitution. It should be readily apparent that United States Senators, once appointed by the state legislature, would have no need for campaign financing whatsoever.
> —John MacMullin, *Mises Daily,* Monday, October 23, 2000 (Ludwig von Mises Institute)

On June 8, the method of suffrage appropriated to the two branches of the national Legislature was again discussed. Although it had been agreed to that the people should elect one branch and the state legislatures the other, the amount of representation afforded each state was still undecided. David Brearly of New Jersey proposed an entirely new approach that, although overruled, summarized many of the difficulties to be overcome in developing a system that would be agreeable to both large and small states.

> Mr. BREARLY: He was sorry he said that any question on this point was brought into view. It had been very much agitated in Congress at the time of forming the Confederation, and was then rightly settled by allowing to each sovereign State an equal vote. Otherwise the smaller States must have been destroyed instead of being saved. The substitution of a ratio, he admitted carried fairness on the face of it; but on a deeper examination was unfair and unjust. Judging of the disparity of the States by the quota of Congress, Virginia would have 16 votes, and Georgia but one. A like proportion to the others will make the whole number ninety. There will be 3 large states, and 10 small ones. The large States by which he meant Mass., Penn, & Virg. Will carry every thing before them. It had been admitted, and was known to him from facts within N. Jersey that

75

where large & small counties were united into a district for electing representatives for the district, the large counties always carried their point, and consequently the large States would do so. While Georgia with her solitary vote, and the other little States will be obliged to throw themselves constantly into the scale of some large one, in order to have any weight at all. He had come to the convention with a view of being as useful as he could in giving energy and stability to the federal Government. When the proposition for destroying the equality of votes came forward, he was astonished, he was alarmed. Is it fair that it will be asked that Georgia should have an equal vote with Virg.? He would not say it was. What remedy then? One only, that a map of the U.S. be spread out, that all the existing boundaries be erased, and that a new partition of the whole be made into 13 equal parts."
—James Madison, *Notes of Debates in the Federal Convention of 1787* Ohio University Press, 1966, pp. 94–95

This proposal was voted down but the suggestion does however demonstrate the diversity of alternatives often discussed by many of the representatives at the convention.

Mr. Paterson considered the proposition for a proportional representation "as striking at the existence of the lesser States." He went on to explain that this convention was authorized under an act of the Congress of the Confederation and "that the articles of the Confederation were therefore the proper basis of all the proceedings of the Convention; we ought to keep within its limits, or we should be charged by our Constituents with usurpation, that the people of America were sharpsighted and not to be deceived." He went on to make the distinction between federal government, one that derives its power from the states, and national government, one that derives its power from the people. He was adamant in his opposition to proportional representation in the national legislature: "He would rather submit to a monarch, to a despot, than to such a fate. He would not only oppose the plan here but on his return home do every thing in his power to defeat it there."*

Mr. James Wilson from Pennsylvania, in contrast, favored representation based upon states' populations: "Equal numbers of people ought to have an equal number of representatives, and different numbers of people different numbers of representatives. We have been told that each State being sovereign, all are equal. So each man is naturally a sovereign over himself, and all men are therefore naturally equal. Can he retain this equality when he becomes a member of a Civil Government? He can not. If New Jersey [Mr. Patterson's state] will not part with her Sovereignty it is in vain to talk of [a new national] Gov. A new partition of the States is desireable, but evidently and

---

*James Madison, *Notes of Debates in the Federal Convention of 1787* (Ohio University Press, 1966, pp. 95–97)

totally impracticable." Because of the severity of the disagreement over individual states' representations, it was decided to adjourn and postpone the vote.

Madison added a different light to the issue regarding individual states' representation in the Senate: "The great danger to our general government is, that the southern and northern interests of the continent are opposed to each other, not from their difference of size, but from the climate, and principally from the effects of their having or not having slaves." Our Civil War some seventy years later seems to bear out Madison's foresight.

On June 11, Roger Sherman suggested what has become known as the Connecticut Compromise, whereby "the proportion of suffrage in the 1st branch should be according to the respective numbers of free inhabitants [excluding slaves]; and that in the second branch or Senate, each State should have one vote and no more." This simple proposal was to become the foundation of our unique national legislature and resolved the issue of equal state representation in at least one branch of Congress, which could have permanently stalled our Constitutional Convention.

> Next to Franklin, the oldest man in the convention, like Franklin he [Sherman] had had no education but in the common school of his birthplace; and as the one learned the trade of a tallow-chandler, so the other had been apprenticed to a shoemaker.
>
> Left at nineteen an orphan on the father's side, he ministered to his mother during her long life; and having suffered from the want of a liberal education, he provided it for his younger brothers.
>
> There was in him kind-heartedness and industry, penetration and close reasoning, an unclouded intellect, superiority to passion, intrepid patriotism, solid judgment, and a directness which went straight to its end. For nineteen years he was annually chosen one of the fourteen assistants, or upper house of the legislature; a judge of the court of common pleas; for twenty-three years, a judge of the superior court.
> —George Bancroft, *History of the Formation of the Constitution of the United States of America*, Vol. II
> D. Appleton and Company, 1882, p. 49

Also on June 11, John Dickinson made a unique proposal suggesting that "actual contributions [taxes submitted to the national government] of the states as the rule of their representation & suffrage in the first branch." By thus connecting "the interest of the States with their duty, the latter would be sure to be performed." I think this idea still has merit.

Rufus King of Massachusetts and Pierce Butler of South Carolina both thought property should be the basis of representation. This would have been difficult to implement, considering what should be considered property and who should determine its value.

June 11 was a pivotal day for the delegates. Up to this point, most of the discussions had been of a general nature: should the Articles of Confederation be modified or abolished, should the executive branch be a single person or a committee, should the members of Congress be appointed by the state legislatures or elected by the people, should the states be given equal representation or should representation be based on a state's size or wealth, should the executive branch have veto power over the legislative branch? Many questions had been asked, but few acceptable answers had been proposed. On this day, however, the motion by Mr. Wilson and Mr. Cotesworth Pinckney that "equitable ratio of representation, in proportion to the whole number of white & other free Citizens & inhabitants of every age, sex, and condition including those bound to servitude for a term of years, and three fifths of all other persons not comprehended in the foregoing description, except Indians not paying taxes, in each State," which is very similar to Article I, Section 2.3, was agreed to in principle. This was a very small step toward drafting our entire Constitution, but as Confucius is credited with saying, "Even the longest journey begins with first step."

On June 12, Richard Spaight, from North Carolina, and William Pierce, from Georgia, proposed that the Senate should be elected every seven years. Mr. Sherman, who preferred five years, thought seven years was too long: "If they did their duty well, they would be re-elected," and if they "acted amiss, an earlier opportunity [failure to be reelected rather than impeachment] should be allowed for getting rid of them." Mr. Pierce reasoned that "the democratic licentiousness of the State Legislatures proved the necessity of a firm Senate. The object of this 2nd branch is to controul [sic] the democratic branch of the National Legislature. If it be not a firm body, the other branch being more numerous, and coming immediately from the people, will overwhelm it. The Senate of Maryland constituted on like principles had been scarcely able to stem the popular torrent." I find it amusing that even in 1787, our government representatives referred to the citizens' wishes as "popular torrent." I suspect this must have been a "closed-door" session. ("If we're not careful, these dang voters will be telling *us* what to do.") The Senate's term was temporarily left at seven years.

The next discussions to resolve term lengths took place on June 26. The proposals ranged from four years to nine years. Many of the delegates made their recommendations based upon what they perceived to be the wishes of the people. James Wilson surmised that "every nation may be regarded in two relations: 1 to its own citizens and 2 to foreign nations. It is therefore not only liable to anarchy and tyranny within, but has wars to avoid and treaties to obtain from abroad. The Senate will probably be the depository of the powers concerning the latter objects. It ought therefore to be made respectable in the eyes of foreign nations. The true reason why Great Britain has not yet listened to a commercial treaty with us has been, because she had no confidence in the stability or efficacy of our Government." He thought nine years with a rotation would provide those desirable qualities. The states voted to set the term at six years.

We have spent much time reviewing the differing positions of the convention representatives regarding suffrage in the national legislature. The small states wanted equal representation, and the large states favored representation proportional to population or wealth. Some feared union by the large states against the smaller ones, while other delegates presented evidences that equally powerful bodies more often than not were adversaries instead of allies. Connecticut's Samuel Johnson reiterated earlier suggestions at compromise when on June 29 he shared with the other delegates, "On the whole I think that as in some respects the States are to be considered in their political capacity, and in others as districts of individual citizens, the two ideas embraced on different sides, instead of being opposed to each other, out [sic] to be combined; that in one branch the people out [sic] to be represented; in the other the States."

The debates over suffrage in the two branches of the national legislature and over the system of electing each branch continued unresolved until July 2. It was decided that a committee of one member from each state should be chosen and that the recommendations of the committees would be earnestly considered.

The report submitted on July 5 contained the following provisions:

1. The first branch should be allowed one member for every 40,000 free inhabitants.
2. All bills for appropriating or raising money, including salaries of the legislators, should originate in the first branch and be unamendable by the second branch.
3. No money shall be drawn from the national treasury except by appropriations of the first branch.
4. In the second branch, each state shall have an equal vote.

The committee's report did nothing more than focus on the areas of disagreement. Mr. Morris thought "the form as well as the matter of the Report objectionable. I came here to represent America; I came here in some degree as a Representative of the whole human race; for the whole human race will be affected by the proceedings of this Convention. I wish you gentlemen to extend your views beyond the present moment of time; beyond the narrow limits of place from which you derive your political origin. This Country must be united. If persuasion does not unite it, the sword will."

The Founding Fathers based their compromises on the assumption that the representatives of each state in both the Senate and the House of Representatives would vote as a unit because of the strong allegiances to their states. No one surmised that members of Congress would eventually be swayed more by their party affiliations than by the local wishes of their own constituents.

Section 3.2   [Article I] Immediately after they shall be assembled in consequence of the first election, they shall be divided as equally as may be into three classes. The seats of the senators of the first class shall be vacated at the expiration of the second year, of the second class at the expiration of the fourth year, and of the third class at the expiration of the sixth year, so that one third may be chosen every second year: and if vacancies happen by resignation, or otherwise, during the recess of the legislature of any State, the executive thereof may make temporary appointments until the next meeting of the legislature, which shall then fill such vacancies.

He has refused, for a long time after such dissolutions, to cause others to be elected; whereby the legislative powers, incapable of annihilation, have returned to the people at large for their exercise; the State remaining, in the meantime, exposed to all the dangers of invasion from without, and convulsions within.
—Declaration of Independence, paragraph 4

From the beginning, most of the delegates agreed that rotation of the elections would be a good way to maintain at least limited seniority and experience in the Senate at all times. The Seventeenth Amendment changed not only how the Senate is to be elected but also how vacancies were to be filled.

Section 3.3   [Article I] No person shall be a senator who shall not have attained to the age of thirty years, and been nine years a citizen of the United States, and who shall not, when elected, be an inhabitant [not a resident] of that State for which he shall be chosen.

The minimum age of thirty for senators was agreed to on June 12 with little debate and with dissension from only three states.

There was some debate about the requirements for prior term of citizenship. Governeur Morris moved "to insert 14 instead of 9 years citizenship: urging the danger of admitting strangers into our public Councils" and was seconded by Mr. Pinckney. Mr. Ellsworth was opposed to increasing to fourteen years as "discouraging meritorious aliens from emigrating to this Country."

Mr. Madison, although not averse to some restrictions, could never agree to fourteen years because "any restriction however in the Constitution would be unnecessary, and improper. Unnecessary because the National Legislature is to have the right of regulating naturalization, and can by virtue thereof fix different periods of residence as conditions of enjoying different privileges of Citizenship: improper because it will give a tincture of **illiberality** to the Constitution, because it will put it out of the power of the Natural Legislature even by special acts of naturalization to confer the full rank of Citizens on meritorious strangers and because it will discourage the most desireable class of people from emigrating to the U.S."

Pierce Butler of South Carolina was opposed to the admission of foreigners without a long residence in the country because "they bring with them, not only attachments to other Countries; but ideas of Government so distinct from ours that in every point of view they are dangerous."

Mr. James Wilson of Pennsylvania said, "To be appointed to a place may be a matter of indifference. To be incapable of being appointed, is a circumstance grating and mortifying."

It was finally agreed that one of the requirements to be elected to the Senate would be "nine years a citizen of the United States," two more than required for the House.

There were also discussions regarding property ownership as a prerequisite for election to the national legislature, a requirement already existing in some state constitutions.

> Mr. PINKNEY. The Committee as he had conceived were instructed to report the proper qualifications of property for the members of the National Legislature; instead of which they have referred the task to the National Legislature itself. Should it be left on this footing, the first Legislature will meet without any particular qualifications of property; and if it should happen to consist of rich men they might fix such qualifications as may be too favorable to the rich; if of poor men, an opposite extreme might be run into. He was opposed to the establishment of an undue aristocratic influence in the Constitution but he thought it essential that the members of the Legislature, the Executive, and the Judges, should be possessed of competent property to make them independent and respectable.
> —James Madison, *Notes of Debates in the Federal Convention of 1787*
> Ohio University Press, 1966, p. 425

> Mr. ELLSWORTH. The different circumstances of different parts of the U.S and the probable differences between the present and future circumstances of the whole, render it improper to have either uniform or fixed qualifications.
> —James Madison, *Notes of Debates in the Federal Convention of 1787*
> Ohio University Press, 1966, p. 426

> Mr. MADISON. A republic may be converted into an aristocracy or **oligarchy** as well by limiting the number capable of being elected, as the number authorized to elect.
> —James Madison, *Notes of Debates in the Federal Convention of 1787*
> Ohio University Press, 1966, p. 427

> Section 3.4   [Article I] The Vice President of the United States shall be President of the Senate, but shall have no vote, unless they be equally divided [in case of a tie vote].

This means the vice president votes only when the Senate is deadlocked in a tie vote. The only other constitutional power given to the vice president is to succeed the president upon his death or removal from office. With this in mind, an important consideration when deciding on a presidential candidate should be the candidate's choice for vice president.

The word "inhabitant" was used as a restriction for Senate eligibility without much discussion, while the word "resident" was preferred in Article II, Section 1.5, regarding requirements to be president.

> Section 3.5   [Article I] The Senate shall chuse [sic] their other officers, and also a president **pro tempore**, in the absence of the Vice President, or when he shall exercise the office of President of the United States.

> Section 3.6   [Article I] The Senate shall have the sole power to try all impeachments. When sitting for that purpose, they shall be on oath or **affirmation**. When the President of the United States is tried, the chief justice shall preside: and no person shall be convicted without the concurrence of two thirds of the members present.

Remember, it says two-thirds of the senators present, not two-thirds of the Senate.

The possibility of impeachment, even after resignation or tenure expiration, probably exists and was specifically mentioned in Section 22 of the Pennsylvania Constitution of 1776: "Every officer of state, whether judicial or executive, shall be liable to be impeached by the general assembly, either when in office, or after his resignation or removal for mar [l]-administration [correct as to the only copy of the Pennsylvania Constitution of 1776 that I have found]."* Because the penalty for impeachment is removal from office (which has already taken place), in addition to prevention from holding any office of honor, trust, or profit under the United States in the future (very unlikely an impeached and convicted officer would run for office again), it is unlikely

that Congress would pursue impeachment following a resignation.
*http://avalon.law.yale.edu/18th_century/pa08.asp

Ben Franklin favored the impeachment authority, stating that the removal of "obnoxious" chief executives had been accomplished by assassination throughout history, and that impeachment would be preferable.

> Section 3.7 [Article I] Judgment in cases of impeachment shall not extend further than to removal from office, and disqualification to hold and enjoy any office of honor, trust or profit under the United States: but the party convicted shall nevertheless be liable and subject to indictment, trial, judgment and punishment, according to law.

It should be observed that "shall not extend further than to removal from office and disqualification to hold and enjoy any office of honor, trust, or profit under the United States" leaves the door open for a sentence, if found guilty, of a lesser punishment. If the only offences worthy of impeachment were "treason, **bribery**, or other high crimes and misdemeanors," which require automatic removal from office as specified in Article II, Section 4, then the above punishment guidelines for an impeachment conviction would not be needed. I therefore believe the writers of the Constitution were allowing impeachment for any offence deemed sufficient by the House.

The Massachusetts Constitution of March 2, 1780, interestingly contains almost identical wording: "Their judgment, however, shall not extend further than to removal from office and disqualification to hold or enjoy any place of honor, trust, or profit, under this Commonwealth; But the party, so convicted, shall be nevertheless, liable to indictment, trial, judgment, and punishment, according to the laws of the land."

During the impeachment proceedings of President Clinton, the question "Can a sitting president be indicted?" was often asked and discussed. The Constitution doesn't clearly answer this question, but if there was a legitimate reason to indict the president we can assume there would be a legitimate reason to first impeach.

> The President of the United States would be liable to be impeached, tried, and upon conviction of treason, bribery, or other high crimes or misdemeanors, removed from office; and *would afterwards* [emphasis added] be liable to prosecution and punishment in the ordinary course of law.
> —Alexander Hamilton, *The Federalist Papers,* Federalist No. 69
> Penguin Group, 1961, p. 416

I do believe, however, that it would be bad public policy to even try to indict a sitting president; such an undertaking would certainly distract from the constitutionally dictated duties of both the indictors and the indicted.

83

Section 4.1   [Article I] The times, places, and manner of holding elections for senators and representatives, shall be prescribed in each State by the legislature thereof; but the Congress may at any time by law make or alter such regulations, except as to the places of choosing senators [meaning the times and manner of holding elections could be changed].

Much authority to self-regulate was given to the national legislature and removed totally from the scope of states' executive or legislative control.

He has called together legislative bodies at places unusual, uncomfortable, and distant from the depository of their public records, for the sole purpose of fatiguing them into compliance with his measures.
—Declaration of Independence, paragraph 7

Mr. KING. If this power [to regulate the times, places and manner of holding the elections of the members of each House be held by the state legislatures] be not given to the National Legislature, their right of judging of the returns of their members may be frustrated. No probability has been suggested of its being abused by them [the national legislature]. Although this scheme of erecting the General Government on the authority of the State Legislatures has been fatal to the federal establishment [under the Articles of Confederation], it would seem as if many gentlemen, still foster the dangerous idea.
—James Madison, *Notes of the Debates in the Federal Convention of 1787*
Ohio University Press, 1966, p. 424

James Madison summarized, "This was meant to give the National Legislature a power not only to alter the provisions of the States, but to make regulations in case the States should fail or refuse altogether."

Section 4.2   [Article I] The Congress shall assemble at least once in every year, and such meeting shall be on the first Monday in December, unless they shall by law appoint a different day.

The Founding Fathers reasoned that unless we were engaged in a war or were in the midst of an economic catastrophe, Congress may decide to meet so infrequently that Article I, Section 4.2, was added. Unfortunately, because many members of Congress are so impressed with their abilities, regard themselves as omnipotent, and love to give speeches and appear on television, they feel the need to convene and legislate constantly and to discuss important matters, such as whether Viagra should be covered by Medicare, what should be the maximum size of legal soft-drink containers, and if Barry Bonds used performance-enhancing drugs. Our federal government just reopened after being closed for two weeks, and the only solution to the budget deficit, which caused the closure in the first place, was for Congress to extend the debt limit. If the only solution our Founding Fathers could come up with at the Constitutional Convention had been to extend the Articles of Confederation, our national language now would probably be Chinese.

The Twentieth Amendment changed this to "noon on the 3rd of January, unless they shall by law appoint a different day."

> Section 5.1   [Article I] Each House shall be the judge of the elections, returns and qualifications of its own members, and a majority of each shall constitute a quorum to do business; but a smaller number may adjourn from day to day, and may be authorized to compel the attendance of absent members, in such manner, and under such penalties as each House may provide.

Again, Congress is given the authority to determine its own affairs without intervention from either the judicial or executive branch or from the state legislatures.

> Section 5.2   [Article I] Each House may determine the rules of its proceedings, punish its members for disorderly behaviour, and, with the concurrence of two thirds, expel a member.

Early drafts of the Constitution did not contain the phrase "with the concurrence of two thirds," but after the suggestion by Mr. Madison that "the right of expulsion was too important to be exercised by a bare majority of a quorum, and in emergencies of faction might be dangerously abused," it was added. I assume this means two-thirds of the total members of each House, not just two-thirds of those present.

> Section 5.3   [Article I] Each House shall keep a journal of its proceedings, and from time to time publish the same, excepting such parts as may in their judgment require secrecy; and the yeas and nays of the members of either House on any question shall, at the desire of one fifth of those present, be entered on the journal.

The Congressional Record publishes the proceedings.

Section 5.4   [Article I] Neither House, during the session of Congress, shall, without the consent of the other, adjourn for more than three days, nor to any other place than that in which the two Houses shall be sitting.

This clause prevents either house from adjourning to purposely stall the legislative process.

Section 6.1   [Article I] The senators and representatives shall receive a compensation for their services, to be ascertained by law, and paid out of the Treasury of the United States. They shall in all cases, except treason, felony and breach of the peace, be privileged from arrest during their attendance at the session of their respective Houses, and in going to and returning from the same; and for any speech or debate in either House, they shall not be questioned in any other place.

This same privilege of "freedom from arrest during their attendance at the session of their respective Houses" existed in many of the state constitutions and had its roots in the unfair usurpations during British rule.

Method and amount of payment to the national legislatures was proposed and discussed on June 12. Both Mr. Madison and Mr. Mason objected to letting each state legislature fix the salaries of its own representatives. "The different States would make different provision for their representatives, and an inequality would be felt among them, they ought to be equal in all respects. The parsimony of the States might reduce the provisions so low that as had already happened in choosing delegates to Congress, the question would be not who were most fit to be chosen, but who were most willing to serve."

The motions to pay these salaries out of the national treasury and to permit members of the national legislature to hold any office under the national government immediately after serving in the legislature were passed on this day without much dissension. Mr. Ellsworth on June 22 again brought up the issue of the source of payment to the national legislators. He favored "payment by the States out of their own Treasuries: the manners of different States were very different in the style of living and in the profits accruing from the exercise of like talents." Mr. Randolph better expressed the majority feelings of the representatives in his reasoning that "if the States were to pay the members of the National Legislature, a dependence would be created that would **vitiate** the whole system. The whole nation has an interest in the attendance & services of the members. The National Treasury therefore is the proper fund for supporting them." Common sense and good judgment again prevailed.

Mr. Gorham of Massachusetts, who seldom spoke during the convention, did suggest that the Constitution should not set the salaries of the legislators but they [Congress] "should provide for their own wages from time to time." Alexander Hamilton was "apprehensive from fixing the wages."

South Carolina's Pierce Butler and John Rutledge proposed that members "of the 2nd branch [the Senate] should be entitled to no salary or compensation for their services." This idea was opposed, the only alternative suggestion being that the "stipends for the second branch should be the same as for the 1st branch." Remember, the amount of payment for members of either house had not yet not been determined by the delegates.

Mr. Jonathan Dayton from New Jersey considered the payment of the Senate by the states as "fatal to their independence."

> Section 6.2   [Article I] No senator or representative shall, during the time for which he was elected, be appointed to any civil office under the authority of the United States, which shall have been created, or the **emoluments** whereof shall have been increased during such time; and no person holding any office under the United States shall be a member of either House during his continuance in office.

This provision is very straightforward—the writers of the Constitution didn't want the legislators creating jobs for themselves—and is very similar to Article V, paragraph 2, of the Articles of Confederation.

> Section 7.1   [Article I] All bills for raising revenue [not to be confused with spending revenue] shall originate in the House of Representatives; but the Senate may propose or concur with amendments as on other bills.

As originally presented as part of the Virginia Plan, either branch could originate any acts; however, after it was decided that only the House would be chosen directly by the people, it was decided that the maxim "no taxation without representation" would be best served by the House.

The Constitution of New Hampshire, January 5, 1776, contained the clause "that all bills, resolves, or votes for raising, levying and collecting money originate in the House of Representatives."

> All money-bills shall originate in the House of Representatives; but the Senate may propose or concur with amendments, as on other bills.
> —Massachusetts Constitution of 1780, Chapter I, Section III, Article VII

Elbridge Gerry first suggested on June 13 that the Senate should be restrained from originating money bills: "The other branch was more immediately the representatives of the people, and it is a maxim that the people ought to hold the purse-strings." South Carolina's Pierce Butler "saw no reason for such a discrimination" and made the prophetic statement that "it will lead the latter into the practice of tacking other clauses to money bills."

Debates concerning the proposal that money bills should originate in the first branch were again resumed on July 6. George Mason speculated that "the 1st branch would be the immediate representatives of the people, the 2nd would not. Should the latter have the power of giving away the people's money they might soon forget the source from whence they received it. We might soon have an aristocracy."

It was agreed to by a majority of the states that "all bills for raising revenue shall originate in the House of Representatives"; the Seventeenth Amendment eliminated the importance of money bills originating in the House, as senators are now elected directly by the people.

Another small item worth mentioning again is the constitutional requirement that all legislation dealing with raising revenue (taxation) must originate in the House of Representatives. As I recall, the Supreme Court ruled that Obama Care was constitutional because it is really a tax. I believe the Obama Care bill originated in the Senate, because the House bill was basically dismantled. If indeed it did originate in the Senate, then it should be ruled unconstitutional. Because it is law, however, it should be enforced by the president, in its totality. Line-item vetoes were ruled unconstitutional by the Supreme Court in the 1998 ruling of Clinton v. City of New York; I think it quite logical, then, that line-item enforcement is not only unconstitutional but also dereliction of presidential duty and certainly could be grounds for impeachment.

> Section 7.2   [Article I] Every bill which shall have passed the House of Representatives and the Senate, shall, before it becomes a law, be presented to the President of the United States; if he approve he shall sign it, but if not he shall return it, with his objections to that House in which it shall have originated, who shall enter the objections at large on their journal, and proceed to reconsider it. If after such reconsideration two thirds of that House shall agree to pass the bill, it shall be sent, together with the objections [of the president], to the other House, by which it shall likewise be reconsidered, and if approved by two thirds of that House, it shall become a law. But in all such cases the votes of both Houses shall be determined by yeas and nays, and the names of the persons voting for and against the bill shall be entered on

the journal of each House respectively. If any bill shall not be returned by the President within ten days (Sundays excepted) [I am surprised the Supreme Court hasn't figured out a way to declare null and void giving special significance to Sunday, the Christian day of worship.] after it shall have been presented to him, the same shall be a law, in like manner as if he had signed it, unless the Congress by their adjournment prevent its return, in which case it shall not be a law [if it was not signed by the president].

This is very significant, for it prevents Congress from adjourning just to circumvent the ten-day return requirement.

The issue of "veto power" or "right to negative" was first discussed on June 4. On this day, Elbridge Gerry proposed "that the National Executive shall have a right to negative any Legislative act which shall not be afterwards passed by -?- parts of each branch of the national Legislature." He also doubted whether the judiciary out to have a part in it, "as they will have a sufficient check against encroachments of their own department by their **exposition** of the laws [judicial review], which involved a power of deciding on their Constitutionality." Rufus King of Massachusetts seconded the motion, observing "that Judges ought to be able to expound the law as it should come before them, free from the bias of having participated in its formation." This discussion lends support to the idea of **judicial review**, or constitutionality determinations of legislative acts by the judicial branch. The February 24, 1803, Supreme Court decision in *Marbury v. Madison* was "the first case to apply the emergent doctrine of judicial review to a congressional statute."*

The doctrine of judicial review was known to many of the delegates and even incorporated into the constitutions of both Pennsylvania and Vermont (not admitted to statehood until 1792).

> The supreme court, and the several courts of common pleas of this commonwealth, shall besides the powers usually exercised by such courts, have the powers of a court of chancery, ... and such other powers as may be found necessary by future general assemblies, not inconsistent with this constitution.
> —Pennsylvania Constitution, September 28, 1776, Section 24

---

*Kermit L. Hall, editor, *The Oxford Companion to the Supreme Court of the United States* (Oxford University Press, 1992, p. 521)

> To be called the Council of Censors; ... And whose duty it
> shall be to enquire whether the constitution has been pre-
> served inviolate in every part; and whether the legislative
> and executive branches of government have performed their
> duty as guardians of the people, or assumed to themselves,
> or exercised other or greater powers than they are intitled
> [sic] to by the constitution.
> —Pennsylvania Constitution, September 28, 1776, Section 47

There was disagreement among some constitutional scholars as to whether the courts
were entitled to the right of judicial review when deciding specific cases. Judge John
Marshall (Chief Justice from February 4, 1801 until his death on July 6, 1835) firmly
established judicial review as a right and duty of the courts in the *Marbury v. Madison*
decision. (See Chapter V.) His justification was based partly on Article VI, Sections 1.2
and 1.3, stipulating that "judicial Officers, both of the United States and of the several
States, shall be bound by Oath or Affirmation, to support this Constitution," and that
"this Constitution, and the Laws of the United States which shall be made in Pursuance
thereof ... shall be the supreme Law of the Land." Marshall argued, "How immoral to
impose upon them [the judicial officers], if they were to be used as the instruments ...
for violating what they swear to support!"

> The interpretation of the laws is the proper and peculiar province of
> the courts. A constitution is, in fact, and must be regarded by the
> judges as, a fundamental law. It not uncommonly happens that
> there are two statutes existing at one time, clashing in whole or in
> part with each other and neither of them containing any repealing
> clause or expression. In such a case, it is the province of the courts
> to liquidate and fix their meaning and operation. So far as they can,
> by any fair construction, be reconciled to each other, reason and
> law conspire to dictate that this should be done; where this is
> impracticable, it becomes a matter of necessity to give effect to one
> in exclusion of the other. The rule which has obtained in the courts
> for determining their relative validity is that the last in order of time
> shall be preferred to the first. But this is a mere rule of construction,
> not derived from any positive law but from the nature and reason of
> the thing. It is a rule not enjoined upon the courts by legislative pro-
> vision but adopted by themselves, as a consonant to truth and pro-
> priety, for the direction of their conduct as interpreters of the law.
> They thought it reasonable that between the interfering acts of an
> equal authority that which was the last indication of its will should
> have the preference.
>
> But in regard to the interfering acts of a superior and subordinate
> authority of an original and derivative power, the nature and rea-
> son of the thing indicate the converse of that rule as proper to be

followed. They teach us that the prior act of a superior ought to be preferred to the subsequent act of an inferior and subordinate authority.

—Alexander Hamilton, *The Federalist Papers*, Federalist No. 78
Penguin Books USA, 1961, p. 468

Mr. Hamilton wrote this in defense of the right of judicial review as it applies to Supreme Court decisions. The Constitution is the superior, and the Supreme Court and the legislature, the subordinate authority. Even though the Supreme Court does indeed have the right of judicial review, it should not be able to legislate or amend the Constitution by the weight of its rulings. Each new case should be considered as it relates to the Constitution, not to prior court rulings. The courts, of course, can rule on the constitutionality of specific legislation, but these rulings should not be the basis for subsequent rulings. Each case dealing with constitutional determinations should be based solely on the wording of the Constitution as it relates to the specific law upon which the Court is ruling, not on previous rulings of a real or supposed similar circumstance. "From the nature of man we may be sure, that those who have power in their hands will not give it up while they can retain it. On the contrary we know they will always when they can rather increase it," said George Mason.

James Wilson was in favor of giving the executive and judiciary branches jointly an absolute negative, with no override provisions.

Gunning Bedford was "opposed to every check (or negative) on the Legislative. It would be sufficient to mark out in the Constitution the boundaries to the Legislative Authority, which would give all the requisite security to the rights of the other departments."

George Mason strongly objected to an absolute negative by the executive branch: "I hope that nothing like a Monarchy would ever be attempted in this Country." "A hatred to its oppressions" had carried the people through the late Revolution. Ben Franklin was against the absolute negative also, and he put forth examples of how the governor of Pennsylvania had refused to sign a bill authorizing military protection to the settlers until the legislature had proposed a bill exempting his estate from taxation.

Roger Sherman was against enabling any one man to stop the will of the whole: "No one man could be found so far above all the rest in wisdom."

James Madison made the proposal (June 4) "that if a proper proportion of each branch would be required to overrule the objections of the Executive, it would answer the same purpose as an absolute negative." On June 6, he again expressed his support for a revision of the laws passed by the legislature to be put into the hands of both the executive and the judiciary branches:

The Executive magistrate would be envied and assailed by disappointed competitors: His firmness therefore would need support. He would not possess those great emoluments from his station, nor that permanent stake in the public interest which would place him out of the reach of foreign corruption: He would stand in need therefore of being controuled [sic] as well as supported. An association of the Judges in his revisionary function would both double the advantage and diminish the danger. It would also enable the Judiciary Department the better to defend itself against Legislative encroachments. A law violating a Treaty, ratified by a pre-existing law, might be respected by the judges; a law violating a constitution established by the people themselves would be considered by the judges as null and void.

Although Mr. Madison makes a good case for inclusion of the judiciary in the veto process, he was overruled by most of the other delegates, especially Mr. Gerry, Mr. King, Mr. Pinckney, and Mr. Dickinson.

Compromise was again the solution, and Article I, Section 7.2 was basically agreed to.

Section 7.3   [Article I] Every order, resolution, or vote to which the concurrence of the Senate and House of Representatives may be necessary (except on a question of adjournment) shall be presented to the President of the United States; and before the same shall take effect, shall be approved by him, or being disapproved by him, shall be repassed by two thirds of the Senate and House of Representatives, according to the rules and limitations prescribed in the case of a bill.

Mr. WILLIAMSON [quoting from James Madison] moved to reconsider the clause requiring three fourth of each House to overrule the negative of the President, in order to strike out ¾ and insert 2/3. He remarked he had himself proposed ¾ instead of 2/3, but he had since been convinced that the latter proportion was the best [In today's pathetic political climate he would have been referred to as "a flip-flopper" instead of just a person who was willing to change his opinion based upon wise reflection]. The former puts too much in the power of the President.
Mr. SHERMAN was of the same opinion; adding that the States would not like to see so small a minority and the President, prevailing over the general voice. In making laws regard should be had to the sense of the people, who are to be bound by them, and it was

more probable that a single man should mistake or betray this sense than the Legislature.
—James Madison, *Notes of the Debates in the Federal Convention of 1787*
Ohio University Press, 1966, pp. 627–628

An excellent source of information regarding congressional protocol and definitions of such terms as **bill, joint resolution**, and **concurrent resolution** can be found at www.votesmart.org and http://thomas.loc.gov/home/thomas.php

> Section 8.1   [Article I] The Congress shall have power to lay and collect taxes, duties, imposts and excises, to pay the debts and provide for the common defense and general welfare of the United States; but all duties, imposts and excises shall be uniform throughout the United States;

We have already learned from Article I, Section 2.3 that direct taxes (as opposed to consumption or indirect taxes) were to be apportioned among the states in direct proportion to population. This makes sense only if the national taxes were to be imposed upon the states and not upon the citizens. Duties, imposts and excises are all indirect taxes and therefore not subject to the apportionment restrictions of Article I, Section 2.3.

> It is a single advantage of taxes on articles of consumption [indirect taxes] that they contain in their own nature a security against excess.* Which means that if the taxes become too excessive, the consumption will slow, and the taxes will diminish.
> —Alexander Hamilton, *The Federalist Papers*, Federalist No. 21
> Penguin Books USA, 1961, p. 142

> It cannot be doubted that this will always be a valuable source of revenue; that for a considerable time it must be a principal source; that at this moment it is an essential one. But we may form very mistaken ideas on this subject, if we do not call to mind in our calculations that the extent of revenue drawn from foreign commerce must vary with the variations, both in the extent and the kind of imports; and that these variations do not correspond with the progress of population, which must be the general measure of the public wants. As long as agriculture continues the sole field of labor, the importation of manufactures [manufactured goods] must increase as the consumers multiply. As soon as domestic manufactures are begun by the hands not called for by agriculture, the imported manufactures will decrease as the numbers of people increase. In a more remote stage, the imports may consist in a

considerable part of raw materials, which will be wrought into articles for exportation, and will, therefore, require rather the
encouragement of bounties than to be loaded with discouraging
duties. A system of government meant for duration ought to con-
template these revolutions and be able to accommodate itself to
them.
—James Madison, *The Federalist Papers*, Federalist No. 41
Penguin Books USA, 1961, p. 262

Herein we find the terms that have probably contributed more to the many usurpations by our federal government than any other section of the entire Constitution:
"provide for the common defense and general welfare of the United States." I suspect the writers of our Constitution, without one exception, would be dismayed at
the contemporary interpretation of "general welfare." Once again, I refer the
reader to the Federalist Papers #41 (we can safely assume Madison was at least
vaguely familiar with the intended meanings of our Constitution) for some historical insight:

Some who have not denied the necessity of the power of taxation
have grounded a very fierce attack against the Constitution, on
the language in which it is defined. It has been urged and echoed
that the power "to lay and collect taxes, duties, imposts, and
excises, to pay the debts, and provide for the common defense
and general welfare of the United States," amounts to an unlimited commission to exercise every power which may be alleged to
be necessary for the common defense or general welfare. No
stronger proof could be given of the distress under which these
writers labor for objections, than their stooping to such a mis-
construction.

Had no other enumeration or definition of the powers of the Congress been found in the Constitution than the general expressions
just cited, the authors of the objections might have had some color
for it; though it would have been difficult to find a reason for so
awkward a form of describing an authority to legislate in all possible
cases. A power to destroy the freedom of the press, the trial by jury,
or even to regulate the course of descents, or the forms of con-
veyances, must be very singularly expressed by the terms "to raise
money for the general welfare."

But what color can the objection have, when a specification of the
objects alluded to by these general terms immediately follows and
is not even separated by a longer pause than a semicolon? If the
different parts of the same instrument ought to be so expounded
as to give meaning to every part which will bear it, shall one part

of the same sentence be excluded altogether from a share in the meaning; and shall the more doubtful and indefinite terms be retained in their full extent, and the clear and precise expressions be denied any signification whatsoever? For what purpose could the enumeration of particular powers be inserted, if these and all others were meant to be included in the preceding general power?

This understanding is paramount to the interpretation of any contract. Remember, the words "common defence, security of liberty and general welfare" came straight out of the Articles of Confederation (Article III). If mentioning generalities granted universal power, then there would have been no reason to amend the Articles of Confederation. This critical issue must never be ignored. In response to a question from Charles Cotesworth Pinckney on May 30 concerning the abolishment of the state governments altogether, Mr. Randolph replied "that he meant by these general propositions merely to introduce the particular ones which explained the outlines of the system he had in view."

Madison continues,

The objection here [the one presented by the anti-federalists that the Constitution gave the national government unlimited power and authority] is the more extraordinary, as it appears that the language used by the convention is a copy from the Articles of Confederation. The objects of the Union among the States, as described in article third, are "their common defense, security of their liberties, and mutual and general welfare." The terms of article eighth are still more identical: "All charges of war and all other expenses that shall be incurred for the common defense or general welfare and allowed by the United States in Congress shall be defrayed out of a common treasury," etc. A similar language again occurs in article ninth. **Construe** either of these articles by the rules which would justify the construction put on the new Constitution, and they vest in the existing Congress a power to legislate in all cases whatsoever. But what would have been thought of that assembly, if, attaching themselves to these general expressions and disregarding the specifications which ascertain and limit their import, they had exercised an unlimited power of providing for the common defense and general welfare? I appeal to the objectors themselves, whether they would in that case have employed the same reasoning in justification of Congress as they now make use of against the convention. How difficult it is for error to escape its own condemnation.

Mr. Sherman on June 6, when discussing whether the national legislature should be elected by the people or by the state legislatures, touched on the subject of limiting the duties and powers of the national government when he said, "The objects of the Union were few—defense against foreign danger, against internal disputes & a resort to force, treaties with foreign nation, regulating foreign commerce and drawing revenue from it, and perhaps a few lesser objects. All other matters civil and criminal would be much better in the hands of the States." I think many of the founders would be shocked to see just how far our national government has expanded its power and its revenue base.

The national government is also hereby authorized to assume the previously existing individual states' debts. Mr. Rutledge motioned on August 18 "that a Grand Committee be appointed to consider the necessity and expediency of the U. States assuming all the State debts—A regular settlement between the Union and the several States would never take place. The assumption would be just as the State debts were contracted in the common defence. It was necessary, as the taxes on imports the only sure source of revenue were to be given up to the Union. It was politic, as by disburdening the people of the State debts it would conciliate them to the plan [the Constitution]."

What follows are the specific authorizations given to Congress to accomplish the generalized goals to "establish justice, insure domestic tranquility, provide for the common defense, promote the general welfare, and secure the blessings of liberty to ourselves and our posterity."

> Section 8.2   [Article I] To borrow money on the credit of the United States;

Initially, this clause also contained the language "and emit bills [of credit]," which was removed after lengthy debate.

> If the United States had credit such bills would be unnecessary; if they had not, unjust & useless. Striking out the words will leave room still for notes of a responsible minister which will do all the good without the mischief. The Monied interest will oppose the plan of Government, if paper emissions be not prohibited.
> —James Madison, *Notes of the Debates in the Federal Convention of 1787* Ohio University Press, 1966, p. 470

Nathaniel Gorham of Massachusetts was "for striking out, without inserting any prohibition. If the words stand they may suggest and lead to the measure."

The motion to remove "and emit bills" passed with dissension from only New Jersey and Maryland.

...nor emit bills, nor borrow money on the credit of the United States, unless by the votes of a majority of the United States in Congress assembled.
—Articles of Confederation, Article IX.7

Section 8.3 [Article I] To regulate commerce [see *Gibbons v. Ogden*] with foreign nations, and among the several States, and with the Indian tribes;

For cutting off our trade with all parts of the world... *

If the new Constitution be examined with accuracy and candor, it will be found that the change which it proposes consists much less in the addition of NEW POWERS to the Union than in the invigoration of its ORIGINAL POWERS. The regulation of commerce, it is true, is a new power; but that seems to be an addition which few oppose and from which no apprehensions are entertained.
—James Madison, *The Federalist Papers*, Federalist No. 45
Penguin Books USA, 1961, p. 293

Section 8.4 [Article I] To establish a uniform rule of naturalization, and uniform laws on the subject of bankruptcies throughout the United States;

He has endeavored to prevent the population of these States; for that purpose obstructing the laws for naturalization of foreigners... **

I think it is disgraceful that our national and state legislatures are more concerned with whether gays can get married, which in reality affects less than five percent of our population, than with establishing an effective naturalization policy. The Paterson Plan in 1787 proposed that "a singular policy for naturalization should be established." Here it is 226 years later and we still don't have one that works. Other than to be more concerned with supporting party politics than finding a fair, lasting immigration policy, there is no reason to demand that immigration reform won't include amnesty for illegal immigrants. I am not in favor of automatically throwing out illegals who have entered this country willing to work, to support their families, to obey our laws, and to earn their way to citizenship. Automatically throwing under the bus those aliens who are living in our country and have violated our naturalizations laws, doesn't appear to me to be the wisest choice. And what are we going to do to prevent them from reentering, brand their heads with a scarlet A? By the way, I think anyone who understands the Fourteenth Amendment would realize that, of course,

---

*Declaration of Independence
**Ibid

gays are entitled to marriage certificates. The real question is why anyone needs a marriage certificate in the first place, other than those issues caused by that damn pesky income tax.

I think we are still waiting for that rule of naturalization.

> Section 8.5   [Article I] To coin money, regulate the value thereof, and of foreign coin, and fix the standard of weights and measures;

> *The United States in Congress assembled shall never coin money, nor regulate the value thereof, unless by the majority votes of the United States in Congress assembled.**

> Section 8.6   [Article I] To provide for the punishment of counterfeiting the securities and current coin of the United States;

> Section 8.7   [Article I] To establish post offices and post roads;

We've certainly attempted that, but it seems the United States Post Office is having trouble competing with FedEx and UPS. I know of very few people who, if it has to be delivered on time, will choose the US Mail. Our government has a very difficult time trying to compete with private enterprise, and now we are trying to implement federal health care. I am hopeful, but my money is on increased costs and chaos.

> Section 8.8   [Article I] To promote the progress of science and useful arts by securing for limited times to authors and inventors the exclusive right to their respective writings and discoveries;

Congress is currently discussing contributing money to promote the "arts"; an occasional reading of the Constitution, and adherence to it, would make their work much easier.

> Section 8.9   [Article I] To constitute **tribunals** inferior to the supreme Court;

Mr. Rutledge wished that this be expunged (removed entirely), arguing that the "State Tribunals might and ought to be left in all cases to decide in the first instance the right

---

*Articles of Confederation, Article IX. paragraph 6

of appeal to the supreme national tribunal, that it was making an unnecessary encroachment of the jurisdiction of the States and creating unnecessary obstacles to their adoption of the new system." Mr. Sherman seconded the motion.

Mr. Madison was strongly in favor of inferior tribunals. He surmised "that unless inferior tribunals were dispersed throughout the Republic with final jurisdiction in many cases, appeals would be multiplied to a most oppressive degree."

Mr. Dickinson contended that if there was to be a national legislature, there ought to be a national judiciary, and that the former ought to have authority to institute the latter. This suggestion, with support from both Madison and Wilson, resulted in the final language as found in Article III, Section 1.

The First Congress in 1789 created United States district courts in every state and in 1891 established intermediate courts of appeals.

> Section 8.10   [Article I] To define and punish piracies and felonies committed on the high seas, and offenses against the law of nations;

The original proposal, "To declare the law and punishment of piracies and felonies" was changed to "To define and punish piracies and felonies" because of the remarks by James Madison:
> Felony at **common law** is vague. It is also defective. If the laws of the States were to prevail on this subject, the citizens of different States would be subject to different punishments for the same offence at sea. There would be neither uniformity nor stability in the law—The proper remedy for all these difficulties was to vest the power proposed by the term 'define' in the National Legislature.
> —James Madison, *Notes of the Debates in the Federal Convention of 1787*
> Ohio University Press, 1966, pp. 473–474

> Section 8.11   [Article I] To declare war, grant letters of marque and reprisal, and make rules concerning captures on land and water

Mr. MADISON and Mr. GERRY moved to insert "declare" striking out "make" war; leaving to the Executive the power to repel sudden attacks.

Mr. MASON was ag [sic] giving the power of war to the Executive, because not safely to be trusted with it; or to the Senate, because

not so constructed as to be entitled to it. He was for clogging rather than facilitating war; but for facilitating peace. He preferred "declare" to "make."
—James Madison, *Notes of the Debates in the Federal Convention of 1787*
Ohio University Press, 1966, p. 476

The United States in Congress assembled shall never engage in war, nor grant letters of marque and reprisal in time of peace … unless by the votes of a majority of the United States in Congress assembled.
—Articles of Confederation, Article IX, paragraph 6

In 1973 Congress adopted the War Powers Resolution, in spite of the veto by President Nixon, in an attempt to more clearly define the differences between their authority to "declare war" and "to raise and support armies," and the president's power to be "Commander in Chief of the Army and Navy of the United States, and of the militia of the several states."

The president may introduce troops into hostilities, according to Congress's interpretation, only pursuant to statutory authorization or to a declaration of war, or in the event of an attack on the United States or its armed forces. This construction binds neither the president nor the judges, who under *Marbury v. Madison* must interpret the Constitution for themselves. The views of Congress, however, are surely of importance when other branches undertake the task of interpretation.

Before the president takes military action, the resolution requires him "in every possible instance" to "consult with Congress." This provision raises interesting questions. In the Libyan controversy, for example, the president disclosed his plans only after the bombers were in the air, and only to a few leading members of Congress. A few members are arguably not Congress; they had precious little time to reflect on the merits of the project, and it is unclear what would have happened if they had objected to the bombing. If consultation is deemed not "possible" because of the ever-present need for secrecy, moreover, the entire provision [relating to prior notification of Congress] is without practical significance.

Whether or not prior consultation is possible, the resolution also requires the president to inform Congress within forty-eight hours after introducing troops on his own initiative. At the end of sixty days he must withdraw the troops unless Congress has declared war or extended the deadline, or is unable to meet. Even during this sixty-day period, moreover, he is required to withdraw them if Congress directs him to do so.

Are these provisions constitutional? Congress relied upon Article I, Section 8, which authorizes it to enact all laws necessary and proper to exercise of the President's as well as its own powers. ... The War Powers Resolution is full in accord with this interpretation.

—David Currie, *The Constitution of the United States: A Primer for the People*
University of Chicago Press, 1988, pp. 39–40

Section 8.12   [Article I] To raise and support armies, but no appropriation of money to that use shall be for a longer term than two years [it can be for less than two years, however];

"[B]ut no appropriation of money to that use shall be for a longer term than two years" was added to appease those many delegates who were fearful of "maintaining standing armies in time of peace."

Security against foreign danger is one of the primitive objects of civil society. Next to the effectual establishment of the Union, the best possible precaution against danger from standing armies is a limitation of the term for which revenue may be appropriated to their support. *

Section 8.13   [Article I] To provide and maintain a navy;

The palpable necessity of the power to provide and maintain a navy has protected that part of the Constitution against a spirit of censure which spared few other parts. It must, indeed, be numbered among the greatest blessings of America that as her Union will be the only source of her maritime [of navigation, shipping] strength, so this will be a principal source of her security against danger from abroad.

—James Madison, *The Federalist Papers,* Federalist No. 41
Penguin Books USA, 1961, p. 260

Section 8.14   [Article I] To make rules for the government and regulation of the land and naval forces;

Section 8.15   [Article I] To provide for calling forth the militia to execute the laws of the union, suppress insurrections and repel invasions;

---

*James Madison, The *Federalist Papers*, Federalist No. 41 (Penguin Books USA, 1961, p. 256)

The term "militia" refers to the soldiers trained and maintained within the individual states and that are now more commonly called the National Guard. The constitutional delegates were fearful of permanently sustaining a "national army" and wanted the national government to have control of the state militias.

> Section 8.16 [Article I] To provide for organizing, arming, and disciplining the militia, and for governing such part of them as may be employed in the service of the United States, reserving to the States respectively the appointment of the officers, and the authority of training the militia according to the discipline prescribed by Congress.

> Mr. DICKENSON. We are come now to a most important matter, that of the sword. His opinion was that the States never would nor ought to give up all authority over the Militia. He proposed to restrain the general power to one fourth part at a time, which by rotation would discipline the whole Militia.
> —James Madison, *Notes of the Debates in the Federal Convention of 1787*
> Ohio University Press, 1966, p. 483

The states were fearful of giving too much power to the national government but, it was agreed that "uniformity was essential and necessary in the regulation of the Militia throughout the Union."

Mr. Mason suggested "to make laws for the regulation and discipline of the militia of the several States reserving to the States the appointment of the officers." Mr. Ellsworth thought the motion of Mr. Mason went too far, and he offered as an alternative, "The militia should have the same arms and exercise and be under rules established by the General Government when in actual service of the U. States and when States neglect to provide regulations for militia, it should be regulated and established by the Legislature of the U.S. The whole authority over the Militia ought by no means to be taken away from the States whose consequence would pine away to nothing after such a sacrifice of power."

As the states' paranoia regarding the authority of the national government subsided, the importance of the state militias diminished and the national armed forces grew in size and strength.

> Section 8.17 [Article I] To exercise exclusive legislation in all cases whatsoever, over such district (not exceeding ten miles square) as may, by cession of the particular States and the acceptance of Congress, become the seat of government of the United States, and to exercise like authority over all places

purchased by the consent of the legislature of the State in which the same shall be, for the erection of forts, magazines, arsenals, dockyards, and other needful buildings; and

Mr. Gerry feared that the power to purchase land from the states for the building of forts, magazines, arsenals, and other necessary buildings might "be made use of to enslave any particular State by buying up its territory, and that the strongholds proposed would be a means of awing the State into an undue obedience to the General Government," so the restriction "by the consent of the legislature of the State in which the same shall be" was added.

The United States ultimately established Washington, DC on land acquired from Maryland.

> Section 8.18   [Article I] To make all laws which shall be necessary and proper for carrying into execution the foregoing powers, and all other powers vested by this Constitution in the government of the United States, or any department or officer thereof.

The Founding Fathers were trying to correct the weaknesses of the Articles of Confederation by granting specific powers to the national government that had been withheld from the Federated Congress. This clause hereby directs Congress to pass laws that will effect the powers granted in clauses 1 through 17 of Article I, Section 8.

The Supreme Court, in the *McCulloch v. Maryland* decision, unanimously ruled that the national government did have the constitutional power to establish a national bank, being granted under Article I, Section 8.18, "which shall be necessary and proper for carrying into execution the foregoing powers," which powers included "to regulate commerce with foreign nations, and among the several States" (Article I, Section 8.3) and that the states could not tax these national banks.

> Marshall next addressed the issue "whether the state of Maryland may, without violating the Constitution," tax a branch of the Bank of the United States. Since the Constitution and federal law were supreme under the Supremacy Clause of Article VI (This Constitution, and the Laws of the United States which shall be made in Pursuance thereof, and all Treaties made, or which shall be made, under the Authority of the United States, shall be the **supreme** Law of the Land;), they took precedence over the laws of the states. The state power to tax, although important and vital, is subordinate to the Constitution. A state cannot tax those subjects to which its sovereign powers do not extend. Marshall pointed out "that the power to tax involves the power to destroy". If a state had power to tax the bank, it could also tax other agencies of the federal

government: the mail, the mint, patents, the customs houses, and the federal courts. In this manner the states could totally defeat "all the ends of government" determined by the people when they created the United States Constitution.

—Kermit L. Hall, editor, *The Oxford Companion to the Supreme Court of the United States*

Oxford University Press, 1992, pp. 537–538

The only issue that was debated and discussed more than representation afforded in the two-branch legislature was the determination of states' rights versus national rights. The Articles of Confederation had delegated too little authority to the Federal Congress and left too much power with the states; however, many delegates felt uncomfortable in creating a powerful national government and expressed concerns similar to those of Pierce Butler from South Carolina when he said, "We are running into an extreme in taking away the powers of the States" and called upon Mr. Randolph for an explanation of his Virginia Plan.

Mr. Randolph disclaimed any intention "to give indefinite powers to the national Legislature," declaring "he was entirely opposed to such an inroad on the State jurisdictions" and that he "did not think any considerations whatever could ever change his determination." Quoting Madison, "His opinion was fixed on this point."

Madison also proclaimed "that he had brought with him into the Convention a strong bias in favor of an enumeration and definition of the powers necessary to be exercised by the national Legislature; but had also brought doubts concerning its practicability. His wishes remained unaltered; but his doubts had become stronger. What his opinion might ultimately be he could not yet tell. But he should shrink from nothing which should be found essential to such a form of Gov as would provide for the safety, liberty and happiness of the community. This being the end [goal] of all our deliberations, all the necessary means for attaining it must, however reluctantly, be submitted to."

> Section 9.1   [Article I] The migration or importation of such persons as any of the States now existing shall think proper to admit, shall not be prohibited by the Congress prior to the year one thousand eight hundred and eight, but a tax or duty may be imposed on such importation, not exceeding ten dollars for each person.

"Such persons" is, of course, referring to slaves. Section 9.1 was a necessary compromise to the southern states that relied heavily on slave labor. Article V prohibits changing, by amendment, Section 9.1 and 9.4 before the year 1808.

Some delegates, George Mason (August 22, Constitutional Convention) in particular, objected to slavery as "producing the most **pernicious** effect on manners. Every mas-

104

ter of slaves is born a petty tyrant. They bring the judgment of heaven on a Country. As nations can not be rewarded or punished in the next world they must be in this. By an inevitable chain of causes & effects providence punishes national sins, by national calamities." Mr. Mason also referred to the importation of slaves as being "nefarious [very wicked] traffic." Oliver Ellsworth, in contrast, surmised, "Let every State import what it pleases. The morality or wisdom of slavery are considerations belonging to the States themselves. What enriches a part enriches the whole, and the States are the best judges of their particular interest." It was finally accepted and agreed to by the majority of the delegates that the importation of slaves would not be prohibited prior to 1808 but that the National Congress could charge an import tax not exceeding ten dollars for each person.

Prior to its final ratified form, this clause contained the wording "nor shall such migration or importation be prohibited." The unanimously approved wording "as any of the States now existing shall think proper to admit" was proposed by John Dickinson to let it be known that some of the states' delegates already objected to slavery.

> Section 9.2   [Article I] The privilege of the writ of **habeas corpus** shall not be suspended, unless when in cases of rebellion or invasion the public safety may require it.

The principle of the writ of habeas corpus was first introduced into English law during the tenure of King Charles I (1625–1649). This right was, however, only sporadically granted to the colonists.

> Section 9.3   [Article I] No **bill of attainder** or **ex post facto** law shall be passed.

"No bill of attainder" prevents citizens from being charged and punished by acts of the legislature without judicial process as had been done by the English parliament.

Mr. Dickinson mentioned to the convention "that on examining Blackstone's Commentaries, he found that the terms, 'ex post facto' related to criminal cases only."

> Laws made to punish for actions done before the existence of such laws, and which have not been declared crimes by preceding laws, are unjust, oppressive, and inconsistent with the fundamental principles of a free government.
> —Massachusetts Constitution, March 1780, Bill of Rights, Article XXIV

> Section 9.4   [Article I] No capitation, or other direct, Tax shall be laid [on the states], unless in proportion to the census or enumeration herein before directed to be taken.

This provision merely establishes the procedure to be used when "apportioning" among the several states those "direct taxes" authorized to Congress in Article I, Section 2.3 and specifically defines a capitation tax (a tax of equal amount that is charged for each person) as a direct tax and prohibits their implementation until the first census has been taken.

George Mason, still sulking from the outcome of Constitutional Convention, remarked during his attempts to thwart ratification of the Constitution during the Virginia Ratifying Convention

> that gentlemen might think themselves secured by the restriction in the fourth clause, that no capitation or other direct tax should be laid but in proportion to the census before directed to be taken. But that when maturely considered it would be found to be no security whatsoever. It was nothing but a direct assertion, or mere confirmation of the clause which fixed the ratio of taxes and representation. It only meant that the quantum to be raised of each state, should be in proportion to their numbers in the manner therein directed. But the general government was not precluded from laying the proportion of any particular state on any one species of property they might think proper.
> —Philip Kurland and Ralph Lerner, *The Founders' Constitution,* Vol. 3 University of Chicago Press, 1987, p. 356

Considering the huge amount of taxes we now pay and the volumes of conflicting expert dissertations written about direct taxes, I believe ole George Mason may have been on to something.

> It is evident from the state of the country, from the habits of the people, from the experience we have had on the point itself that it is impracticable to raise any very considerable sums by direct taxation. Tax laws have in vain been multiplied; new methods to enforce the collection have in vain been tried; the public expectation has been uniformly disappointed, and the treasuries of the States have remained empty.
>
> In so opulent a nation as that of Britain, where direct taxes from superior wealth must be much more tolerable, and from the vigor of the government, much more practicable revenue is derived from taxes of the indirect kind, from imposts and from excises. Duties on imported articles form a large branch of this latter description.
> —Alexander Hamilton, *The Federalist Papers,* Federalist No. 12 Penguin Books USA, 1961, pp. 92–93

On August 20, Rufus King asked what "was the precise meaning of *direct* taxation?" [emphasis added], and no one answered. I'm not sure if no one knew the answer or if everyone other than Mr. King thought the question to be so self-explanatory that no answer was needed. Two hundred twenty-six years have transpired, and the question has still not been answered.

> Section 9.5 [Article I] No tax or duty shall be laid on articles exported from any State.

The states that exported many of their products didn't want to be taxed more than states that had few goods to export.

To specifically prohibit taxing exports was a major concession by the northern states. Rufus King of Massachusetts summed up his feeling:

> In two great points the hands of the Legislature were absolutely tied. The importation of slaves could not be prohibited—exports could not be taxed. Is this reasonable? What are the great objects of the General System? 1. Defence against foreign invasion. 2. Defence against internal sedition. Shall all the States then be bound to defend each; & shall each be at liberty to introduce a weakness which will render defence more difficult? Shall one part of the U.S. be bound to defend another part, and that other part be at liberty not only to increase its own danger [by importing more slaves for example], but to withhold the compensation for the burden? If slaves are to be imported shall not the exports produced by their labor, supply a revenue the better to enable the General Government to defend their masters? There was so much inequality & unreasonableness in all this, that the people of the Northern States could never be reconciled to it.

Rufus King did however ultimately approve and sign the Constitution.

> Mr. GOUVERNEUR MORRIS considered such a proviso as inadmissible any where. It was so radically objectionable, that it might cost the whole system the support of some members. He contended that it would not in some cases be equitable to tax imports without taxing exports; and that taxes on exports would be often the most easy and proper of the two. The taxing on imports, however, may be looked at as an incentive for domestic production of the imported articles.

> Mr. MADISON 1. The power of taxing exports is proper in itself, and as the States can not with propriety exercise it separately, it ought

to be vested in them collectively. 2. It might with particular advantage be exercised with regard to articles in which America was not rivaled in foreign markets, as Tob [sic] &c. 3. It would be unjust to the States whose produce was exported by their neighbours [sic], to leave it subject to be taxed by the latter.
—James Madison, *Notes of the Debates in the Federal Convention of 1787*
Ohio University Press, 1966, p. 467

Mr. Hugh Williamson of North Carolina "considered the clause proposed against taxes on exports as reasonable and necessary."

The decision to prohibit taxes on exports was a compromise (being able to count slaves as three-fifths when determining direct taxes) between the northern states that wanted to tax exports (primarily on articles produced or grown in the south) and the southern states that realized export taxes would unfairly burden them.

Section 9.6   [Article I] No preference shall be given by any regulation of commerce or revenue to the ports of one state over those of another; nor shall vessels bound to, or from, one state, be obliged to enter, clear, or pay duties in another.

It was agreed to that no particular state should benefit financially solely because of its natural geographic conveniences.

Section 9.7   [Article I] No money shall be drawn from the Treasury, but in consequence of appropriations made by law; and a regular statement and account of the receipts and expenditures of all public money shall be published from time to time.

Section 9.8   [Article I] No title of nobility shall be granted by the United States; and no person holding any office of profit or trust under them, shall, without the consent of the Congress, accept of any present, emolument, office, or title, of any kind whatever, from any king, prince, or foreign State.

Section 10.1   [Article I] No State shall enter into any treaty, alliance, or confederation; grant letters of marque and reprisal; coin money; emit bills of credit; make any thing but gold and silver coin a tender in payment of debts; pass any bill of attainder, ex post facto law, or law impairing the obligation of contracts, or grant any title of nobility.

This was done to avoid conflicts of interest between the individual states and the national government, and to establish us abroad as a nation and not just a confederation.

> Section 10.2   [Article I] No State shall, without the consent of the Congress, lay any imposts_or duties on imports or exports, except what may be absolutely necessary for executing its inspection laws; and the net produce of all duties and imposts, laid by any State on imports or exports, shall be for the use of the Treasury of the United States; and all such laws shall be subject to the revision and control of the Congress.

> Section 10.3   [Article I] No State shall, without the consent of Congress, lay any duty of tonnage, or ships of war in time of peace, enter into any agreement or compact with another State or with a foreign power, or engage in war, unless actually invaded, or in such imminent danger as will not admit of delay.

On June 8, Mr. Pinckney moved "that the National Legislature shall have authority to negative all laws which they shall judge to be improper." He was referring to all laws passed by any of the states. Mr. Pinckney made the case that the acts of Congress under the Articles of Confederation had been undermined by the states and that "this negative was in fact the corner stone of an efficient national Government; that under the British Government the negative of the Crown had been found beneficial, and the States are more one nation now, than the Colonies were then."

Mr. Madison seconded the motion, reminding the delegates that without a negative by the national government on the acts of the states, the state legislatures had a tendency to "encroach on the federal authority, to violate national Treaties, to infringe the rights and interests of each other, to oppress the weaker party within their respective jurisdictions." He thought a negative was "the mildest expedient that could be devised for preventing these mischiefs." He also believed this "negative" would render the use of force unnecessary.

Hugh Williamson was against the negative on the grounds that it "might restrain the States from regulating their internal police." Mr. Gerry was also opposed to such a power and was "against every power that was not necessary." He had no objection to a negative against certain measures, however. Mr. Sherman seemed to agree when he said, "The cases in which the negative out [sic] to be exercised, might be defined."

The idea to give the federal government the right to overrule any state law was abandoned, and Article I, Sections 10.1 through 10.3 were agreed to. The Tenth Amendment, adopted on December 15, 1791, went even further in guaranteeing states' rights: "The powers not delegated to the United States by the Constitution, nor pro-hibited by it [the Constitution] to the States, are reserved to the States respectively, or to the people."

John Dickinson from Delaware "deemed it impossible to draw a line between the cases proper and improper for the exercise of the negative." He went on to say, "We must take our choice of two things. We must either subject the States to the danger of being injured by the power of the National Government or the latter to the danger of being injured by that of the States." He thought the danger greater from the States. Mr. Bedford, also from Delaware, was concerned that the small states would be over-whelmed by the national government through majority representation of the larger states in the national legislature or from the larger states directly. Here again we find one of the major hurdles confronting the convention, that of protecting the small states from encroachments by the large states, and preventing the national govern-ment from intruding on the states' rights. Creating a new national government was a very difficult job indeed; the Federated Congress was too weak to function effectively under the Articles of Confederation, and the delegates were wary of creating a national government that might easily assume the powers of another monarchy.

The convention on July 17 took up consideration of the proposal that the national leg-islature would have the power "to negative all laws passed by the several States con-travening in the opinion of the National Legislature the articles of Union, or any treaties subsisting under the authority of the Union." As always, arguments were made for and against the motion. Mr. Sherman thought "it unnecessary, as the Courts of the States would not consider as valid any law contravening the Authority of the Union, and which the legislature [the national legislature] would wish to be nega-tived." James Madison, in contrast, considered "the negative on the laws of the States as essential to the efficacy and security of the General Government. The necessity of a General Government proceeds from the propensity of the States to pursue their par-ticular interests in opposition to the general interest. This propensity will continue to disturb the system, unless effectually controuled [sic]." Unfortunately, the judicial sys-tem has assigned to the Supreme Court the right to "negative" any act by any branch, either state or national, and then effectually legislate their own unelected opinions into law.

There was a brief discussion regarding Resolution 6 of the Virginia Plan "authorizing an exertion of the force of the whole against a delinquent State." James Madison summed up the feelings of the convention when he stated that "the more he reflected on the use of force, the more he doubted the practicability, the justice and the efficacy [effectiveness] of it when applied to people collectively and not individually. A union of the States containing such an ingredient seemed to provide for its own destruction. The use of force against a State, would look more like a declaration of war, than an infliction of punishment, and would probably be considered by the party attacked as a dissolution of all previous compacts by which it might be bound."

Some of the rights and powers that had under the Articles of Confederation been retained by the states were now being granted to the new national government.

ARTICLE II

Section 1.1   The executive Power shall be vested in a President of the United States of America. He shall hold his Office during the term of four Years, and, together with the Vice President, chosen for the same Term, be elected, as follows:

Prior to determining the election procedure, there was much discussion about whether the executive power should be placed in the hands of one or more than one person. Mr. Wilson preferred a single magistrate "as giving most energy dispatch and responsibility to the office." Mr. Gerry favored the policy of annexing a council to the executive "in order to give weight and inspire confidence." Mr. Randolph strenuously opposed a unity in the executive power. He regarded it "as the fetus of monarchy"; in turn, Mr. Wilson replied "that unity in the Executive instead of being the fetus of monarchy would be the best safeguard against tyranny." The motion for a single magistrate was postponed by common consent until the extent of executive authority was determined. Wise men usually refrain from making decisions until hearing all the options and their respective consequences.

John Rutledge of South Carolina made the astute observation that "they supposed themselves precluded by having frankly disclosed their opinions from afterwards changing them, which he did not take to be at all the case." Unfortunately, today's political climate encourages the term "flip-flopper" to be applied to those wise enough to change their minds.

On June 2, Pierce Butler of South Carolina "contended strongly for a single magistrate as most likely to answer the purpose of the remote parts. If one man should be appointed he would be responsible to the whole, and would be impartial to its interests. If three or more should be taken from as many districts, there would be a constant struggle for local advantages. In Military matters this would be particularly mischievous."

Mr. Rutledge and Mr. Cotesworth Pinckney surmised, "the blank for the number of persons in the Executive be filled with the words 'one person'" and they supposed the reasons "to be so obvious and conclusive in favor of one that no member would oppose the motion." Mr. Randolph opposed it so vigorously that he eventually left the convention and refused to sign the Constitution in part because of this objection.

James Wilson thought the principal reason for unity in the executive power was that "officers might be appointed by a single, responsible person."

The motion proposing a single magistrate was passed on June 4 by vote of 7-3 and passed unanimously on July 17.

Section 1.2   [Article II] Each State shall appoint, in such Manner as the Legislature thereof may direct [one of many attempts to retain the states' involvement in the national government], a number of Electors, equal to the whole Number of Senators and Representatives to which the State may be entitled in the Congress; but no Senator or Representative, or Person holding an Office of Trust or profit under the United States, shall be appointed an Elector.

The purpose of Section 1.2 of Article II of the Constitution was to promote separation between the executive and legislative branches of the federal government by having the state legislatures appoint the presidential electors, in contrast to having Congress elect the president.

Section 1.3   [Article II] The Electors shall meet in their respective States, and vote by Ballot for two persons, of whom one at least shall not be an Inhabitant of the same State with themselves. And they shall make a List of all the Persons voted for, and of the Number of Votes for each; which List they shall sign and certify, and transmit sealed to the Seat of the Government of the United States, directed to the President of the Senate. The President of the Senate shall, in the Presence of the Senate and House of Representatives, open all the Certificates, and the Votes shall then be counted. The Person having the greatest Number of Votes shall be the President, if such Number be a Majority of the whole Number of Electors appointed; and if there be more than one who have such a majority, and have an equal Number of Votes, then the House of Representatives shall immediately chuse [sic] by Ballot one of them for President; and if no Person have a majority, then from the five highest on the List the said house shall in like Manner chuse [sic] the President. But in chusing [sic] the President, the Votes shall be taken by the States, the Representation from each State having one Vote; A quorum for this Purpose shall consist of a Member or Members from two thirds of the States, and a Majority of all the States shall be necessary to a Choice. In every Case, after the Choice of the President, the Person having the greatest Number of Votes of the Electors shall be the Vice President. But if there should remain two or more who have equal Votes, the Senate shall chuse [sic] from them by Ballot for the Vice President.

It was agreed between most of the delegates that because the electors could not choose both candidates from their own state, the large states would have less influence on the election outcome and increase the odds for a majority, keeping the selection in the hands of the electors and not in Congress. Gouverneur Morris said "Besides

112

as one vote is to be given to a man out of the State, and as this vote will not be thrown away, ½ the votes will fall on characters eminent and generally known."*

The Senate was originally delegated to decide ties, but overwhelming objection on the grounds of too close a connection between the Senate and the president and possibly "aristocracy," the job to decide ties was given to the House, as suggested by Roger Sherman, with the Senate to cast the deciding votes in case of a tie for vice president.

Alexander Hamilton wished to remove the word "majority" from the election process, thereby preventing the Senate (subsequently changed to the House) from "taking the candidate having the smallest number of votes, and make him President."

Remember, a majority of all the votes cast may not amount to a majority of the number of electors appointed. The word "appointed" was added "to remove ambiguity from the intention of the clause" in case some of the electors chose not to vote.

Roger Sherman, expressing his opinion about election of the "national magistrate" (June 1) remarked, "An independence of the Executive on the supreme Legislature, was the very essence of tyranny if there was any such thing." He believed that because the primary duty of the executive power would be "for carrying the will of the Legislature into effect," "the person or persons ought to be appointed by and accountable to the Legislature only." Mr. Sherman seems to have favored a more cohesive national government than the majority of the delegates were willing to create.

Gouverneur Morris (July 17) indicated that perhaps just the opposite might be the case when he said, "If the Executive be chosen by the National Legislature, he will not be independent on [from] it; and if not independent, usurpation and tyranny on the part of the Legislature will be the consequence."

James Wilson favored direct election by the people as "both a convenient and successful mode," at least in theory. He also favored "deriving not only both branches of the Legislature from the people, without the intervention of the State Legislatures but the Executive also; in order to make them as independent as possible of each other, as well as of the States." The method eventually agreed upon by the delegates, of appointing electors from among the citizens as directed by the state legislatures, seems to be a compromise not only of method but also of state government involvement in the national government.

Elbridge Gerry of Massachusetts "opposed the election by the national legislature," fearing "there would be constant intrigue kept up for the appointment" and "votes would be given by the former under promises or expectations from the latter, of recompensing them by services to members of the Legislature or to their friends." He

---

*James Madison, *Notes of Debates in the Federal Convention of 1787* (Ohio University Press, 1966, p. 583)

favored Mr. Wilson's motion but feared it would alarm the states' partisans as tending to supersede altogether the state authorities.

Again on June 9, the discussions regarding the election process of the president (the national executive) were resumed. Mr. Gerry moved "that the National Executive should be elected by the Executives [governors] of the States whose proportion of votes should be the same with that allowed to the States in the election of the Senate." There were numerous objections to this idea, delegates surmising that a national executive appointed by the state executives would be prone to support the states on encroachments of the national power and that the state executives "will not cherish the great Oak which is to reduce them to paltry shrubs." Mr. Gerry's motion was unanimously defeated, and a counter-resolution was postponed until a later date.

The proposition that the national executive should "be chosen by the National Legislature" came under discussion again on July 17. Gouverneur Morris was "pointedly against his being so chosen. He will be the mere creature of the Legislature: if appointed and impeachable by that body. He ought to be elected by the people at large, by the freeholders of the Country. If the Legislature elect, it will be the work of intrigue, of **cabal**, and of faction." Roger Sherman "thought that the sense of the Nation would be better expressed by the Legislature, than by the people at large. The latter will never be sufficiently informed of characters, and besides, will never give a majority of votes to any one man. They will generally vote for some man in their own State, and the largest State will have the best chance for the appointment."

As a result of the tie in the electoral vote (for the 1801–1805 term) between Thomas Jefferson and Aaron Burr, (who only four years later shot and killed Alexander Hamilton), the election procedure for president and vice president was changed by the Twelfth Amendment (adopted September 25, 1804), stipulating that votes must now be cast separately for president and vice president. If no majority (of the whole number of electors appointed) is received for the office of president, the House will vote as before from among the three (originally five) candidates receiving the most votes.

The probability of a tie vote in the general election has been greatly reduced as the number of states, and consequently the number of appointed electors, has increased.

> The mode of appointment of the Chief Magistrate of the United States is almost the only part of the system, of any consequence, which has escaped without severe censure or which has received the slightest mark of approbation from its opponents. The most plausible of these, who has appeared in print, has even deigned to admit that the election of the President is pretty well guarded. … It was desirable that the sense of the people should operate in the choice of the person to whom so important a trust was to be confided. This end will be answered by committing the right of making it, not to any pre-established body, but to men chosen by

the people for the special purpose, and at the particular conjunc-
ture. ... A small number of persons, selected by their fellow-citi-
zens from the general mass, will be most likely to possess the
information and discernment requisite to so complicated an
investigation.
—Alexander Hamilton, *The Federalist Papers,* Federalist No. 68
Penguin Books USA, 1961, pp. 411–412

The Twentieth Amendment changes the termination date for the offices of president
and vice president from March 4 to noon on January 20.

There were no term limits set for the office of president until ratification of the
Twenty-second Amendment in 1951. The president cannot now be elected for more
than two terms, and only one term if the person "acted as President, for more than
two years of a term to which some other person was elected President."

> Section 1.4   [Article II] The Congress may determine the
> Time of chusing [sic] the Electors, and the Day on which they
> shall give their Votes; which Day shall be the same throughout
> the United States.

In 1872 Congress chose the first Tuesday after the first Monday in November of every
fourth year to be Election Day. When we vote on Election Day, we are not actually
casting a vote for the candidate of our choice but merely casting a vote to choose the
electors representing our states. Most of the states require that their electors vote as
a unit for the candidate receiving the most votes.

> Section 1.5   [Article II] No Person except a **natural born
> Citizen**, or a Citizen of the United States, at the time of the
> Adoption of the Constitution, shall be eligible to the Office
> of President, neither shall any Person be eligible to that
> Office who shall not have attained to the Age of thirty-five
> Years, and been fourteen Years a Resident within the United
> States.

There were no requirements stipulated for the office of vice president because that
office was merely given to the presidential candidate receiving the second greatest
number of votes. The Twelfth Amendment, which calls for the electors to vote separately for the president and vice president, establishes the same restrictions for both
offices, "but no person constitutionally ineligible to the office of President shall be eligible to that of Vice President of the United States."

The word "resident" was chosen over "inhabitant" to include persons only residing
within the United States who may have their permanent homes elsewhere. The

definitions of the two words are quite similar, and the preference of either term by a few of the delegates (Madison and Sherman primarily) is perhaps insignificant.

The term "natural born" was probably most familiar to the Founding Fathers from the "Commentaries on the Laws of England," written by Sir William Blackstone (an English jurist, judge, and Tory politician of the eighteenth century) between 1765 and 1769, when discussing the meaning of the term "natural born subject," which he identified as "such as are born within the dominions of the crown of England." The term "natural born citizen" was also used in the Declarations and Resolves, and Resolutions of the Continental Congresses.

Although the exact meaning of the term "natural-born citizen" has recently been questioned and debated, who exactly qualifies as a natural born citizen was never discussed during the Constitutional Convention. Until a definitive constitutional amendment is proposed and ratified, it will be impossible to exclude anyone claiming United States citizenship at birth from being elected president, and the original intent of the Founding Fathers is superfluous.

> Section 1.6   [Article II] In Case of the Removal of the President from Office, or of his Death, Resignation, or Inability to discharge the Powers and Duties of the said Office, the Same shall **devolve** on the Vice President, and the Congress may by Law provide for the Case of Removal, Death, Resignation or Inability, both of the President and Vice President, declaring what Officer shall then act as President, and such Officer shall act accordingly, until the Disability be removed, or a President shall be elected.

The Twenty-fifth Amendment (1967) requires that "whenever there is a vacancy in the office of the Vice President [including if the president was removed or resigned from office and was succeeded by the vice president, leaving the office of vice president vacant], the President shall [not "may"] nominate a Vice President who shall take office upon confirmation by a majority [a majority of the members, not a majority of those present] vote of both Houses of Congress.

> Section 1.7   [Article II] The President shall, at stated Times, receive for his Services, a Compensation, which shall neither be increased nor diminished during the Period for which he shall have been elected, and he shall not receive within that Period any other Emolument from the United States, or any of them [the states].

The rich, old (81 years), and wise Mr. Ben Franklin was opposed to paying the president for his services. His proposal:

Whose necessary expences shall be defrayed, but who shall receive no salary, stipend fee or reward whatsoever for their services. There are two passions which have a powerful influence on the affairs of men. These are ambition and avarice; the love of power, and the love of money. Separately each of these has great force in prompting men to action; but when united in view of the same object, they have in many minds the most violent effects. Place before the eyes of such men, a post of honour that shall be at the same time a place of profit, and they will move heaven and earth to obtain it. It will be the bold and the violent, the men of strong passions and indefatigable activity in their selfish pursuits. These will thrust themselves into your Government and be your rulers. And these too will be mistaken in the expected happiness of their situation: For their vanquished competitors of the same spirit, and from the same motives will perpetually be endeavouring to distress their administration, thwart their measures, and render them **odious** to the people.

Section 1.8   [Article II] Before he enter on the Execution of his Office, he shall take the following Oath or Affirmation: - "I do solemnly swear [affirm] that I will faithfully execute the office of President of the United States, and will to the best of my Ability, preserve, protect and defend the Constitution of the United States."

Section 2.1   [Article II] The President shall be Commander in Chief of the Army and Navy of the United States, and of the militia of the several states, when called into the actual Service of the United States; he may require the Opinion, in writing, of the principal Officer in each of the executive Departments, upon any Subject relating to the Duties of their respective Offices, and he shall have Power to grant Reprieves and Pardons for Offences against the United States, except in Cases of Impeachment.

The president shall be commander in chief of the armed forces when they are called into actual service by Congress, pursuant to their power to "declare war" and "raise and support armies" as authorized by Article I, Sections 8.11 and 8.12. In an attempt to more clearly define the boundary between Congress and the president regarding military actions, Congress in 1973 approved the War Powers Resolution (a **joint resolution**). The resolution states that the president may introduce United States Armed

---

*James Madison, *Notes of Debates in the Federal Convention of 1787* (Ohio University Press, 1966, pp. 52–53)

Forces into hostilities pursuant to a declaration of war, to a specific statutory authorization, or a national emergency created by attack upon the United States, its territories or possessions, or its armed forces. The president "in every possible instance shall consult with Congress before introducing United States Armed Forces into hostilities," and the president shall submit to the Speaker of the House and to the president pro tempore of the Senate within forty-eight hours a detailed report explaining why and under what authorization the troops were used.

* *http://avalon.law.yale.edu/20th_century/warpower.asp*

> That the governor and Council…they possess the power of granting pardons to criminals, after condemnation, in all cases of treason, felony, or other offences.*

The North Carolina Constitution established the governor as the "captain-general" with the power to "grant pardons and reprieves."

The Georgia Constitution of 1777 specifically prohibited the governor from granting pardons ("in the case of pardons and remission of fines, which he shall in no instance grant").

> But he shall, with the advice of the Council of State [or Privy Council, consisting of eight Members, chosen by joint Ballot of both Houses of Assembly], have the power of granting reprieves or pardons, except where the prosecution shall have been carried on by the House of Delegates, or the Law shall otherwise particularly direct; in which Cases, no reprieve or Pardon shall be granted but by resolve of the House of Delegates.**

Pardons, of course, can be granted prior to a conviction. Luther Martin of Maryland on August 27 moved "to insert the words "after conviction" after the words "reprieves and pardons" but was objected to by Mr. Wilson on the grounds "that pardon before conviction might be necessary in order to obtain the testimony of accomplices."

> Section 2.2   [Article II] He shall have Power, by and with the Advice and Consent of the Senate, to make Treaties [See Article 9 of the 1754 Albany Plan], provided two thirds of the Senators present concur; and he shall nominate, and by and with the Advice and Consent of the Senate [a simple majority], shall appoint Ambassadors, other public Ministers and Consuls,

---

*New Jersey Constitution, 1776, Article IX
**Virginia Constitution, 1776

Judges of the supreme Court, and all other Officers of the United States, whose Appointments are not herein otherwise provided for, and which shall be established by Law; but the Congress may by Law vest the Appointment of such inferior Officers, as they think proper, in the President alone, in the Courts of Law, or in the Heads of Departments.

The initial suggestions regarding the authority and power of the executive were made by James Madison "that a national Executive ought to be instituted with power to carry into effect the national laws, to appoint to offices in cases not otherwise provided for, and to execute such other powers not Legislative nor Judiciary in their nature, as may from time to time be delegated by the national Legislature." James Wilson seconded this motion. Charles C. Pinckney then proposed that the words "and to execute such other powers not Legislative nor Judiciary in their nature as may from time to time be delegated" be removed as unnecessary, the object of them being included in the "power to carry into effect the national laws." Mr. Madison then surmised that he "did not however see any inconveniency in retaining them, and cases might happen in which they might serve to prevent doubts and misconstructions."

> Mr. WILSON said According to the plan as it now stands, the President will not be the man of the people as he ought to be, but the Minion of the Senate. He cannot even appoint a tide-waiter without the Senate.
> —James Madison, *Notes of the Debates in the Federal Convention of 1787*
> Ohio University Press, 1966, p. 588

The first discussions at the convention about appointing judges came on June 5 when James Wilson opposed the appointment of judges by the national legislature: "Intrigue, partiality, and concealment were the necessary consequences. A principal reason for unity in the Executive was that officers might be appointed by a single, responsible person."

Mr. Rutledge "was by no means disposed" to grant so great a power to any single person, meaning the chief executive. Ben Franklin wished "such other modes to be suggested as might occur to other gentlemen: it being a point of great moment."

James Madison disliked "the election of the Judges by the Legislature or any numerous [large in number] body. Besides the danger of intrigue and partiality, many of the members were not judges of the requisite qualifications. The Legislative talents, which were very different from those of a Judge, commonly recommended men to the favor of Legislative Assemblies. It was known too that the accidental circumstances of presence and absence, of being a member or not a member, had a very undue influence on the appointment." He also "was not satisfied with referring the appointment to the Executive." He was "rather inclined to give it to the Senatorial branch, as numerous enough to be confided in-as not so numerous as to be governed by the motives of the other branch; and as being sufficiently stable and independent to follow their deliberate judgments."

Charles Pinckney and Roger Sherman discussed appointment of the national judiciary on June 13 with their motion that "the Judges of the supreme tribunal should be appointed by the 1st branch of the National Legislature." James Madison objected on the grounds that "they [the legislatures] were too much influenced by their partialities. The candidate who was present, who had displayed a talent for business in the legislative field, who had perhaps assisted ignorant members in business of their own, or of their Constituents, or used other winning means, would without any of the essential qualifications for an expositor of the laws prevail over a competitor not having these recommendations, but possessed of every necessary accomplishment." In other words, Madison feared that the House, which was elected by the people, would be more prone to support a judicial candidate based on their "campaign contributions" than on their expertise of the law. He preferred that the appointment should be made "by the Senate, which as a less numerous and more select body, would be more competent judges, and which was sufficiently numerous to justify such a confidence in them."

It was on July 18 that Mr. Gorham told the convention that he "would prefer an appointment by the second branch to an appointment by the whole Legislature; but he thought even that branch too numerous, and too little personally responsible, to ensure a good choice. I suggest that the Judges be appointed by the Executive with the advice and consent of the second branch." It was this proposal that was eventually agreed to by the majority of the delegates, a compromise that included ideas from numerous proposals.

> Section 2.3　　[Article II] The President shall have power to fill up all Vacancies that may happen during the Recess of the Senate, by granting Commissions which shall expire at the End of their [the Senate's] next Session.

This gives to the president the authority to temporarily fill vacancies that would normally require the approval of the Senate, such as Cabinet members or Supreme Court justices. (See Article II, Section 2.2.)

> Section 3　　[Article II] He shall from time to time give to the Congress Information of the State of the Union, and recommend to their Consideration such Measures as he shall judge necessary and expedient; he may, on extraordinary Occasions, convene both Houses, or either of them, and in Case of Disagreement between them, with Respect to the Time of Adjournment, he may adjourn them to such Time as he shall think proper; he shall receive Ambassadors and other public

Ministers; he shall take Care that the Laws be faithfully executed, and shall **Commission** all the Officers of the United
States.

The president, of course, does not actually choose all the "officers of the United
States," but he does sign all of their commission papers.

Section 4 [Article II] The President, Vice President and all
civil Officers of the United States, shall be removed from Office
on Impeachment for, and Conviction of, Treason, Bribery [giv-
ing or receiving bribes], or other high Crimes and [high] Misdemeanors.

This means that if there is an impeachment and subsequent conviction for "Treason,
Bribery [either bribing or being bribed], or other high Crimes and Misdemeanors,"
removal from office is a mandate, not an option. Impeachment for any other reasons
falls under Article I, Section 3.7.

That the Governor, and other officers, offending against the
State, by violating any part of this Constitution, mal-administration, or corruption, may be prosecuted, on the impeachment of the General Assembly...
—North Carolina Constitution, 1776

The Governour, when he is out of Office, and others offending
against the State, either by Mal-administration, Corruption, or
other Means, by which the safety of the State may be endan-
gered, shall be impeachable by the House of Delegates. If
found guilty, he or they shall be either for ever disabled to hold
any Office under Government, or removed from such Office
Pro tempore, or subjected to such Pains or Penalties as the
laws shall direct.*

Gunning Bedford of Delaware on June 1 made the first mention of impeachment of
the executive during discussions about term duration of the national executive. Mr.
Bedford was opposed to so long a term as seven years. "He begged the committee to
consider what the situation of the Country would be, in case the first magistrate
should be saddled on it for such a period and it should be found on trial that he did not
possess the qualifications ascribed to him, or should lose them after his appointment.
An impeachment would be no cure for this evil, as an impeachment would reach misfeasance (misdeeds or offence) only, not incapacity"—in other words, sins of commission as opposed to sins of omission.

---

*Virginia Constitution, 1776

John Dickinson of Delaware (formerly from Pennsylvania) on June 2 talked about removal of the chief executive: "that the Executive be made removable by the National Legislature on the request of a majority of the Legislatures of individual States." He did not like the plan of impeaching the great officers of state, and he did not wish to abolish the state governments "as some gentlemen seemed inclined to do. The happiness of this Country required considerable powers to be left in the hands of the States." It must be remembered that no decisions about the national legislature (regarding either the number of branches or the weight of representation) had even been made yet. How the national legislature would be chosen, the number of branches it would contain, and whether representation would be based equally among the states (as Congress was in the Articles of Confederation) or on some type of population or "contributory" determination between the states had not been decided yet. Most delegates realized that to rest the fate of the executive on an as yet undetermined entity would be a bit premature.

George Mason favored "some mode of displacing an unfit magistrate, because of both the fallibility of those who choose, as well as by the corruptibility of the man chosen."

Mr. Wilson and Mr. Madison observed "that it [involving the state legislatures] would leave an equality of agency in the small with the great States; that it would enable a minority of the people to prevent the removal of an officer who had rendered himself justly criminal in the eyes of a majority; that it would open a door for intrigues against him in States where his administration might just be unpopular, and might tempt him to pay court to particular States whose leading partizans he might fear." This reasoning prevailed in the final procedural method agreed to for removal by impeachment (Article I, Section 2.5 authorizing the House to impeach, and Article I, Section 3.6 authorizing the Senate to try to remove with a two-thirds conviction vote). The House, which is elected by the people and apportioned according to the individual state's population, requires only a simple majority to impeach [discredit]. The Senate, which prior to the Seventeenth Amendment was chosen by the state legislatures, needs a two-thirds majority to convict. The two-thirds majority is a safeguard against minority rule. (A simple majority in the Senate could theoretically allow twenty-six of our states, even though they may represent much less than fifty percent of the United States population, to inflict their will upon the majority.)

Hugh Williamson of North Carolina was the first to propose "and be removable on impeachment and conviction of **mal-practice** or neglect of duty." This motion was agreed to, and considering what on the same day was spoken by Mr. Randolph, "that the permanent temper of the people was adverse to the very semblance of Monarchy," I find it highly likely that the phrase "high Crimes and Misdemeanors" was intended in the broadest terms, not the narrowest. John Dickinson proposed that "the Executive be removeable by the National Legislature at the request of a majority of State Legislatures."

Let's first dismiss the notion that "high" refers to the offender and not the crime. The second paragraph of Article IV of the Articles of Confederation contains the phrase "treason, felony, or other high misdemeanor" in reference to crimes and punishment of "any person," with absolutely no restriction to high-ranking civil officers. Because all of the delegates were familiar with the Articles of Confederation, I believe the same reasoning should apply to the Constitution also.

The safeguards against politically motivated impeachment and conviction are assured through the procedure, not the boundaries placed on the interpretations of the specified crimes. The outcome of the Clinton impeachment and trial is **vindication** of the system.

The Committee of the Whole presented its first draft of the Constitution to the delegates on June 13. The article dealing with impeachment ("& to be removeable on impeachment and conviction of malpractices or neglect of duty") was amended numerous times before reaching the form eventually agreed to by the delegates. It is interesting that "against the United States" was to be inserted after "misdemeanors" as agreed to unanimously by the delegates on September 8 but was inadvertently left off the final draft; it does appear in Article II, Section 2.1 in reference to granting reprieves and pardons.

ARTICLE III

Section 1   The judicial Power of the United States, shall be vested in one Supreme Court, and in such inferior Courts as the Congress may from time to time ordain and establish. The judges, both of the supreme and inferior Courts, shall hold their Offices during good Behaviour, and shall, at stated Times, receive for their Services, a Compensation, which shall not be diminished during their Continuance in Office.

Article III overcame one of the complaints against the king set forth in the Declaration of Independence that stated, "He [the king] has obstructed the administration of justice, by refusing his assent to laws for establishing judiciary powers."

Many of the state constitutions contained similar language related to tenure in office, specifically the Virginia Constitution (1776) and the North Carolina Constitution (1776), which stated, "shall hold their offices during good behavior" and "and hold their offices during good behavior," respectively.

The phrase "shall hold their Offices during good Behavior and shall receive for their services, a compensation" was basically unchanged from the original proposal advanced by Randolph in his Virginia Plan. Article III, Section 1 was included in our Constitution (and most of the then existing state constitutions) as a safeguard to prevent the grievance listed in the Declaration of Independence ("He has made judges dependent on his will alone for the tenure of their offices, and the amount and payment of their salaries.") from occurring within our new national government.

The First Congress, in 1789, established a chief justice (John Jay being the first) and five additional judges for the Supreme Court, which was later increased to eight additional judges.

> Section 2.1   [Article III] The judicial Power [of the United States Supreme Court as well as inferior national courts] shall extend to all Cases [criminal and civil], in Law and **Equity**, arising under this Constitution, the Laws of the United States, and Treaties made, or which shall be made, under their [the United States] Authority;—to all Cases affecting Ambassadors, other public ministers and Consuls [the Supreme Court shall have original jurisdiction, as set forth in Article III, Section 2.2 below];—to all Cases of admiralty and maritime Jurisdiction:—to Controversies to which the United States shall be a Party;—to Controversies between two or more States [the Supreme Court shall have original jurisdiction];—between a State and Citizens of another State;—between Citizens of different States;—between Citizens of the same State claiming lands under Grants of different States, and between a State, or the Citizens thereof, and foreign States, Citizens or Subjects.

Although the Eleventh Amendment excluded from federal jurisdiction any lawsuit "commenced or prosecuted against one of the United States by Citizens of another State, or by Citizens or Subjects of any Foreign State," it did not remove from federal jurisdiction lawsuits initiated by any of the states against citizens of other states.

The judicial branch received less discussion during the convention than did the other two branches. Creating the judiciary did satisfy a complaint in the Declaration of Independence that "he has obstructed the administration of justice, by refusing his assent to laws for establishing judiciary powers." Congress was left with the task of establishing most of the procedural guidelines of the judicial branch.

This section of Article III specifically designates which disputes the national (federal) government has the jurisdiction to settle. The following section sets forth in which instances the Supreme Court has either original or appellate jurisdiction.

Article IX, paragraph 2 of the Articles of Confederation provided for "the United States in Congress assembled" to settle boundary disputes between two or more states.

On June 13, Virginia's Randolph and Madison moved "that the jurisdiction of the National Judiciary shall extend to cases, which respect the collection of the national revenue, impeachments of any national officers, and questions which involve the national peace and harmony," which was agreed to. The jurisdiction to impeach and to judge impeachments was later given to the House and to the Senate, respectively.

> The interpretation of the laws is the proper and peculiar province of the courts. A constitution is, in fact, and must be regarded by the judges as, a fundamental law. It therefore belongs to them to ascertain its meaning as well as the meaning of any particular act proceeding from the legislative body. If there should happen to be an irreconcilable variance between the two, that which has the superior obligation and validity ought, of course, to be preferred; or, in other words, the Constitution ought to be preferred to the statute, the intention of the people to the intention of their agents.
> —Alexander Hamilton, *The Federalist Papers,* Federalist No. 78
> Penguin Books USA, 1961, p. 467

Section 2.2   [Article III] In all Cases affecting Ambassadors, other public Ministers and Consuls, and those in which a State shall be Party, the supreme Court shall have original jurisdiction. In all the other Cases before mentioned [Section 2.1 above], the supreme Court shall have appellate jurisdiction, both as to Law and Fact, with such Exceptions, and under such Regulations, as the Congress shall make.

This section does not give Congress the authority to legislatively change the cases over which the Supreme Court shall have original jurisdiction; however, Congress may exempt certain cases from the appellate jurisdiction of the Supreme Court.

Section 2.2 of the Constitution, specifically where original jurisdiction is being granted to the Supreme Court, was used by Chief Justice John Marshall to rule that Section 13 of the Judiciary Act of 1789 was unconstitutional.

Section 2.3   [Article III] The Trial of all Crimes [does not include civil or equity cases], except in Cases of Impeachment, shall be by Jury; and such Trial shall be held in the State where the said Crimes shall have been committed; but when not committed within any State, the Trial shall be at such Place or Places as the Congress may by Law have directed.

For depriving us in many cases, of the benefits of trial by jury…*

For transporting us beyond seas to be tried for pretended offenses…**

The object here was to provide for a trial by jury of criminal offences committed either within or outside of any State jurisdiction.

> Mr. WILLIAMSON, observed that no provision was yet made for juries in Civil cases and suggested the necessity of it.
>
> Mr. GERRY urged the necessity of Juries to guard agst. corrupt Judges. He proposed that the Committee last appointed [at the Convention] should be directed to provide a clause for securing the trial by Juries.
>
> Mr. GORHAM. It is not possible to discriminate equity cases from those in which juries are proper. The Representatives of the people may be safely trusted in this matter.
>
> Col: MASON the difficulty mentioned by Mr. Gorham. The jury cases can not be specified. A general principle laid down on this and some other points would be sufficient. He wished the plan had been prefaced with a Bill of Rights, [and] would second a Motion if made for the purpose. It would give great quiet to the people; and with the aid of the State declarations [many of the state constitutions already contained bills of rights], a bill might be prepared in a few hours.
>
> —James Madison, *Notes of the Debates in the Federal Convention of 1787*
> Ohio University Press, 1966, p. 630

Section 3.1   [Article III] Treason against the United States, shall consist only in levying War against them [individually or collectively], or in adhering to their Enemies, giving them Aid and Comfort. No Person shall be convicted of Treason unless on the Testimony of two Witnesses to the same overt Act, or on Confession in open Court.

Remember, we had just finished a war to gain our independence, and the spirit of nationalism was a very passionate emotion among the delegates. Because conviction of treason would most assuredly result in severe punishment, probably death, it was felt necessary to narrowly define its meaning and also to firmly establish the prerequisites necessary for a conviction.

---

*Declaration of Independence
**Ibid

It was then moved to insert after "two witnesses" the words "to the same overt act."

Doc. FRANKLIN wished this amendment to take place—prosecutions for treason were generally **virulent**; and perjury too easily made use of against innocence.

—James Madison, *Notes of the Debates in the Federal Convention of 1787*

Ohio University Press, 1966, p. 492

Section 3.2 [Article III] The Congress shall have Power to declare the Punishment of Treason, but no **Attainder** of Treason shall work Corruption of Blood [apply to relatives], or Forfeiture except during the Life of the Person attainted.

Prior to our Constitution, the British parliament had issued bills of attainder (which are specifically prohibited under Article I, Section 9.3) without any corresponding conviction in the courts. These bills of attainder resulted not only in the execution of the person attainted but also in the permanent confiscation of the person's personal property and some sort of punishment to their posterity. Capital punishment was certainly still permissible, for treason or any other crime as prescribed by Congress, but it could only be carried out through the jurisdiction of the courts and not by a legislative act.

Mr. KING observed that the controversy relating to Treason might be of less magnitude than was supposed; as the Legislature might punish capitally under other names than Treason.

—James Madison, *Notes of the Debates in the Federal Convention of 1787*

Ohio University Press, 1966, p. 492

Congress in 1790 prescribed the punishment for treason to be death by hanging, and in 1862 as death and loss of slaves or, at a minimum, five years in prison and fines of at least $10,000. Conviction of treason prohibits the person from holding government office.

The more I read Article III, the more I am reminded of the priest who late in life admitted to only two certainties: "There is a God, and I am not Him." I have come to two conclusions about our judicial system: there are laws, and I am not a lawyer.

Although Article III affected the judicial branch, it left to Congress the task of establishing the many details of the newly created national court system.

The Judiciary Act of 1789 ranks as one of the most important enactments Congress has ever undertaken, more akin to a constitutive act [although subject to revocation by the Supreme Court] than to

ordinary legislation. The task was arduous, given the weakness of the new government and the extreme political sensitivity of many features of the court system. Congress struggled with the problem during the whole of its long first session, and the act that finally emerged in September 1789 was thought by many to be a sound but temporary compromise [as some thought also of the Constitution]. Yet, thanks to a combination of astute political foresight, hard work, and luck [the harder I work, the luckier I get], most of the important features of the national judiciary established by the act are with us today.
—Kermit L. Hall, editor, *The Oxford Companion to the Supreme Court of the United States*
Oxford University Press, 1992, p. 472

ARTICLE IV

Section 1   Full Faith and Credit shall be given in each State to the public Acts, Records, and judicial Proceedings of every other State. And the Congress may by general Laws prescribe the manner in which such Acts, Records and Proceedings shall be proved, and the Effect thereof.

Full faith and credit shall be given [they will be relied upon as truthful and factual] *in each of these states to the records, acts and judicial proceedings of the courts and magistrates of every other state.*
—Articles of Confederation, Article IV

Section 2.1   [Article IV] The Citizens [Citizens clearly did not include slaves.] of each State shall be entitled to all Privileges and Immunities of Citizens in the several [United] States.

This means that no state shall deny to its citizens rights or privileges that are guaranteed to United States citizens by the Constitution.

The Thirteenth Amendment (adopted December 18, 1865) abolished slavery, and the Fourteenth Amendment guaranteed citizenship, both in federal and state, to all persons born or naturalized in the United States.

Section 2.2   [Article IV] A Person charged in any State with Treason, Felony, or other Crime, who shall flee from Justice, and be found in another State, shall on Demand of the executive Authority of the State from which he fled, be delivered up, to be removed to the State having Jurisdiction of the Crime.

Section 2.3   [Article IV] No Person held to Service or Labour in one State, under the Laws thereof, escaping into another, shall, in Consequence of any Law or Regulation therein [meaning into a State outlawing slavery] be discharged from such Service or Labour, but shall be delivered up on Claim of the Party to whom such Service or Labour may be due.

This clause was added at the insistence of delegates from the southern states, primarily Pierce Butler, to prevent their slaves from escaping to, and claiming sanctuary in, slave-free states. The Thirteenth and Fourteenth Amendments somewhat reduced the ramifications of this clause of the Constitution.

This clause originally stated, "No Person legally held" but was changed to "under the Laws thereof," in compliance of the wishes of those who thought the term "legally held" was "**equivocal**, and favoring the idea that slavery was legal in a moral view."

Section 3.1   [Article IV] New States may be admitted by the Congress into this union; but no new State shall be formed or erected within the jurisdiction of any other State; nor any State be formed by the Junction of two or more States, or Parts of States, without the Consent of the Legislatures of the States concerned as well as of the Congress.

The word "jurisdiction" was chosen over "limits" to deter New York from preventing statehood for Vermont.

On April 11, 1862, West Virginia, which had been part of Virginia, was granted statehood. Virginia, on April 17, 1861, seceded from the United States, joined South Carolina, Mississippi, Florida, Alabama, Georgia, Louisiana, and Texas in the Confederacy and forfeited the rights protected by Section 3.1.

Section 3.2   [Article IV] The Congress shall have Power to dispose of and make all needful Rules and Regulations respecting the Territory or other Property belonging to the United States; and nothing in this Constitution shall be so construed as to Prejudice any Claims of the United States, or of any particular State.

This clause gives power to Congress to dispose of lands gained from England during and before the Revolutionary War that weren't legally claimed by any of the existing states. This settled one of the many weaknesses of the Articles of Confederation.

Concurrent with the writing of the Constitution at the Constitutional Convention, the United States in Congress Assembled, still in session, was preparing the **Northwest Ordinance** of July 13 1787, which in general outlined the procedures to establish representative government in the territories (excluding the lands claimed by the existing states) owned by the United States, and specifically guaranteed writs of habeas corpus, trial by jury, no cruel or unusual punishments, freedom of religious worship, and explained, "There shall be neither slavery nor involuntary servitude in the said territory, otherwise than in the punishment of crimes, whereof the party shall have been duly convicted."* It was signed into law by President George Washington on July 7, 1789

The Northwest Ordinance dealt only with lands east of the Mississippi River; the territory west of the Mississippi wasn't acquired by the United States until the Louisiana Purchase in 1803. Although Congress was given authority to "make all needful rules and regulations respecting the Territory or other Property belonging to the United States," the Supreme Court in the *Scott v. Sandford* (1857) ruling evidentially decided that prohibiting slavery wasn't a "needful rule or regulation." I assume the definition of needful depended upon whether you were a southern or northern judge.

> Section 4   [Article IV] The United States shall guarantee to every State in this Union a Republican Form of Government, and shall protect each of them against Invasion; and on Application of the Legislature, or of the Executive [in case the Legislature will not or cannot be convened] against domestic Violence.

"Or of the Executive" was added at the suggestion of Mr. Dickinson on the grounds that "the occasion itself might hinder the Legislature from meeting."

ARTICLE V

> The Congress, whenever two thirds of both Houses shall deem it necessary, shall propose Amendments to this Constitution, or, on the Application of the Legislatures of two thirds of the several States, shall call a Convention for proposing Amendments, which, in either Case, shall be valid to all Intents and Purposes, as Part of this Constitution, when ratified by the Legislatures of three fourths of the several States, or by Convention in three fourths thereof, as the one or the other Mode of Ratification may be proposed by the Congress; Provided that no Amendment which may be made prior to the Year One thousand eight hundred and

---

Northwest Ordinance, Article VI

eight shall in any Manner affect the first and fourth Clauses in the ninth Section of the first Article; and that no State, without its Consent, shall be deprived of its equal Suffrage in the Senate.

The Virginia Plan, as presented to the Convention on May 29, contained in Article 13 the proposal "that provision ought to be made for the amendment of the Articles of Union whensoever it shall seem necessary, and that the assent of the National Legislature ought not to be required."

> Mr. PINKNEY doubted the propriety or necessity of it.
> Mr. GERRY favored it. The novelty & difficulty of the experiment requires periodical revision. The prospect of such a revision would also give intermediate stability to the Gov. Nothing had yet happened in the States where this provision [in the states' constitutions] existed to prove its impropriety.
> —James Madison, *Notes of the Debates in the Federal Convention of 1787*
> Ohio University Press, 1966, p. 68

Regarding the possibility of amending the Constitution without the consent of the national legislature, Colonel Mason "urged the necessity of such a provision. The plan now to be formed will certainly be defective, as the Confederation has been found on trial to be. Amendments therefore will be necessary, and it will be better to provide for them, in an easy, regular and Constitutional way than to trust to chance and violence. It would be improper to require the consent of the Nat. Legislature, because they may abuse their power, and refuse their consent on that very account."*

On Sept 10, Mr. Madison proposed and Mr. Hamilton seconded the amendment procedure that was ultimately agreed to and accepted, with the subsequent addition that prohibited amending Sections 9.1 and 9.4 of Article I, prior to 1808.

The first and fourth clauses of Article I, Section 9 dealt with Congress being unable to prohibit any state from importing slaves before 1808 and the three-fifths rule for including slaves when determining state populations. Article V prohibits amending these two clauses prior to 1808, which was added to the amendment procedure on demand by Mr. Rutledge of South Carolina—again, not a vote favoring slavery, but a necessary compromise.

Mr. Gerry favored amendment without requiring the approval of the national legislature. He felt "the novelty and difficulty of the experiment requires periodical revision:

---

*James Madison, *Notes of the Debates in the Federal Convention of 1787* (Ohio University Press, 1966, p. 104)

The prospect of such a revision would also give intermediate stability to the Government."

Article V specifically sets forth the procedures to amend the United States Constitution, and not included as one of those methods is a Supreme Court ruling based on judicial review. Perhaps an amendment stating "Rulings by the courts, including the Supreme Court of the United States, on the constitutionality of a specific piece of legislation, will apply only to that specific legislative act upon which they have rendered a decision. Prior rulings of the Supreme Court, based on constitutionality issues, may not be used in determining the constitutionality of any prior or subsequent similar legislation. Court decisions regarding constitutionality issues will not effectually "amend" the Constitution of the United States, nor that of any of the individual states. In addition, ruling any piece of legislation unconstitutional will require the decision to be favored by at least seven of the Supreme Court judges. If less than seven judges are in attendance, no rulings may be made regarding constitutionality" would put curbs on judicial review.

The Supreme Court judges are appointed for life, are completely insulated from the consequences of their decisions, and are practically immune from removal. Samuel Chase was the only Supreme Court justice in history to be impeached, and he was found innocent (three votes short of the required twenty-two) by the Senate.

Article V places no time limit for a proposed amendment to be approved.

ARTICLE VI

Section 1.1   All Debts contracted and Engagements entered into, before the Adoption of this Constitution, shall be as valid against the United States under this Constitution, as under the Confederation.

In 1787, the United States owed more than seventy-five million dollars, most of which had been borrowed to support the Revolutionary War. This clause in our Constitution was a prerequisite to maintaining creditability with other nations. In addition, the Paris Peace Treaty of 1783 between England and the United States, contained the wording, "It is agreed that creditors on either side shall meet with no lawful impediments to recovery of the full value in sterling money of all bona fide debts heretofore contracted."

Section 1.2   [Article VI] This Constitution, and the Laws of the United States which shall be made in Pursuance thereof, and all Treaties made, or which shall be made, under the Authority of the United States, shall be the supreme Law of the Land; and judges in every State shall be bound thereby, any Thing in the Constitution or Laws of any State to the Contrary notwithstanding [in spite of anything to the contrary in any state law or state constitution].

John Rutledge of South Carolina on August 23, proposed this clause almost verbatim.

The Supreme Court (*Marbury v. Madison,* for one example) has established that "in pursuance thereof" has a broader meaning than just "subsequent to"; for laws to become "the supreme Law of the Land," they must also be authorized by and not violate this Constitution. "Because unconstitutional statutes are not the 'law of the land,' every judge must refuse to enforce them. This obligation assures that the courts themselves cannot be used as instruments for infringing the constitutional rights of the individual."*

> Section 1.3   [Article VI] The Senators and Representatives before mentioned, and the Members of the several State Legislatures, and all executive and judicial Officers, both of the United States and of the several States, shall be bound by Oath or Affirmation, to support this Constitution; but no religious Test shall ever be required as a Qualification to any Office or public Trust under the United States.

Requiring oaths in support of the national constitution from the members of the state legislatures, like almost every other section of the Constitution, found both proponents and opponents within the delegation. Mr. Sherman thought of it "as unnecessarily intruding into the State jurisdictions." Mr. Randolph, in contrast, considered it "necessary to prevent that competition between the National Constitution and laws and those of the particular States, which had already been felt. The officers of the States are already under oath to the States. To preserve a due impartiality they ought to be equally bound to the national Government. The National authority needs every support we can give it."

Mr. Gerry did not like the clause. He thought "there was as much reason for requiring an oath of fidelity to the States, from National officers, as vice versa." The motion to include the oath of support passed by the narrow margin of 6-5.

The "no religious Test" language was proposed by Charles Pinckney of South Carolina.

---

*David P. Currie, *The Constitution of the United States: A Primer for the People* (University of Chicago Press, 1988, p. 18)

133

ARTICLE VII

The ratification of the conventions of nine States, shall be sufficient for the establishment of this Constitution between the States so ratifying the same.

The ratification by conventions from nine states was a departure from the Articles of Confederation (Article 13), which required the approval of all the state legislatures to ratify or amend.

Mr. Sherman and Mr. King thought ratification by conventions was unnecessary, but James Madison thought it was essential. "Hence in conflicts between acts of the States, and of Congress, especially where the former are of posterior [later] date, and the decision is to be made by State tribunals, an uncertainty must necessarily prevail, or rather perhaps a certain decision in favor of the State authority." He was also concerned that a breach of any one Article, by any State, absolved the other States from the whole obligation. For these reasons, he thought "it indispensable that the new Constitution should be ratified in the most unexceptionable [least likely to displease] form, and by the supreme authority of the people themselves."

Mr. Pinckney hoped "that in case the experiment should not unanimously take place, nine States might be authorized to unite under the same Government." Any state not ratifying the Constitution would flounder alone.

It is interesting to note that Article 13 of the Articles of Confederation required unanimous approval by all thirteen states to amend the Articles; the Constitution thus gave more power to nine states than the Articles of Confederation did to thirteen.

Ratification by nine states was chosen because "Nine States had been required in all great cases under the Confederation & that number was on that account preferable," according to George Mason (August 31).

Ben Franklin wrote a speech that was delivered by James Wilson on the last day of the convention. I think it is a wonderful summary of the emotions, the compromises, the fears, and the hopes that had been expressed, debated, and kindled during the convention. This speech is presented below, as reproduced by James Madison.

> I confess that there are several parts of this constitution which I do not at present approve, but I am not sure I shall never approve them: For having lived long, I have experienced many instances of being obliged by better information, or fuller consideration, to change opinions even on important subjects, which I once thought right, but found to be otherwise. It is therefore that the older I grow, the more apt I am to doubt my own judgment, and

to pay more respect to the judgment of others. Most men indeed as well as most sects in Religion, think themselves in possession of all truth, and that wherever others differ from them it is so far error. Steele a Protestant in a Dedication tells the Pope that the only difference between our Churches in their opinions of the certainty of their doctrines is, the Church of Rome is infallible and the Church of England is never in the wrong. But though many private persons think almost as highly of their own infallibility as of that of their sect, few express it so naturally as a certain French lady, who in a dispute with her sister, said "I don't know how it happens, Sister, but I meet with no body but myself, that's always in the right."

In these sentiments, Sir, I agree to this Constitution with all its faults, if they are such; because I think a general Government necessary for us, and there is no form of Government but what may be a blessing to the people if well administered, and believe farther that this is likely to be well administered for a course of years, and can only end in Despotism, as other forms have done before it, when the people shall become so corrupted as to need despotic Government, being incapable of any other. I doubt too whether any other Convention we can obtain, may be able to make a better Constitution. For when you assemble a number of men to have the advantage of their joint wisdom, you inevitable [sic] assemble with those men, all their prejudices, their passions, their errors of opinion, their local interests, and their selfish views. From such an assembly can a perfect production be expected? It therefore astonishes me, Sir, to find this system approaching so near to perfection as it does; and I think it will astonish our enemies, who are waiting with confidence to hear that our councils are confounded like those of the Builders of Babel; and that our States are on the point of separation, only to meet hereafter for the purpose of cutting one another's throats. Thus I consent, Sir, to this Constitution because I expect no better, and because I am not sure, that it is not the best. The opinions I have had of its errors, I sacrifice to the public good. I have never whispered a syllable of them abroad. Within these walls they were born, and here they shall die. If every one of us in returning to our Constituents were to report the objections he has had to it, and endeavor to gain partisans in support of them, we might prevent its being generally received, and thereby lose all the **salutary** effects and great advantages resulting naturally in our favor among foreign Nations as well as among ourselves, from our real or apparent unanimity. Much of the strength and efficiency of any Government in procuring and securing happiness to the people, depends, on opinion, on the general opinion of the goodness of the Government, as well as of the wisdom and integrity of its Governors. I hope therefore that for our sakes as a part of the people, and for the sake of **posterity**, we shall act heartily and unanimously in recommending this Constitution (if approved by Congress and confirmed by the Conventions) wherever our influence may extend, and turn our future thoughts and endeavors to the means of having it well administered.

On the whole, Sir, I can not help expressing a wish that every member of the Convention who may still have objections to it, would with me, on this occasion doubt a little of his own infallibility, and to make manifest our unanimity, put his name to this instrument. [Good advice on any occasion]
—James Madison, *Notes of the Debates in the Federal Convention of 1787*
Ohio University Press, 1966, pp. 653–654

The only three men present on this day who refused to sign the Constitution were George Mason and Edmund Randolph of Virginia, and Elbridge Gerry of Massachusetts. The specific reasons for their refusals will be discussed in Chapter VII, The Founding Fathers. Little did they realize the great and enduring honor they were forfeiting.

As the last members were signing our new Constitution, Ben Franklin, while looking at the back of the president's chair on which the sun happened to be painted, remarked, "I have said often and often in the course of the Session, and the vicissitudes of my hopes and fears as to its issue, looked at that behind the President without being able to tell whether it was rising or setting: But now at length I have the happiness to know that it is a rising and not a setting Sun."

I heartily recommend reading James Madison's "Notes of Debates in the Federal Convention of 1787" to everyone interested not only in learning more about our Constitution but also as a unique opportunity to enjoy and learn from the diverse viewpoints of great men assembled together with the difficult and indispensable task of uniting the separate colonial governments.

Done in Convention by the Unanimous Consent of the States present the Seventeenth Day of September in the Year of our Lord, one thousand seven hundred and Eighty seven and of the independence of the United States of America the twelfth. In witness whereof we have hereunto subscribed our names,

Go: Washington—Presidt. and Deputy from Virginia

New Hampshire
John Langdon
Nicholas Gilman

Massachusetts
Nathaniel Gorham
Rufus King

Connecticut
Wm. Saml. Johnson
Roger Sherman

New York
Alexander Hamilton

New Jersey
Wil: Livingston
David Brearley
Wm. Paterson
Jona: Dayton

Pennsylvania
B. Franklin
Thomas Mifflin
Robt. Morris
Geo. Clymer
Thos. Fitzsimons
Jared Ingersoll
James Wilson
Gouv Morris

Delaware
Geo: Read
Gunning Bedford Jun
John Dickinson
Richard Bassett
Jaco: Broom

Maryland
James McHenry
Dan of St. Thos Jenifer
Danl. Carroll

Virginia
John Blair
James Madison Jr.

North Carolina
Wm. Blount
Richd. Dobbs Spaight
Hugh (Hu) Williamson

South Carolina
J. Rutledge,
Charles Cotesworth &
Charles Pinckney
Pierce Butler

Georgia
William Few
Abr Baldwin

Attest
William Jackson, Secretary

Order of Ratification:

Delaware	Dec 7	1787	*Unanimous*
Pennsylvania	Dec 12	1787	*46-23*
New Jersey	Dec 18	1787	*Unanimous*
Georgia	Jan 1	1788	*Unanimous*
Connecticut	Jan 9	1788	*128-40*

Massachusetts	Feb 6	1788	187-168
Maryland	April 28	1788	63-11
S. Carolina	May 23	1788	149-73
New Hampshire*	June 21	1788	57-47
Virginia	June 26	1788	89-79
New York	July 26	1788	30-27
N. Carolina	Nov 21	1789	194-77
Rhode Island	May 29	1790	34-32

*New Hampshire, being the ninth state to ratify, thereby effected the Constitution and the United States of America. Because it was the duty of the Continental Congress to acknowledge the ratification of the new Constitution by the various states, the new national government did not become official until March 4, 1789, with the seating of the First Constitutional Congress.

THE AMENDMENTS

(Amendments I through X proposed September 25, 1789, adopted December 15, 1791)

AMENDMENT I

Congress shall make no law respecting an establishment of religion, or prohibiting the free exercise thereof; or **abridging** the freedom of speech, or of the press; or the right of the people peaceably to assemble, and to petition the Government for a redress of grievances.

The theory of "separation of church and state" first gained notoriety after Locke's "Letter on Toleration" (1689). There is not one reference in Amendment I, not one reference in the entire Constitution, relating to church and state. Supreme Court decisions have not only mistaken "no law respecting an establishment of religion" for "separation of church and state," but have ruled we must interchange "religion" with "God," while completely forgetting "or prohibiting the free exercise thereof." Are you atheists really more afraid of seeing the Ten Commandments displayed on government property than a vampire is of eating garlic bread? I haven't read the Ten Commandments in a long time, but I seem to remember the so-called Ten Commandments contained some good guidelines, even for Jews, Christians, Muslims, and atheists.

The constitutional delegates were certainly familiar with the word "expression," and if they intended freedom of speech to include every act known to man, I doubt they would have felt the need to also specifically mention freedom of the press. Also, I think it is important to notice the use of the word "abridging" in the first Amendment and the word "infringed" in the second Amendment. I think the Founding Fathers wanted to make restricting our freedom to keep and bear arms just as difficult as restricting our freedom of speech and freedom of the press. I think the stretch from "speech" to "expression" might exceed most elastic limits. I'm also not convinced that the right to burn our national flag, in violation of laws prohibiting such, should be protected under freedom-of-speech rights. The real problem is why some legislators felt the need to even pass anti-flag-burning laws; anyone who wants to burn our flag, as long as it is their own flag, should be free to do so. I never anticipated that flag burning would become a national obsession.

The First Amendment could be interrupted to only prohibit Congress from legislatively infringing upon specific rights; "The Supreme Court [*New York Times Co. v. United States*] has held, however, that other branches of the federal government also lack power to infringe the rights the amendment protects."
—David P. Currie, *The Constitution of the United States: A Primer for the People* University of Chicago Press, 1988, p. 79

The Fourteenth Amendment has been used (*Everson v. Board of Education of Ewing Township*) to extend the First Amendment protections against "respecting an establishment of religion" to include state statute encroachments. *Engel v. Vitale* (1962) and *Abington School District v. Schempp* (1963) used the Establishment Clause to prevent prayer in public schools.

Other cases, such as *Stromberg v. California* (1931), *O'Brien v. United States* (1968), and *Schenck v. United States* (1919) have redefined freedom of speech and have standardized rules for legislative invasions.

The House of Representatives, convening for the first time in 1789, quickly took up the question of amending the Constitution by adding our Bill of Rights. James Madison began the debate as follows:

> This day, Mr. Speaker, is the day assigned for taking into consideration the subject of amendments to the Constitution... I will state my reasons why I think it proper to propose amendments, and state the amendments themselves, so far as I think they ought to be proposed. If I thought I could fulfill the duty which I owe to myself and my constituents, to let the subject pass over in silence, I most certainly should not trespass upon the indulgence of this House. But I cannot do this, and am therefore compelled to beg a patient hearing to what I have to lay before you. And I do most sincerely believe, that if Congress will devote but one day to this subject, so far as to satisfy the public that we do not disregard their wishes, it will have a salutary influence on the public councils, and prepare the way for a favorable reception of our future measures.
> —Philip B. Kurland and Ralph Lerner, editors, *The Founders' Constitution*, Vol. V
> University of Chicago Press, 1987, pp. 20, 24

Although a few of the delegates wished to include a bill of rights in the finished draft of the Constitution, I believe that because many of the state constitutions already included their own bills of rights and that nothing in our new constitution abrogated those rights, many of the delegates decided that including them as part of their united effort might be superfluous.

> As to religion, I hold it to be the indispensable duty of every government, to protect all conscientious professors thereof, and I know of no other business which government hath to do therewith.
> —Thomas Paine, *Common Sense*
> Penguin Books, 1986, pp. 108–109

That the people have a right to freedom of speech, and of writing, and publishing their sentiments; therefore the freedom of the press ought not to be restrained.
—Pennsylvania Constitution, 1776, Section XII

The liberty of the press is essential to the security of freedom in a state; it ought not, therefore, to be restrained in this Commonwealth.
—Massachusetts Constitution, 2 Mar. 1780, Section XVI

That the people have a right to assemble together...
—North Carolina Constitution, December 18, 1776, Section XVIII

That the people have a right to assemble together...
—Pennsylvania Constitution, September 28, 1776, Section XVI

That freedom of the press is one of the great bulwarks of liberty, and therefore ought never to be restrained.
—North Carolina Constitution, December 18, 1776, Section XV

There shall be no establishment of any one religious sect in this State in preference to another.
—Delaware Constitution, 1776, Article 29

That freedom of speech and debates—ought not to be impeached in any other court or judicature.
—Maryland Constitution, November 11, 1776, Section VIII

We should be aware that even though we have freedom of the press, printing of libelous or harmful material does not dismiss one from the potential consequences of abusing that freedom.

Nor does our constitution or declaration of rights abrogate the common law in this respect, as some have insisted. The 16th Article [Massachusetts Constitution, 1780] declares, that "the liberty of the press is essential to the security of freedom in a state; it ought not, there, to be restrained in this commonwealth. In the 11th Article it is declared, that every "subject of the commonwealth ought to find a certain remedy, by having recourse to the laws, for all injuries or wrongs which he may receive in his person, property or character." And thus the general declaration in the 16th article is qualified. Besides, it is well understood, and received as a commentary on this provision for the liberty of the press, that it was intended to prevent all such previous restraints upon publication as had been practiced by other governments, and in early times here, to stifle the efforts of patriots towards enlightening their fellow subjects upon their rights and the duties of rulers. The liberty of the press was to be unrestrained, but he who used it was to be responsible in case of its abuse; like the right to keep fire arms, which does not protect him who uses them for annoyance or destruction.

—Philip B. Kurland and Ralph Lerner, editors, *The Founders' Constitution*, Vol. 5

University of Chicago Press, 1987, p. 177

AMENDMENT II

A well regulated militia, being necessary to the security of a free State, the right of the people to keep and bear arms, shall not be infringed.

This amendment clearly states "the right of the *People*." It doesn't say the right of the people when serving in the militia. This right is not restricted to times of war and ends with "shall not be infringed" instead of "unless restricted by any government statute."

Amendment II says, "A well regulated militia, being necessary to the security of a free State, the right to keep and bear [to carry, transport, to have or show] arms shall not be infringed." Gun-control advocates seem to always omit the part about how those rights "shall not be infringed." This means that there should be no laws restricting our right to keep and bear arms, such as concealed-weapons permits, such as trying to restrict the size of the clips, such as setting restrictions regarding which days of the week we can bear them. I suppose because one of our commanders in chief wasn't sure what the definition of "is" is, it's not surprising that the word infringed is (or should I use the simple words "may be") difficult to define. Mexico has laws against private citizens carrying guns, but the drug lords seem to have no trouble finding assault weapons (even before Mr. Holder freely handed them out). Killings in this country are not the result of a lack of legislated gun controls; we already have many laws outlawing murder, without much effect.

> This was an indictment founded on the act of the legislature of this State [Kentucky], "to prevent persons in this common-wealth from wearing concealed arms."

> Whether or not an act of the legislature conflicts with the constitution [in this case the State Constitution], is, at all times, a question of great delicacy, and deserves the most mature and deliberate consideration of the court. But though a question of delicacy, yet as it is a judicial one, the court would be unworthy its station, were it to shrink from deciding it, whenever in the course of judicial examination, a decision becomes material to the right in contest. The court should never, on slight implication or vague conjecture, pronounce the legislature to have transcended its authority in the enactment of law; but when a clear and strong

142

conviction is entertained, that an act of the legislature is incompatible with the constitution, there is no alternative for the court to pursue, but to declare that conviction, and pronounce the act inoperative and void. And such is the conviction entertained by a majority of the court (Judge Mills dissenting, [sic]) in relation to the act in question.
—Philip B. Kurland and Ralph Lerner, editors, *The Founders' Constitution,* Vol. V
University of Chicago Press, 1987, p. 213

That the people have a right to bear arms for the defence of themselves and the state.
—Pennsylvania Constitution, 1776, Section XIII

AMENDMENT III

No soldier shall, in time of peace be quartered in any house, without the consent of the owner, nor in time of war, but in a manner to be prescribed by law.

No soldier in time of peace, shall be quartered in any house, without the consent of the owner; and in time of war, such quarters ought not to be made but by the civil authorities in a manner ordained by the legislature.
—New Hampshire Constitution, 1776, Article 27, Quartering of Soldiers

He has kept among us in times of peace, standing armies, without the consent of our legislature.
—Declaration of Independence

AMENDMENT IV

The right of the people to be secure in their persons, houses, papers, and effects, against unreasonable searches and seizures, shall not be violated, and no warrants shall issue, but upon probable cause, supported by oath or affirmation, and particularly describing the place to be searched, and the persons or things to be seized.

Massachusetts Constitution, 2 March, 1780, Section XIV: "Every subject has a right to be secure from all unreasonable searches, and seizures of his person, his houses, his papers, and all his possessions."

> Pennsylvania Constitution, September 28, 1776, Section X: "That the people have a right to hold themselves—and possessions free from search and seizure…"

The Fourth Amendment prevented Writs of Assistance, which had been issued to help enforce British trade regulations proclaimed under the Townshend Act of 1767.

> What is clear is that, in the New England colonies, the writs entered popular and political rhetoric as despotic instruments that allowed brutal customs officers to raid the homes of innocent families and were seen as similar to the general warrants used in London against John Wilkes, friend of America and another victim of oppression and corruption. General warrants were condemned as illegal in Britain both by the Court of Common Pleas and by parliamentary resolution. The use in America of writs of assistance, which so closely resembled them, added to colonial grievances, to the sense of unequal treatment.
> —Jack P. Greene and J. R. Pole, editors, *The Blackwell Encyclopedia of the American Revolution*
> Blackwell Publishers, 1994, p. 167

AMENDMENT V

No person shall be held to answer for a capital, or otherwise **infamous** crime, unless on a presentment or indictment of a grand jury, except in cases arising in the land or naval forces, or in the militia, when in actual service in time of war or public danger; nor shall any person be subject for the same offense to be twice put in jeopardy of life or limb; nor shall be compelled in any criminal case to be a witness against himself, nor be deprived of life, liberty, or property, without **due process of law**; nor shall private property be taken for public use without just compensation.

Because of the right not to "be compelled in any criminal case to be a witness against himself," the Supreme Court in the *Miranda v. Arizona* case in 1966 ruled that any statement made by a suspect while under interrogation will not be admissible in court unless the suspect has previously been notified of his Fifth Amendment rights.

> In one of its most famous decisions, Miranda v. Arizona (1966), the Warren Court required police to advise criminal suspects of particular constitutional rights prior to interrogation. These Miranda warnings consisted of four items: (1) the right to remain silent; (2) the reminder that anything said could be used against the suspect;

(3) the right to counsel; and (4) the related reminder that counsel would be provided for indigents.

Miranda warnings apply when suspects are in police custody and under interrogation. In decisions subsequent to *Miranda*, the Court has emphasized that custody consists of the restriction of freedom of movement by the police.

—Kermit L. Hall, editor, *The Oxford Companion to the Supreme Court of the United States*
Oxford University Press, 1992, p. 555

VII. That, in all criminal prosecutions, every man has a right to be informed of the accusation against him, and to confront the accusers and witnesses with other testimony, and shall not be compelled to give evidence against himself.
—North Carolina Constitution, December 18, 1776

VIII. That every member of society hath a right to be protected in the enjoyment of life, liberty and property, and therefore is bound to contribute his proportion towards the expense of that protection and yield his personal service when necessary, or an equivalent thereto: But no part of a man's property can be justly taken from him, or applied to public uses, without his own consent, or that of his legal representatives.
—Pennsylvania Constitution, September 28, 1776

The Sixteenth Amendment (in only thirty words) has voided the last clause of the Fifth Amendment "nor shall private property [our personal income] be taken for public use without just compensation." How many of us consider buying jets for foreign governments, whether they be democratic or not, as just compensation for taking part of our income?

AMENDMENT VI

In all criminal prosecutions, the accused shall enjoy the right to a speedy and public trial, by an impartial jury of the State and district wherein the crime shall have been committed, which district shall have been previously ascertained by law, and to be informed of the nature and cause of the accusation; to be confronted with the witnesses against him; to have compulsory process for obtaining witnesses in his favor, and to have the assistance of counsel for his defense.

That, in all criminal prosecutions, every man hath a right to be informed of the accusation against him.
—Maryland Constitution, November 11, 1776, Section XIX

8. That in all capital or criminal prosecutions a man hath a right to demand the cause and nature of his accusation, to be confronted with the accusers and witnesses, to call for evidence in his favour, and to a speedy trial by an impartial jury of his vicinage, without whose unanimous consent he cannot be found guilty, nor can he be compelled to give evidence against himself; that no man be deprived of his liberty except by the law of the land, or the judgment of his peers.
—Virginia Declaration of Rights, June 12, 1776

AMENDMENT VII

In suits at common law where the value in controversy shall exceed twenty dollars, the right of trial by jury shall be preserved, and no fact tried by a jury shall be otherwise reexamined in any court of the United States, than according to the rules of the common law.

11. That in controversies respecting property, and in suits between man and man, the ancient trial by jury is preferable to any other, and ought to be held sacred.
—Virginia Declaration of Rights, June 12, 1776

SECT. 25. Trials shall be by jury as heretofore: And it is recommended to the legislature of this state, to provide by law against every corruption or partiality in the choice, return, or appointment of juries.
—Pennsylvania Constitution, September 28, 1776

Agreement as to what "the rules of common law" specifically are, may present some problems.

AMENDMENT VIII

Excessive bail shall not be required, nor excessive fines imposed, nor cruel and unusual punishments inflicted.

Cruel *and* unusual is quite different from cruel *or* unusual, and certainly did not prohibit the death penalty (life and limb, attainder) in 1787. Duels to the death were quite common—ask Alexander Hamilton.

Furman v. Georgia (1976, 5-4) was the first time the Supreme Court struck down the death penalty pursuant to the "cruel and unusual punishment" clause of the Eighth Amendment, three of the justices finding not the death penalty per se to be cruel and unusual, but that the discretion of the jury produced a random pattern among who received the death penalty and the randomness itself was cruel and unusual. I think most will agree that death is cruel but as to whether it is also unusual will depend upon ever-changing contemporary interpretations. What I find random is the way the Supreme Court interprets the Constitution. Remember, the president appoints the Supreme Court judges, and that fact should be considered when choosing our presidents.

> XXVI.   No magistrate or court of law shall demand excessive bail or sureties, impose excessive fines, or inflict cruel or unusual punishments.
> —Massachusetts Constitution, March 2, 1780

> X.   That excessive bail should not be required, nor excessive fines imposed, nor cruel or unusual punishments inflicted.
> —North Carolina Constitution, December 18, 1776

AMENDMENT IX

The enumeration in the Constitution of certain rights shall not be construed to deny or **disparage** others retained by the people.

Samuel Adams, in his "The Rights of the Colonists," written on November 20, 1772 (four years before the Declaration of Independence) stated:

> In short it is the greatest absurdity to suppose it in the power of one or any number of men at the entering into society, to renounce their essential natural rights, or the means of preserving those rights when the great end of civil government from the very nature of its institution is for the support, protection and defence of those very rights: the principal of which as is before observed, are life liberty and property. If men through fear, fraud or mistake, should in terms renounce and give up any essential natural right, the eternal law of reason and the great end of society, would absolutely vacate such renunciation; the right to freedom being the gift of God Almighty, it is not in the power of Man to alienate this gift, and voluntarily become a slave.
> —Philip B. Kurland and Ralph Lerner, editors, *The Founders' Constitution,* Vol. 5
> University of Chicago Press, 1987, pp. 395–396

AMENDMENT X

The powers not delegated to the United States by the Constitution, nor prohibited by it [the Constitution] to the States, are reserved to the States respectively, or to the people.

The first ten amendments are collectively referred to as the Bill of Rights. James Madison (Representative from Virginia) proposed to the House that amendments should be considered on June 1, 1789, during the First Session of Congress. A few of the constitutional delegates had desired a Bill of Rights during the convention, George Mason in particular, and many of the states during their ratifying process had suggested also that a Bill of Rights should be included in the Constitution.

> Each State retains its sovereignty, freedom, and independence, and every power, jurisdiction and right, which is not by this confederation *expressly* [emphasis added] delegated to the United States, in Congress assembled.
> —Articles of Confederation, Article II

The omission of the word "expressly" from the Tenth Amendment was instrumental in the decision of *McCulloch v. Maryland,* whereby the Court (elaborated by Justice Marshall) ruled that the Constitution granted "incidental or implied powers" to our national government. This is quite a stretch, because there was overwhelming sentiment among the delegates that their mission was to improve upon the Articles of Confederation (which did contain the word "expressly") while keeping the powers of the new federal government to a minimum. I believe this an example of a highly educated man (Marshall) becoming so impressed with his own intelligence that he abandoned his common sense.

> Sir, I think there is another subject with regard to which this Constitution deserves approbation. I mean the accuracy with which the line is drawn between the powers of the general government and those of the particular state governments. We have heard some general observations, on this subject, from the gentlemen who conduct the opposition. They have asserted that these powers are unlimited and undefined. These words are as easily pronounced as limited and defined. ... Whoever views the matter in a true light, will see that the powers are as minutely enumerated and defined as was possible, and will also discover that the general clause ["provide for the common defense, promote the general welfare, and secure the blessing of liberty to ourselves and our posterity"], against which so much exception is taken, is nothing more than what was necessary to render effectual the particular powers that are granted.
> —James Wilson, *Pennsylvania Ratifying Convention,* 4 December 1787

The Tenth Amendment is the most ignored (by our federal legislature) component of the Bill of Rights, probably because it was intended to limit those who most frequently usurp it.

I have mentioned a few articles from various state Constitutions that had already enumerated similar personal protections to those found in the US Constitution's Bill of Rights, just to demonstrate that our Constitution was as much an amalgamation of existing ideas as it was a result of new and original concepts.

The Supreme Court in *Barron v. Baltimore* (1833) by vote of 7-0, concluded that the Bill of Rights restrained only the national government, not the state or local governments. It wasn't until 1925, with *Gitlow v. New York*, that the Barron decision began to lose its preemptive status. Ratification of the Fourteenth Amendment, specifically restricting states' authority under the clause "No State shall make or enforce any law that shall abridge the privileges or immunities of citizens of the United States" helps support the contemporary mood of the courts that the Bill of Rights does indeed also restrict the states. Being the simple minded guy that I am, I had presumed that Article VI, Section 1.2, of the Constitution "This Constitution, and the Laws of the United States which shall be made in Pursuance thereof, and all Treaties made, or which shall be made, under the Authority of the United States, shall be the supreme Law of the Land; and judges in every State shall be bound thereby, any Thing in the Constitution or Laws of any State to the Contrary notwithstanding" had already made this idea pretty clear.

AMENDMENT XI
(Proposed September 5, 1794, adopted January 8, 1798)
The judicial power of the United States shall not be construed to extend to any suit in law or equity, commenced or prosecuted against one of the United States by Citizens of another State, or by Citizens or Subjects of any Foreign State.

A default judgment ruling by the Supreme Court in *Chisholm v. Georgia,* whereby Chisholm, after losing in the State Court, was awarded monies from Georgia for the value of clothing supplied by Chisholm during the Revolutionary War, Georgia losing in spite of claiming immunity from the suit on grounds of its being "a sovereign and independent state," precipitated proposing the Eleventh Amendment. Congress, being fearful of "creditors flocking to the federal courts,"* passed this amendment. This was the first time a Supreme Court decision had been superseded by a constitutional amendment.

AMENDMENT XII
(Proposed December 12, 1803, adopted September 25, 1804)
The Electors shall meet in their respective states, and vote by ballot for President and Vice-President, one of whom, at least, shall not be an inhabitant of the same state with themselves;

---

*Kermit L. Hall, editor, *The Oxford Companion to the Supreme Court of the United States* (Oxford University Press, 1992, p. 144)

they shall name in their ballots the person voted for as President, and in distinct ballots the person voted for as Vice-President, and they shall make distinct lists of all persons voted for
as President, and of all persons voted for as Vice-President,
and of the number of votes for each, which lists they shall sign
and certify, and transmit sealed to the seat of the government
of the United States, directed to the President of the Senate; —
The President of the Senate shall, in the presence of the Senate
and House of Representatives, open all the certificates and the
votes shall then be counted; — The person having the greatest
number of votes for President, shall be the President, and if
such number be a majority of the whole number of Electors
appointed; and if no person have such majority, then from the
persons having the highest numbers not exceeding three on
the list of those voted for as President, the house of Representatives shall choose immediately, by ballot, the President. But
in choosing the President, the votes shall be taken by states,
the representation from each state having one vote; and quorum for this purpose shall consist of a member or members
from two-thirds of the states, and a majority of all the states
shall be necessary to a choice. And if the house of Representatives shall not choose a President whenever the right of choice
shall devolve upon them, before the fourth day of March next
following [changed to January 20 by the Twentieth Amendment in 1933], then the Vice-President shall act as President, as
in the case of the death or other constitutional disability of the
President. — The person having the greatest number of votes as
Vice-President, shall be the Vice-President, if such number be
a majority of the whole number of Electors appointed, and if
no person have a majority, then from the two highest numbers
on the list, the Senate shall choose the Vice-President; a quorum for the purpose shall consist of two-thirds of the whole
number of Senators, and a majority of the whole number shall
be necessary to a choice. But no person constitutionally ineligible to the office of President shall be eligible to that of Vice-
President of the United States.

This amendment was implemented primarily because of the tie votes cast for Thomas
Jefferson and Aaron Burr in the 1801 presidential election. See Article II, Section 1.3
for a detailed explanation of the original procedural mechanics.

But Mr. President, I have never yet seen the great inconvenience
that has been so much clamored about, and that will be provided
against in future by substituting this amendment. There was,

indeed, a time when it became necessary for the House of Representatives to elect, by ballot, a President of the United States from
the two highest in vote, and they were engaged here some days, as
I have been told, in a very good-humored way, in the exercise of
that Constitutional right; they at length decided; and what was the
consequence: The people were satisfied, and here the thing ended.
What does this prove? That the Constitution is defective? No sir, but
rather the wisdom and efficiency of the very provision intended to
be stricken out, and that the people are acquainted with the nature
of their Government; and give me leave to say, if fortune had smiled
upon another man, and that election had eventuated in another
way, the consequence would have been precisely the same; the
great mass of the people would have been content and quiet; and
those factious restless disorganizers, that are the eternal disturbers
of all well administered Governments, and who then talked of resistance, would have had too much prudence to hazard their necks in
so dangerous an enterprise. I will not undertake to say that there
was no danger apprehended on that occasion. I know many of the
friends of the Constitution had their fears; the experiment however,
proved them groundless; but what was the danger apprehended
pending the election in the House of Representatives? Was it that
they might choose Colonel Burr or Mr. Jefferson President? Not at
all; they had, notwithstanding what had been said on the subject by
the gentleman from Maryland [Mr. Wright] a clear Constitutional
right to choose either of them, as much so as the Electors in the several States had to vote for them in the first instance;
—Philip B. Kurland and Ralph Lerner, editors, *The Founders' Constitution,* Vol. V
University of Chicago Press, 1987, p. 457

The Electoral College has gained a lot of attention lately because of the outcome of
the presidential election of 2000: Bush won the electoral vote and was elected president; Gore possibly won the popular vote and a paid trip back to Tennessee, and the
Supreme Court eventually allocated the electoral votes in Florida. The Constitution
has stood strong even in the face of microscopic scrutiny and bombardment by the
uninformed, the misinformed, the disenchanted, and the ACLU.

I believe the Electoral College system is fair, and it helps to protect the rights of the
less populous states. This method of electing the president was implemented as a
compromise to the small states, to protect their citizens from being overrun by those
of the more populous states. Don't be duped into believing that a president not
receiving the majority of the popular votes doesn't have a "mandate of the people."
The inconsistencies that have developed in our presidential election process are not
due to the electoral concept but are the result of partisan politics dictating electoral
selection and their subsequent voting restrictions, as directed by the state legisla-

tures. We all need to know how our electors are nominated, when they are chosen, and if they are legally bound to vote as a unit. The problems need to be solved at the state, not the national, level.

AMENDMENT XIII
(Proposed February 1, 1865, adopted December 18, 1865)

Section 1   Neither slavery nor involuntary servitude, except as a punishment for crime whereof the party shall have been duly convicted, shall exist within the United States, or any place subject to their jurisdiction

Section 1 legally ended slavery throughout the entire United States, subsequent to the end of the Civil War on May 10, 1865.

Section 2   Congress shall have power to enforce this article by appropriate legislation.

In March of 1857, approximately four years before the beginning of the Civil War, the US Supreme Court, in the *Scott v. Sandford* case, handed down the most partisan and controversial decision in their history. In addition to being a catalyst for the Civil War, the decision in this case sparked passage of the Thirteenth, Fourteenth and Fifteenth Amendments.

AMENDMENT XIV
(Proposed June 16, 1868, adopted July 28, 1868)

Section 1   All persons born or naturalized in the United States, and subject to the jurisdiction thereof, are citizens of the United States and of the State wherein they reside. No State shall make or enforce any law that shall abridge the privileges or immunities of citizens of the United States; nor shall any State deprive any person of life, liberty, or property, without due process of law [The Fifth Amendment guaranteed us protection from the federal government by due process of law; the protection of these same rights is hereby extended to include actions by the state governments.]; nor deny to any person within its jurisdiction the equal protection of the laws.

Article IV, Section 2.1 of the Constitution had merely granted certain rights to citizens (which did not include slaves). The Fourteenth Amendment granted citizenship to slaves residing within the United States and therefore entitled them to the rights granted by Article IV, Section 2.1.

Two important cases decided on the basis of "due process of law," *Lochner v. New York* (1905) and *Roe v. Wade* (1973), demonstrate the wide-reaching power used by the Supreme Court to "expound the Constitution." The courts define not only words or phrases (liberty, property, due process) but additionally, when and to whom those definitions apply.

The Supreme Court in both the abovementioned cases declared state statutes to be unconstitutional on grounds that they deprived individuals of liberty without due process. The government does not, however, have the authority to deprive citizens of life, liberty, or property *with due process,* if by doing so, it deprives them of any other of their constitutionally protected rights.

> Section 2   Representatives shall be apportioned among the several States according to their [the states'] respective numbers, counting the whole number of persons in each State, excluding Indians not taxed. But when the right to vote at any election for the choice of electors for President and Vice-President of the United States, Representatives in Congress, the Executive and Judicial officers of a State, or the members of the Legislature thereof, is denied to any of the male inhabitants of such State, being twenty-one years of age, and citizens of the United States, or in any way abridged, except for participation in rebellion, or other crime, the basis of representation therein shall be reduced in the proportion which the number of such male citizens shall bear to the whole number of males citizens twenty-one years of age in such State.

Women still didn't have the right to vote (and rightfully so), but slavery had been legally abolished. A state could still prohibit males above the age of twenty-one from voting, but by doing so, the state would thereby reduce its representation in Congress. Now that slavery had been abolished, only "Indians not taxed" were still excluded from being counted when determining each state's representation in the House. Freeing the slaves greatly increased the representative power in Congress of the southern states while simultaneously increasing their burden for payment of direct taxes.

> Section 3   No person shall be a Senator or Representative in Congress, or elector of President and Vice-President, or hold any office, civil or military, under the United States, or under any State, who, having previously taken an oath, as a member of Congress, or as an officer of the United States, or as a member of any State legislature, or as an executive or judicial officer of any State, to support the Constitution of the United States, shall have engaged in insurrection or rebellion against

the same, or given aid or comfort to the enemies thereof. But Congress may by vote of two-thirds of each house, remove such disability.

Section 4   The validity of the public debt of the United States, authorized by law, including debts incurred for payment of pensions and bounties for services in suppressing insurrection or rebellion, shall not be questioned. But neither the United States nor any State shall assume or pay any debt or obligation incurred in aid of insurrection or rebellion against the United States, or any claim for the loss or emancipation of any slave; but all such debts, obligations and claims shall be held illegal and void.

Section 4 absolves the national government, or any of the states, from responsibility to pay the debts of states involved in "insurrection or rebellion against the United States," specifically the Confederate States.

Section 5   The Congress shall have power to enforce, by appropriate legislation, the provision of this article.

It is important to realize that the Fourteenth Amendment protects the citizens from the states, not from each other. Nothing in the amendment prohibits private discrimination.

AMENDMENT XV
(Proposed February 27, 1869, adopted March 30, 1870)
Section 1   The right of citizens of the United States to vote shall not be denied or abridged by the United States or by any State on account of race, color, or previous condition of servitude.

Even after the ratification of the Fourteenth Amendment, the states could—even though by doing so, they would forfeit part of their representation in the House—still restrict voting rights among their male citizens. This amendment was focused at those states who, in spite of the Fourteenth Amendment, still chose to prohibit black Americans from voting.

Some states, such as Texas, still attempted to thwart black voters by excluding them from voting in primaries where political parties chose their candidates. Instead of using the simple and straightforward reasoning that "to vote" really meant "to vote," the Supreme Court applied the "equal protection" clause of the Fourteenth Amendment to declare unconstitutional the exclusion of blacks from state primaries.

Section 2   The Congress shall have power to enforce this article by appropriate legislation.

AMENDMENT XVI
(Proposed July 12, 1909, adopted February 25, 1913)
The Congress shall have power to lay and collect taxes on incomes, from whatever source derived, without apportionment among the several States, and without regard to any census or enumeration

Now this is my favorite amendment. It has caused more chaos than wars, divorces, or natural disasters. I cannot imagine how we were duped into permitting approval of the Sixteenth Amendment, and its repeal should be the focus of every American citizen. Repeal would eliminate many accountants, the IRS, and the significance of April 15; reduce federal government spending; and have more effect on our lives than even, say, the mandatory helmet laws or the required posting of the caloric content of Twinkies. We are led by the nose like a bunch of sheep. Our tax laws are too complex; tax deduction regulations contain hidden agendas that subsidize uneconomic ventures at our expense (ethanol in our gasoline, for example). Alternative minimum taxes, capital gains taxes, and every other special-interest tax hidden in the maze of yearly tax reform needs to be eliminated. Our congressional members talk quite often about tax reform, which to them seems to mean simply changing depreciation from five years to seven years, changing the maximum rate charged on long-term capital gains from 16% to 17.5%, and on and on. This is not tax reform and does nothing more than thicken our tax code regulations. We've got to repeal the Sixteenth Amendment, creating a revenue crisis for our government, to get meaningful tax reform. Why is it so difficult to have a national sales tax (and let the retailers submit our taxes) or a percentage tax on gross income? We can discuss which should come first, the chicken (repealing the Sixteenth Amendment) or the egg (tax reform), but I believe that until we create an unavoidable necessity for reform, it will never happen.

Current tax laws control how we save money, how we spend money, and how we invest money. The tax laws have changed every year since 1913, not once becoming simpler, always becoming more complex, requiring us to hire accountants, requiring the government to hire more IRS employees, hire more attorneys to settle disputes, and always, without one exception, increasing the costs to run our government.

Perhaps a new amendment might read, "The Sixteenth Amendment is hereby revoked and declared null and void in its entirety. In addition, taxing of one's personal income, by either local, state, or federal governments, or their legal representative, is in violation of this amendment. This amendment won't take effect until ninety days subsequent to its ratification." We can never expect two-thirds of both the Senate and the House to propose this amendment; the only chance we have to get this done is to demand that our state legislatures (two-thirds of them, as is set forth in Article V of the Constitution) "shall call a Convention for proposing Amendments, which, in either

Case, shall be valid to all Intents and Purposes, as Part of this Constitution, when ratified by the Legislatures of three fourths of the several States, or by Convention in three fourths thereof." This power to amend was retained by the individual states, without the need of any support from the federal government, either the executive, legislative, or judicial branch.

The few words comprising the Sixteenth Amendment have given more power to the Federal Government and taken more power away from us than 226 years of legislation, both state and federal.

In the *Maryland v. McCulloch* decision, Justice John Marshall made the statement "The power to tax involves the power to destroy." This is very true; our income tax is killing me.

AMENDMENT XVII
(Proposed May 16, 1912, adopted May 31, 1913)

The Senate of the United States shall be composed of two Senators from each State, elected by the people thereof, for six years; and each Senator shall have one vote. The electors in each State shall have the qualifications requisite for electors of the most numerous branch of the State legislatures.

When vacancies happen in the representation of any State in the Senate, the executive authority of such State shall issue writs of election to fill such vacancies: provided, that the legislature of any State may empower the executive thereof to make temporary appointments until the people fill the vacancies by election, as the legislature may direct.

This amendment shall not be so construed as to affect the election or term of any Senator chosen before it becomes valid as part of the Constitution.

This amendment drastically altered one of the most debated concepts proposed during the convention—that of determining the composition of the national legislature and the method of their election. The Senators prior to this amendment had been chosen by their own state legislatures, and in a manner controlled by the individual states.

James Wilson, who on May 31 motioned, "both branches of the national Legislature ought to be chosen by the people," also favored the election method created by the Seventeenth Amendment.

Now that the Senate is also elected directly by the people, the restriction that money bills must originate in the House is somewhat superficial.

AMENDMENT XVIII
(Proposed December 3, 1917, adopted January 29, 1919)

Section 1   After one year from the ratification of this article the manufacture, sale, or transportation of intoxicating liquors within, the importation thereof into, or the exportation thereof from the United States and all territory subject to the jurisdiction thereof for beverage purposes is hereby prohibited.

Section 2   The Congress and the several States shall have concurrent power to enforce this article by appropriate legislation.

Section 3   This article shall be inoperative unless it shall have been ratified as an amendment to the Constitution by the legislatures of the several States, as provided in the Constitution, within seven years from the date of the submission thereof to the States by the Congress.

This amendment was somewhat counterproductive and was subsequently revoked just fourteen years later by the Twenty-first Amendment. When the federal government realized that liquor was going to be produced and sold in spite of this amendment and that they (the federal government) were losing valuable tax income, they quickly repealed this amendment. This is similar to when the federal government abhorred betting on horse races, portrayed as badly as devil worshiping, but now that both horse racing has become a source for taxation, it is promoted as great family fun.

AMENDMENT XIX
(Proposed May 19, 1919, adopted August 26, 1920)

Section 1   The right of citizens of the United States to vote shall not be denied or abridged by the United States or by any State on account of sex.

Section 2   The Congress shall have power by appropriate legislation to enforce the Provisions of this article.

Women hereby gained the right to vote throughout the United States. I'm surprised, knowing how the Supreme Court has interpreted the meaning of single words, or the omission of words, that "gender" wasn't chosen over "sex."

AMENDMENT XX
(Proposed March 3, 1932, adopted February 6, 1933)

Section 1   The terms of the President and Vice-President shall end at noon on the twentieth day of January, and the terms of Senators and Representatives at noon on the third day of January, of the years in which such terms would have ended if this article had not been ratified; and the terms of their successors shall then begin.

Section 2   The Congress shall assemble at least once in every year, and such meeting shall begin at noon on the third day of January [(changed from the first Monday in December as established by Article I, Section 4.2], unless they shall by law appoint a different day [(if not for this language it would take another amendment to change the day again].

Section 3   If, at the time fixed for the beginning of the term of the President, the President-elect shall have died, the Vice-President-elect shall become President. If a President shall not have been chosen before the time fixed for the beginning of his term, or if the President-elect shall have failed to qualify, then the Vice-President-elect shall act as President until a President shall have qualified; and the Congress may by law provide for the case wherein neither a President-elect nor a Vice-President-elect shall have qualified, declaring who shall then act as President, or the manner in which one who is to act shall be selected, and such person shall act accordingly until a President or Vice-President shall have qualified.

Section 4   The Congress may by law provide for the case of the death of any of the persons from whom the House of Representatives may choose a President whenever the right of choice shall have devolved upon them, and for the case of the death of any of the persons from whom the Senate may choose as Vice-President whenever the right of choice shall have devolved upon them.

Section 5   SECTIONS 1 and 2 shall take effect on the 15th day of October following the ratification of this article.

Section 6   This article shall be inoperative unless it shall have been ratified as an amendment to the Constitution by the legislatures of three-fourths of the several States within seven years from the date of its submission.

This is one of the few amendments that has a ratification expiration date. Notice that the last amendment ratified (the twenty-seventh) was proposed on September 25, 1789, and not ratified until May 19, 1992.

158

AMENDMENT XXI
(Proposed February 20, 1933, adopted December 5, 1933)

Section 1   The eighteenth article of amendment to the Constitution of the United States is hereby repealed.

Section 2   The transportation or importation into any State, Territory, or possession of the United States for delivery or use therein of intoxicating liquors, in violation of the laws thereof [the states' laws], is hereby prohibited.

The Eighteenth Amendment was repealed for two primary reasons: first, the members of Congress were having problems finding reliable bootleggers, and second, they (members of Congress) wanted to appease the Seagram Company for the campaign contributions that Congress had probably extorted from the company.

Section 3   This article shall be inoperative unless it shall have been ratified as an amendment to the Constitution by conventions in the several States, as provided in the Constitution, within seven years from the date of the submission thereof to the States by the Congress.

AMENDMENT XXII
(Proposed March 24, 1947, adopted March 1, 1951)

Section 1   No person shall be elected to the office of the President more than twice, and no person who has held the office of President, or acted as President, for more than two years of a term to which some other person was elected President shall be elected to the office of the President more than once. But this Article shall not apply to any person holding the office of President when this Article was proposed by Congress, and shall not prevent any person who may be holding the office of President, or acting as President, during the term within which this Article becomes operative from holding the office of President or acting as President during the remainder of such term.

This sets the maximum time for any person to be elected to the office of president at ten years. He could serve more if he assumed the office again under conditions not requiring an election.

Section 2   The article shall be inoperative unless it shall have been ratified as an amendment to the Constitution by the legislatures of three-fourths of the several States within seven years from the date of its submission to the States by the Congress.

AMENDMENT XXIII
(Proposed June 16, 1960, adopted April 3, 1961)
Section 1.1   The District constituting the seat of Government of the United States shall appoint in such manner as the Congress may direct:

Section 1.2   A number of electors of President and Vice-President equal to the whole number of Senators and Representatives in Congress to which the District would be entitled if it were a State, but in no event more than the least populous State; they shall be in addition to those appointed by the States, but they shall be considered, for the purpose of the election of President and Vice President, to be electors appointed by a State; and they shall meet in the District and perform such duties as provided by the twelfth article of amendment.

Section 2   The Congress shall have power to enforce this article by appropriate legislation.

This amendment gives the residents of the District of Columbia the right to vote in presidential elections.

AMENDMENT XXIV
(Proposed August 27, 1962, adopted January 23, 1964)
Section 1   The right of citizens of the United States to vote in any primary or other election for President or Vice President, for electors for President or Vice President, or for Senator or Representative in Congress, shall not be denied or abridged by the United States or any State by reason of failure to pay any poll tax or other tax.

The Supreme Court in *Harper v. Virginia State Board of Elections* ruled that the Twenty-fourth Amendment also applies to prohibiting voting in state elections because of failure to pay any tax, subsequent to the Equal Protection clause of the Fourteenth Amendment. Most states had already eliminated all poll taxes, so the Harper decision therefore had limited effect.

Section 2   The Congress shall have power to enforce this article by appropriate legislation.

AMENDMENT XXV
(Proposed July 6, 1965, adopted February 23, 1967)

Section 1   In case of the removal of the President from office or his death or resignation, the Vice President shall become President.

Section 2   Whenever there is a vacancy in the office of the Vice President, the President shall nominate a Vice President who shall take the office upon confirmation by a majority vote of both houses of Congress.

This amendment was passed primarily as a result of the assassination of President John F. Kennedy, which caused us to be without a vice president for nearly fourteen months.

Section 3   Whenever the President transmits to the President pro tempore of the Senate and the Speaker of the House of Representatives his written declaration that he is unable to discharge the powers and duties of his office, and until he transmits to them a written declaration to the contrary, such powers and duties shall be discharged by the Vice President as Acting President.

Section 4.1   Whenever the Vice President and a majority of either the principal officers of the executive departments or of such other body as Congress may by law provide, transmit to the President pro tempore of the Senate and the Speaker of the House of Representatives their written declaration that the President is unable to discharge the powers and duties of his office, the Vice President shall immediately assume the powers and duties of the office as Acting President.

Section 4.2   Thereafter, when the President transmits to the President pro tempore of the Senate and the Speaker of the House of Representatives his written declaration that no inability exists, he shall resume the powers and duties of his office unless the Vice President and a majority of either the principal officers of the executive departments or of such other body as Congress may by law provide, transmit within four days to the President pro tempore of the Senate and the Speaker of the House of Representatives their written declaration that the President us unable to discharge the powers and duties of his office. Thereupon Congress shall decide the issue, assembling within forty-eight hours for that purpose if not in session. If the Congress, within twenty-one days after receipt of the latter written declaration, or, if Congress is not in session, within twenty-one days after Congress is required to assemble, determines by two-thirds vote of both Houses that the President is unable to discharge the power and duties of his office, the Vice President shall continue to discharge the same as Acting President; otherwise, the President shall resume the powers and duties of his office.

AMENDMENT XXVI
(Proposed March 23, 1971, adopted July 5, 1971)

Section 1   The right of citizens of the United States, who are eighteen years of age or older, to vote shall not be denied or abridged by the United States or by any State on account of age.

Section 2   The Congress shall have power to enforce this article by appropriate legislation.

This amendment was passed in response to the Court decision in *Oregon v. Mitchell* (1970) that limited the power of congressional legislation to only federal elections, leaving the states to regulate their own local elections. This amendment legally took power from the states, a somewhat fearful trend.

AMENDMENT XXVII
(Proposed September 25, 1789, adopted May 19, 1992)

No law, varying the compensation for the services of the Senators and Representatives, shall take effect, until an election of Representatives shall have intervened.

The Constitution (Article II, Section 1.7 and Article III, Section 1) had placed restrictions on varying the compensation of both the executive and judicial members but not on the legislative branch. This amendment had been proposed during the First Session of Congress in 1789 but was not ratified until 1992. Unfortunately, because we have no term limit restriction for congressional members, this amendment is a joke.

CHAPTER V

SUPREME COURT INTERPRETATIONS

Brandenburg v. Ohio **(1969, 9-0)** The court unanimously overturned a lower court conviction of Clarence Brandenburg for violating an Ohio statute by advocating racial conflict during a televised Ku Klux Klan rally. In this case, the court extended our First Amendment protection of free speech by replacing the *"clear and present danger"* rule, established in *Schneck v. United States,* with punishment of advocacy of illegal action only if "such advocacy is directed to inciting or producing imminent lawless action and is likely to incite or produce such action." "*Brandenburg* is the lynchpin of the modern doctrine of free speech, which seeks to give special protection to politically relevant speech and to distinguish speech from action."
> —Kermit L. Hall, editor, *The Oxford Companion to the Supreme Court of the United States*
> Oxford University Press, 1992, p. 86

Brown v. Board of Education **(1954, 9-0)** This unanimous decision in favor of the NAACP reversed the doctrine established by *Plessy v. Ferguson* (1896, 7-1) that laws requiring "equal but separate accommodations for the white and colored races" were constitutional. Chief Justice Earl Warren, in the Brown case, ruled, "In the field of public education, separate but equal has no place," and the court determined that the protection guaranteed by the Fourteenth Amendment of "equal protection" extended to public education. Because the decision didn't provide any specific funds to implement integration, any meaningful relief from segregation was slow in coming. *Brown v. Board of Education* was, however, instrumental in the Civil Rights Act of 1964 and the Voting Rights Act of 1965.

> Laws requiring children to attend school in their own neighborhoods obviously serve legitimate interests in efficiency. Should they nevertheless be condemned as racially discriminatory because they have the effect of separating pupils of different races? What the Constitution forbids, the Court has concluded, is differential treatment *on grounds of* race; it does not require affirmative efforts to achieve racial balance. ... The Constitution merely protects the individual against wrongful action by government; the state need not eliminate **de facto** differences that it did not cause.
> —David Currie, *The Constitution of the United States: A Primer for the People*
> University of Chicago Press, 1988, pp. 60–61

Chisholm v. Georgia **(1793, 4-1)** Chisholm, a citizen of South Carolina, sued Georgia on behalf of a South Carolina merchant, claiming monies for the value of clothing supplied to Georgia by the merchant during the Revolutionary War. Georgia refused to appear, claiming immunity as a sovereign and independent state. Article III, Section

2.1 specifically grants federal jurisdiction to suits between "a State and citizens of another State," and the Supreme Court ruled in favor of the plaintiff, Mr. Chisholm. Congress subsequently proposed the Eleventh Amendment, which removed cases of this nature from federal jurisdiction.

***Dennis v. United States* (1951, 6-2)** Eleven Communist Party leaders had been convicted in federal court for violation of certain statutes of the Smith Act (Alien Registration Act of 1940), which "made it a crime to teach or advocate the violent [or forceful] overthrow of any government in the United States, to set up an organization to engage in such teaching or advocacy, or to conspire to teach, advocate, or organize the violent [or forceful] overthrow of any government in the United States."* In affirming the convictions, the court, through Chief Justice Fred Vinson, modified the *"clear and present danger"* guidelines set forth in *Schneck v. United States* to the even more invasive *"grave and probable danger"* guidelines. "In each case," Vinson wrote, courts "must ask whether the gravity of the evil discounted by its improbability, justifies such invasion of free speech as is necessary to avoid the danger."* Fortunately, more recent rulings such as in *Yates v. United States* (1957) and *Brandenburg v. Ohio* (1969) have tempered this judicial assault on our First Amendment "freedom of speech" rights, but they have failed to rule the Smith Act unconstitutional.

***Engel v. Vitale* (1962, 7-1)** The court decided to maintain the "wall of separation" between church and state that was first mentioned by Thomas Jefferson (although not to be found anywhere in the Constitution or subsequent amendments) and later fortified by the Supreme Court in *Everson v. Board of Education of Ewing Township* (1947, 5-4). The court extended the First Amendment protection of "Congress shall make no law respecting an establishment of religion" to the states and the local school boards under the infamous Fourteenth Amendment's "equal protection of the laws" clause and discarded the "shall make no law prohibiting the free exercise thereof" section. Although it appears to me that the court has attempted to equate "no law respecting an establishment of religion" with "no law respecting an establishment of god," the court's opinions are the only ones that matter.

***Everson v. Board of Education* (1947, 5-4)** New Jersey had authorized its boards of education to reimburse parents, including those whose children went to Catholic schools, for the cost of bus transportation to and from school. Arch Everson, a taxpayer and New Jersey resident, wanted this statute declared unconstitutional because it violated the "establishment of religion" clause of the First Amendment. Even though the Fourteenth Amendment extends the First Amendment rights ("*Congress* shall make no law") to the states, the court ruled the New Jersey statute to be constitutional "because it did no more than provide a general program to help parents get their children, regardless of their religion, safely and expeditiously to and from accred-

---

*Kermit L. Hall, editor, *The Oxford Companion to the Supreme Court of the United States* (Oxford University Press, 1992, p. 225)

ited schools"[1] and "has not in the slightest breached a wall between church and state. Its [New Jersey's] statute is therefore constitutional."[2] The fact that the decision wasn't unanimous, I find absurd.

Gibbons v. Ogden **(1824, 6-0)** The first case decided by the Supreme Court dealing solely with the constitutional powers of Congress to regulate interstate and foreign commerce (Article I, Section 8.3). The New York courts had repeatedly upheld their own authority to issue navigation licenses, effectively creating monopolies, as opposed to rights created by congressional navigation permits. Daniel Webster made the argument for Gibbons, the holder of the federal license, setting out as options to be considered when deciding constitutional matters concerning the overlap of state and national powers regarding regulation of interstate commerce, the following: "(1) exclusive national power; (2) fully concurrent state and national powers; (3) partially concurrent state power not reaching 'higher branches' of that commerce; and (4) supremacy of a national statute over a contrary state statute."[3] The court ruled that the federal license of Gibbons nullified the New York grant of monopoly. Although the definition of "commerce" was expanded to include much more than the mere exchange of goods, the determination of national versus state supremacy was ambiguous, and subsequent rulings by the Supreme Court have depended more upon the moods of the judges than on any precedent set in *Gibbons*.

Gitlow v. New York **(1925, 7-2)** Benjamin Gitlow was a left-wing member of the Socialist Party who had been convicted in New York state court for advocating the violent overthrow of the government, in violation of the New York Criminal Anarchy Law of 1902. Although the Court upheld the concept that the First Amendment rights should be extended to the states, it ruled against Gitlow on the grounds that "a state may punish utterances endangering the foundations of organized government and threatening its overthrow by unlawful means." Judge Oliver Wendell Holmes, along with Justice Louis D. Brandeis, in dissension declared, "The only difference between the expression of an opinion and an incitement in the narrower sense is the speaker's enthusiasm for the result. Eloquence may set fire to a reason. But whatever may be thought of the redundant discourse before us, it had no chance of starting a present conflagration."[4] *Stromberg v. California* (1931) was the first time the Supreme Court actually ruled unconstitutional a state law for prohibiting free speech in violation of the First Amendment.

---

[1]Kermit L. Hall, editor, *The Oxford Companion to the Supreme Court of the United States* (Oxford University Press, 1992, p. 263)
[2]Ibid
[3]Ibid., p. 337
[4]Ibid., p. 340

Hylton v. United States **(1796, 3-0)** Daniel Hylton sued in the federal court of Virginia, claiming that a required duty or "carriage tax" was unconstitutional on the grounds that the tax violated Article I, Section 9.4 of the US Constitution. The Supreme Court upheld the decision by the lower court that the tax was indeed constitutional, on the grounds that the particular "carriage tax" was an excise tax and therefore was an "indirect tax," not a direct tax, and as such did not violate Article I, Section 9.4.

Katzenbach v. McClung **(1964, 9-0)** The court ruled that because a locally owned restaurant, Ollie's Barbecue, bought some of its supplies from a source that received some of their food products from out of state, Congress had the authority under the "regulate commerce" clause to pass legislation prohibiting the racially discriminating seating practices of the restaurant. "Thus, *Katzenbach* stands as authority for an apparently unlimited power in Congress to regulate any local activity if some aggregate economic impact on interstate commerce can be plausibly posited [postulated]."* The decision rendered in Katzenbach v. McClung, granting almost unrestricted powers to Congress pursuant to Article I, Section 8.3 of the US Constitutuin (regulate commerce among the several States) as grounds for the constitutionality of the Civil Rights Act of 1964, is quite disturbing. I agree with the consequences of the decision but the rationale of allowing Congress to control the business decisions of a small, locally owned enterprise based on their authority to regulate interstate commerce is totally absurd.

Malloy v. Hogan **(1964, 5-4)** Malloy had previously pleaded guilty to participating in an illegal gambling operation. After serving time in jail and while on probation, he was called to testify as part of a State of Connecticut inquiry into gambling and other crimes. He refused to answer specific questions relating to his earlier conviction, citing his Fifth Amendment protection of self-incrimination. He was subsequently charged with contempt and placed in prison until he agreed to cooperate with the inquiry. In previous cases, such as *Twining v. New Jersey*,** the court had determined that Fifth Amendment rights were to protect the citizens against infringements by the national government, not the state governments. *Malloy* overturned these earlier rulings, sustaining that the states, under Section I of the Fourteenth Amendment, could not violate a citizen's rights as guaranteed by the Fifth Amendment. Justices Byron White and Potter Stewart agreed with the view that the Fourteenth Amendment incorporated the privilege of self-incrimination to the states, but they dissented in Malloy because "in their view the facts in this case didn't warrant the application of the privilege," believing that Malloy was not in danger of self-incrimination. I find it perplexing that anyone, much less Supreme Court justices, would ever believe the Bill of Rights protects us from only the national government.

---

*Kermit L. Hall, editor, *The Oxford Companion to the Supreme Court of the United States* (Oxford University Press, 1992, p. 481)
**Ibid, p. 884

If that is the case, we really have no protection at all. Additionally, anyone who has read Article VI of the Constitution would know "This Constitution, and the Laws of the United States which shall be made in Pursuance thereof, …. shall be the supreme Law of the land."

Marbury v. Madison (1803, 5-0) The landmark Supreme Court decision firmly establishing the right of judicial review (to rule a law unconstitutional). Marbury, who had been appointed a justice of the peace in the District of Columbia, but whose commission had not been delivered, petitioned the Supreme Court to issue a **writ of mandamus** to then Secretary of State James Madison, demanding that he deliver the commission to Marbury. The court found that Marbury had a legal right to the commission, that Madison should deliver it, and that a writ of mandamus was the appropriate remedy. The Supreme Court ruled, however, that under Article III, Section 2.2, the restrictions placed on the original jurisdiction power of the Supreme Court did not allow it to issue the writ. Section 13 of the Judiciary Act of 1789 "The Supreme Court shall also have appellate jurisdiction from the circuit courts and courts of the several states, in the cases herein after specially provided for; and shall have power to issue writs of prohibition to the district courts, when proceeding as courts of admiralty and maritime jurisdiction, and writs of mandamus, in cases warranted by the principles and usages of law, to any courts appointed, or persons holding office, under the authority of the United States" was unconstitutional, and therefore the court would not compel Madison to deliver the justice of the peace commission.

McCulloch v. Maryland (1819, 7-0) In 1816, Congress established the second bank of the United States, in spite of constitutional objections by Thomas Jefferson. Maryland, along with several other states, adopted laws taxing branches of this national bank, and James McCulloch, cashier for the bank, refused to pay the tax. Both the county court and the court of appeals of Maryland affirmed the legality of the tax; the case was then appealed to the United States Supreme Court. Chief Justice John Marshall for the court ruled the Maryland law unconstitutional, arguing "that the government of the Union, though limited in its powers, is supreme within its sphere of action." He further reasoned that because the national government was empowered by Article I, Section 8.3 to regulate commerce and by Article I, Section 8.18 "to make all laws which shall be necessary and proper," the Bank of the United States was constitutional. Marshall next decided that national law, because of the Supremacy Clause of Article VI, took precedence over state laws, and that because the "power to tax involves the power to destroy," the individual states could not tax the United States banks. Now, by gosh, if buying barbecue sauce in Arkansas that was made in Alabama can violate Congress's right to regulate commerce, it can surely create a national bank, in spite of Mr. Jefferson's opinions to the contrary.

Miranda v. Arizona (1966, 5-4) This case involved a confession obtained from Ernesto Miranda during a police interrogation. Miranda's defense claimed his Fifth Amendment rights that "no person be compelled in any criminal case to be a witness against himself, … without due process of law" had been violated. Prior to

Miranda the courts determined the admissibility of a confession in a state criminal case based on whether the confession had been "voluntary." Also, Fifth Amendment protections against self-incrimination did not generally apply during police questioning. Miranda effectuated the current procedure of informing the suspect of his rights to an attorney, to remain silent, that anything said could be used as evidence, and that counsel will be provided for indigents.

***NAACP v. Alabama* (1958, 9-0)** The NAACP had been fined $100,000 by an Alabama trial court for contempt by failing to produce a membership list, as required by Alabama corporate filing laws. The Supreme Court overturned the state court decision on the grounds that it violated the members' First Amendment freedom of association rights. This decision established the *indirect* freedom of association as part of the First Amendment freedom of speech. In the first place, the word "association" does not appear in the First Amendment; neither is it implied, and to jump to "indirect" freedom of association is a joke.

***Plessy v. Ferguson* (1896, 7-1)** The Supreme Court upheld a Louisiana statute that required railroads to provide "equal but separate accommodations for the white and colored races." Plessy, who was less than one-quarter of African descent, purchased a first-class ticket on a train bound from New Orleans, Louisiana, to Covington, Louisiana, and attempted to board a whites-only car. He was arrested and his case was initially tried in the court of John Howard Ferguson. Ferguson ruled that Louisiana had the right to regulate railroads as long as they operated within state boundaries. The case was ultimately heard before the Supreme Court and resulted in the famous "separate but equal" doctrine, which should have been the "equal but separate" doctrine. The effect of this ruling was somewhat reversed in the *Brown v. Board of Education decision.*

***Pollack v. Farmers' Loan and Trust Co* (1895)** This case involved a stockholder who sued to prevent his bank from paying a national income tax prescribed under the newly enacted Income Tax Law of 1894. The court first ruled by 8-0 that a "tax on income from state and municipal bonds was essentially a tax on the state itself, violating the principle of state sovereignty [subsequently reversed in *South Carolina v. Baker* in 1988]." Secondly, the court decided that a tax on income from real property was a direct tax (see Article I, Section 2.3), and thirdly, the court split evenly on the question of whether a general tax on private and corporate incomes was also a direct tax. This decision somewhat contradicts an earlier decision, *Springer v. United States* (1881, 7-0), that declared income taxes not to be direct taxes and thus were constitutional. The uncertainty was finally settled with the passage of the Sixteenth Amendment in 1913, which gave the federal government the power to tax anything and everything—and because those powers weren't enough to stay within a budget, the federal government keeps granting itself the power to continue raising its debt limit. It's similar to if we are overdrawn at the bank and just call our friendly bankers and have them put some more money in our accounts, with the promise that when we are overdrawn again next month, they will loan us some more money—and please, no overdraft charges.

Reynolds v. Simms (1964, 8-1) The court ruled that voting districts within the states must be set to assure equal population and therefore equal representation. The basis for this decision was the widely used Fourteenth Amendment's Equal Protection Clause (Section I, "the equal protection of the laws").

Roe v. Wade (1973, 7-2) This is the decision that has severely restricted legislative attempts by the states to place meaningful restrictions on abortion availability. Texas and Georgia had passed laws that required as a prerequisite for hospital abortions, the imminent danger to the mother's health. The appeal to the Supreme Court to rule these state statutes unconstitutional was brought on behalf of "Jane Roe" in an unsuccessful attempt to conceal the litigant's real name, Norma McCorvey. The court ruled that these state laws were unconstitutional by the invocation of substantive "due process" guaranteed by the Fourteenth Amendment to the woman's right to privacy, perhaps located in the Fourth Amendment clause "the right of the people to be secure in their persons." The judges also established the "trimester" guideline, which determines the constitutionality of state abortion statutes based on potential health risks to the pregnant woman. This expansion of constitutional rights protection was probably more of an attempt to pacify the women's movement than an interpretation of the Constitution. I've searched the Constitution for the word "privacy" and don't find it.

Schenck v. United States (1919, 9-0) The first Supreme Court case involving infringement by national legislation upon First Amendment rights of free speech. Charles Schenck, the general secretary of the Socialist Party, had been convicted of violating the 1917 Espionage Act that prohibited obstruction of military recruiting. Schenck's lawyers argued that the Espionage Act violated First Amendment protections and thus was unconstitutional. Judge Oliver Wendell Holmes herewith established his now famous "clear and present danger" addition to the First Amendment, thereby circumventing the constitutionally established amendment process: "The question in every case is whether the words are used in such circumstances and are of such a nature as to create a *clear and present danger* that they will bring about the substantive evils that Congress has a right to prevent." The court unanimously upheld the lower court ruling and further declared the Espionage Act to be constitutional.

Scott v. Sandford (1857, 7-2) Virginia-born slave Dred Scott filed a freedom suit against Irene Emerson in the St. Louis County Circuit Court under Missouri law. Scott had been sold in 1833 to an army surgeon, Dr. John Emerson. Mr. Scott had married Harriet Robinson while living in the free territory of Wisconsin, her ownership being transferred to Dr. Emerson. In April of 1846, Dred and Harriet Scott initiated their suit against Irene Emerson, the widow of the then deceased Dr. Emerson. When the case was eventually tried in 1850, the Missouri court ordered that Mr. Scott and his wife be freed; but the decision was overturned after John Sandford (Mrs. Emerson's brother) appealed the decision to th Missouri Supreme Court because of wages earned by Mr. Scott but supposedly due to Mrs. Emerson. The case was appealed in federal court and was ultimately decided by the Supreme Court in favor of Mr. Sandford. The court ruled that although blacks could be citizens of specific states, they were not citizens of the United States and therefore had no right to sue in federal court. Secondly, Congress had no authority to forbid or abolish slavery in the new territories (despite Article IV, Section 3.2), and the **Missouri Compromise** was accordingly declared unconstitutional. Finally, the court decided that no matter what the status of a slave might have been in a free state or territory, if the slave voluntarily returned to a slave state, the laws of that state would stand as interpreted by its own courts. This horrendous decision played a minor role in instigating the Civil War and a major role in the enactment of the Thirteenth, Fourteenth, and Fifteenth Amendments.

Stromberg v. California **(1931, 7-2)** This majority decision was considered a landmark case in constitutional law because it was the first time the Fourteenth Amendment had been extended to include First Amendment protection from state legislation. Yetta Stromberg had been convicted in California court for publicly displaying a red flag, in violation of California statute. The court ruled that the "No State shall make or enforce any law that shall abridge the privileges or immunities of citizens of the United States" and the "equal protection of the laws" clauses of the Fourteenth Amendment also prohibited the states from encroaching upon our Bill of Rights freedoms. Prior to the Fourteenth Amendment, the first Ten Amendments, according to the courts, protected us only from federal statutes (which effectually reduced their value to zero).

United States v. O'Brien **(1968, 7-1)** The court ruled that David O'Brien, who had been convicted for burning his draft card in violation of federal statute and then claimed the law violated his First Amendment right of free speech, was guilty and that the statute was constitutional. The court "set out a test for determining when governmental regulation was justified in freedom of expression cases involving symbolic speech. This test required the government interest to be a valid and important one, and one unrelated to the suppression of free speech. Further, the restriction of First Amendment freedoms could be no greater than was essential to the furtherance of that interest."*

Youngstown Sheet & Tube Co. v. Sawyer **(1952, 6-3)** During the Korean War, anticipating that a steelworkers strike would harm US participation in the United Nations' police action against North Korea, President Harry Truman (**Executive Order** 10340) ordered Secretary of Commerce Charles Sawyer to seize and operate the nation's steel mills. The owners of Youngstown Sheet and Tube Co. filed a complaint with the Supreme Court that the Taft-Hartley Act allowed both parties to arrive at a settlement, with intervention by Congress if collective bargaining was unsuccessful and that the president had no authority to seize their mill.

> It is true that Congress has no power to deprive the president of the authority the Constitution gives him. Only the president, for example, may be commander in chief of the armed forces. How the president

---

*Kermit L. Hall, editor, *The Oxford Companion to the Supreme Court of the United States* (Oxford University Press, 1992, p. 602)

executes the laws, on the other hand, may to some extent be determined by legislation pursuant to the Necessary and Proper Clause [of
Article I, Section 8.18 of the Constitution]. Thus in the narrowest
sense the *Youngstown* decision merely confirms that the president
must obey the law and that Congress may limit presidential authority
to seize private property even for the purposes of national security... In directing the president to "take care that the laws be faithfully executed," Jackson wrote, article II "gives a governmental
authority that reaches so far as there is law"; in forbidding depriva-
tions of life, liberty or property without due process, the Fifth
Amendment "gives a private right that authority shall go no further."
—David P. Currie, *The Constitution of the United States: A Primer for
the People*
University of Chicago Press, 1988, pp. 37–38

CHAPTER VI

THE FOUNDING FATHERS

The "Founding Fathers" herein are limited to those men who actually attended the Constitutional Convention of 1787. It may surprise you who was not in attendance.

RICHARD BASSETT (Delaware, April 2, 1745–September 18, 1815) Born in Maryland, studied law, and was admitted to the Delaware Bar. Captain of a Delaware troop in the Colonial Army, member of his state constitutional convention in 1776 and 1792, member of the Delaware Senate (1782) and House of Representatives (1786), and a Delaware representative at the Annapolis Convention of 1786. Although he attended regularly, there is no record he ever spoke during the Constitutional Convention. He served in the United States Senate from March 4, 1789, until March 3, 1793, and is credited with being the first man to cast his vote to locate the capital of the United States in Washington, DC. He was an elector on the Adams presidential ticket in 1797, Governor of Delaware from January 9, 1799, to March 3, 1801, and appointed United States circuit judge in 1801

GUNNING BEDFORD JR. (Delaware, 1747–March 30, 1812) Born in Philadelphia, graduated with honors from Princeton (classmate of James Madison) in 1771, admitted to the bar and began his practice in Dover. He was a member of the Delaware House of Representatives and served as attorney general of Delaware from 1778 to 1789. He was a member of the Continental Congress from March 10, 1783 until November 1788, was presidential elector in 1789 and 1793, was appointed United States district judge by George Washington, which position he held from September 26, 1789, until his death in 1812. He spoke often during the convention, opposed the early proposal of a seven-year term for the president ("An impeachment would be no cure for this evil, as an impeachment would reach misfeasance only, not incapacity"), opposed presidential veto, favored congressional approval of executive appointments, and was a staunch advocate of small states' rights.

JOHN DICKINSON (Delaware and Pennsylvania, November 2, 1732–February 14, 1808) Born near the village of Trappe in Talbot County, Maryland, he received a private education, studied law in Philadelphia, and in 1753 moved to London to continue his studies. Dickinson was one of the wealthiest of the colonists, was a brigadier general in the Pennsylvania militia and coauthored with Thomas Jefferson the "."

Dickinson was a member of the Pennsylvania assembly in 1764; a delegate to the Colonial Congress in 1765; a Pennsylvania delegate to the Continental Congress (1774–1776) and delegate from Delaware (1779–1780); president of Delaware in 1781 and president of Pennsylvania from 1782 to 1785.

Surprisingly, even though Dickinson was a member of the Continental Congress that drafted the Declaration of Independence, he refused to sign, preferring to complete the Articles of Confederation prior to declaring Independence from Britain. He also did not sign the US Constitution; having to leave early, he authorized his friend and fellow delegate George Read to sign for him representing Delaware. He was, however, an active supporter for its ratification.

GEORGE READ (Delaware, September 18, 1783–September 21, 1798) Born in Cecil County, Maryland. His family soon moved to New Castle, Delaware, and at the age of fifteen, he began studying law with a Philadelphia lawyer. He was the only signer of the Declaration of Independence to vote against independence, possibly because he believed reconciliation with England was possible. As a member of the Constitutional Convention, Read was a staunch supporter of a strong national government (especially the executive branch), insisted upon protecting small states' rights, and led the push for ratification, Delaware being the first state to do so.

Read was the attorney general for lower Delaware in 1763, delegate in the Continental Congress (1774–1777), president of the state constitutional convention in 1776, vice president of Delaware under the Constitution, member of the state house of representatives (1779–1780), judge of the United States court of appeals in admiralty cases in 1782; elected to the United States Senate and served from March 4, 1789, to December 2, 1793, when he resigned; also the chief justice of Delaware.

JACOB BROOM (Delaware, October 17, 1752–April 25, 1810) Born at Wilmington, Delaware., to a father who was a blacksmith. Although Broom dabbled in politics, he was primarily a business man involved in shipping and the import trade. At the Constitutional Convention, he favored a powerful national government with veto rights of states' laws. After the convention, Broom returned to Wilmington, becoming its first postmaster in 1790.

ROBERT MORRIS (Pennsylvania, January 20, 1734–May 8, 1806) Born in Liverpool, England, he immigrated to Maryland in 1747, living with his father, who was a tobacco exporter. After some formal education in Philadelphia, he worked for the shipping and banking firm of Thomas and Charles Willing, becoming a partner in 1754.

He was a delegate to the Continental Congress (1776–1778), signer of the Declaration of Independence and representative in the state assembly (1778–1780), and superintendent of finance (1781–1784) under the Articles of Confederation; established the Bank of North America; was a member of the Pennsylvania legislature (1785–1787) and delegate to the Constitutional Convention (1787); and elected to United States Senate (1789–1795). He declined the position of secretary of the treasury under Washington.

Mr. Morris personally helped finance some of the militia during the Revolutionary War but died in poverty after unsuccessful land speculations, which led to his imprisonment for debt from February 1798 to August 1801. He was one of only two men to sign the

Declaration of Independence, the Articles of Confederation, and the United States Constitution.

BEN FRANKLIN (Pennsylvania, January 17, 1706–April 17, 1790) Franklin was born in Boston in 1723 and later moved to Philadelphia, where he worked as a printer. After one year, he moved to London, spending two years there before returning to Philadelphia.

He published the *Pennsylvania Gazette* (1730–1748) and *Poor Richard's Almanac* (1732–1758); was a clerk of the state assembly (1744–1754) and a member of several Indian commissions; was appointed postmaster general of the British North American Colonies in 1753; was agent of Pennsylvania in London (1757–1762, 1764–1775) and a delegate in the Continental Congress (1775–1776); signed and served on the committee that drafted the Declaration of Independence; was president of the Pennsylvania Constitutional Convention of 1776; was sent as a diplomatic commissioner to France by the Continental Congress and later minister to France (1776–1785); was governor of Pennsylvania (1785–1788); and was the oldest delegate at the Constitutional Convention of 1787.

Franklin spent many years of his life in Europe, serving as the First United States Ambassador to France in 1776 and, with John Jay and John Adams, negotiated the Treaty of Paris (1783).

He expressed his desire to abolish slavery as early as 1735. Numerous times during the Constitutional Convention, his prestige and pleas for calm compromises quelled vigorous dissension among some of the delegates. Franklin died less than a year after George Washington became our first president, satisfied with his accomplishments and hoping that our country would prosper under the Constitution that he helped mold.

THOMAS MIFFLIN (Pennsylvania, January 10, 1744–January 20, 1800) Born in Philadelphia, the son of a rich merchant, graduated from the College of Philadelphia (now the University of Pennsylvania), and, after returning from Europe in 1765, established a mercantile business with his brother George Mifflin.

Mifflin, against the wishes of his fellow Quakers, joined the Continental Army, was appointed as a major and then quartermaster general of the Army, rising to brigadier general in May 1776. He was accused of embezzlement while quartermaster and resigned, although an inquiry never took place.

He was a delegate in the Continental Congress from 1774 to 1776 and from 1782 to 1784; chosen member of the Board of War November 7, 1777; speaker of the state house of representatives from 1785 to 1788; delegate to the Constitutional Convention (although attending regularly, he seldom spoke); president of the supreme executive council of Pennsylvania from October 1788 to October 1790; president of the state constitutional convention of 1790; and first governor of Pennsylvania from 1790 to 1799.

GOUVERNEUR MORRIS (Pennsylvania, January 31, 1752–November 6, 1816) Born and died in New York City, graduated from King's College at the age of sixteen, studied law and gained admission to the bar just three years later. His half-brother Lewis was a signer of the Declaration of Independence.

Morris drafted the first constitution of New York in 1776, along with John Jay and Robert Livingston. In August of that year, the British seized his family's estate, and his mother, being a Loyalist, gave their estate to the British for military use. He moved to Philadelphia in 1779 after his defeat for reelection to the Continental Congress, primarily due to his advocacy of a strong national government.

Morris was a delegate to the Continental Congress from 1777 to 1778, where he was a signer of the Articles of Confederation. He was a delegate to the Constitutional Convention from Pennsylvania, speaking more times than any other delegate; was minister plenipotentiary to France from January 12, 1792, to August 15, 1794; was elected as a Federalist to the United States Senate to fill the vacancy caused by the resignation of Philip Schuyler, serving from April 3, 1800, to March 3, 1803; and was chairman of the Erie Canal Commission from 1810 to 1813.

JAMES WILSON (Pennsylvania, September 14, 1742–August 28, 1798) Born at Carskerdo, Scotland, graduated from the University of St. Andrews, then spent two years studying in Glasgow and Edinburg before moving to Philadelphia, where he taught at the Academy and College of Philadelphia, now the University of Pennsylvania. After a brief teaching career, he studied law under John Dickinson, was admitted to the bar in 1767, and one year later opened a private practice in Reading, Pennsylvania.

Wilson soon became involved in Revolutionary politics, attended the first provincial assembly to discuss relations with Britain, and was elected to the Continental Congress from 1775 to 1778, from 1782 to 1783, and from 1785 to 1787. He was a signer of the Declaration of Independence, a signer of the United States Constitution, and a delegate to the Pennsylvania state convention that ratified the Constitution. Next to Gouverneur Morris, Wilson was probably the most prolific speaker at the Constitutional Convention. He was a member of the **Committee of Detail,** which drafted the first version of the Constitution.

Wilson was appointed an associate justice of the first United States Supreme Court by Washington and served from 1789 to 1798. Although at one time a wealthy land owner, Wilson made many bad investments in western territory land deals and died broke. He probably suffered from mental illness.

GEORGE CLYMER (Pennsylvania, March 16, 1739–January 24, 1813) Born in Philadelphia, Pennsylvania, orphaned at one year of age, raised by his uncle and later joined that uncle as a partner in his mercantile business. Although he was quiet and rarely spoke during the Continental Congresses and Constitutional Convention, he was a member of many committees dealing with commerce and finance and was co-treasurer of the Continental Congress.

Clymer was elected to the first Congress, serving in the House of Representatives from Pennsylvania from March 4, 1789, to March 3, 1791. He was one of the commissioners who negotiated a treaty with the Cherokees and Creeks on June 29, 1796, the first president of the Pennsylvania Bank, and an original member of the Pennsylvania Academy of Fine Arts.

THOMAS FITZSIMMONS (Pennsylvania, 174–August 26, 1811) Born in Leinster, Ireland, he moved to America in the late 1750s. Having received little formal education, he joined one of his brothers-in-law in the George Meade (his father-in-law) and Company, specializing in the West Indies Trade.

Fitzsimons joined the Pennsylvania militia, commanded a company of volunteer home guards, and served as a reserve in the Battle of Trenton in 1776. As with many of the Founding Fathers, his involvement in the Revolutionary War had as much to do with protecting their economic interests as with a patriotic desire to gain independence from Britain.

He was a member of the state house of representatives from 1786 to 1787, a delegate to the Continental Congress in 1782 and 1783, and a delegate to the United States Constitutional Convention (was a signer), and although he attended regularly, he seldom spoke, if at all. He was elected to the United States House of Representatives from Pennsylvania, serving from March 4, 1789, to March 3, 1795. Fitzsimons also was a director of the Insurance Company of North America, was president of the Philadelphia Chamber of Commerce, and served as a trustee of the University of Pennsylvania.

JARED INGERSOLL (Pennsylvania, October 24, 1749–October 31, 1822) Born in New Haven, Connecticut, graduated from Yale in 1766, studied law in England at Middle Temple, and was admitted to the Pennsylvania bar in 1773. Ingersoll's father was a Loyalist and served as stamp master for the Colony of Connecticut, as prescribed under the terms of the Stamp Act of 1765. While in Europe, he made the acquaintance of Benjamin Franklin, and that introduction probably help nurture Ingersoll's ultimate desire for independence from Britain.

Ingersoll, once free of his family's Loyalist politics, served in the Continental Congress from 1780 to 1781 and as a delegate to the United States Constitutional Convention. Although inclined to merely amending the Articles of Confederation, he seldom spoke at the convention but was a signer. He later served as the attorney general of Pennsylvania (1790–1799, 1811–1817), was appointed the United States district attorney for the eastern district of Pennsylvania, and lost the election as the Federalist candidate for vice president in 1812 (Dewitt Clinton of New York ran as the presidential candidate, losing to Madison and Elbridge Gerry as vice president).

DAVID BREARLY (New Jersey, June 11, 1745–August 16, 1790) Born near Trenton, New Jersey, he attended the College of New Jersey (now Princeton) and began his law practice in Allentown, New Jersey. He was an early advocate of independence from Great Britain, first serving in the Revolutionary War as a captain in the Monmouth County Militia and rising to colonel in the New Jersey Militia Brigade.

Brearly served as the chief justice of the New Jersey Supreme Court, ruling in the New Jersey State case of *Holmes v. Walton* (1780) that the judiciary had the right to rule on the constitutionality of specific legislative acts, the first such ruling based on the theory of judicial review.

Brearly served as a delegate to the Constitutional Convention. Although a proponent of the New Jersey Plan (favoring equal representation from both the large and small states in Congress), he chaired the Committee on Postponed Matters, was a signer of the United States Constitution, and presided at the New Jersey convention that ratified the Constitution on December 18, 1787 (becoming the third state to ratify). Brearly was appointed by Washington as a federal district judge, serving until his death in 1790, at age forty-five.

JONATHAN DAYTON (New Jersey, October 16, 1760–October 19, 1824) Born in Elizabeth, New Jersey, graduated from the College of New Jersey (now Princeton) in 1776, served under Washington at Valley Forge, and fought at the Battle of Yorktown, Virginia.

Dayton was a member of the New Jersey State Council for several terms and its speaker in 1790. He was a delegate to the Federal Constitutional Constitution, where he spoke frequently and became a signer; was elected to the Second, Third, Fourth, and Fifth United States House of Representatives (March 4, 1791–March 3, 1799); and was elected to the United States Senate (March 3, 1805). He was arrested on charges of conspiring with Aaron Burr in treasonable projects involving western lands but was subsequently released and never brought to trial. He was the youngest delegate at the Constitutional Convention.

WILLIAM PATERSON (New Jersey, December 24, 1745–September 9, 1806) Born in County Antrim, Ireland, he moved with his family to America, finally settling in Princeton, New Jersey, in 1750 after traveling throughout the northern colonies. Patterson graduated from the College of New Jersey (now Princeton) with a master's degree in 1766. He studied law under Richard Stockton (a signer of the Declaration of Independence), was admitted to the bar in 1768, and began his legal practice at New Bromley, New Jersey.

Paterson was selected as a delegate to the first three provincial congresses of New Jersey and, as secretary, recorded the New Jersey State Constitution of 1776. He represented New Jersey at the Constitutional Convention, presenting the New Jersey Plan (the Paterson Plan) but later agreeing to the Great Compromise of equal states' representation in the Senate, with representation based on population in the House of Representatives, He left the convention early but returned to sign the final draft of the Constitution. He was also a member of the New Jersey Convention that unanimously ratified (the third state to do so) the United States Constitution on December 18, 1787.

Paterson was very active in the new federal government, being elected to the United States Senate, serving from March 4, 1789, to March 2, 1790, when he resigned to run for governor. He was elected governor of New Jersey (1791–1793) and was confirmed as a justice of the Supreme Court of the United States, serving from March 4, 1793, until his death in Albany, New York, on September 9, 1806.

WILLIAM C. HOUSTON (New Jersey, 1746–1788) Born in South Carolina, he attended the College of New Jersey (now Princeton), graduated in 1768, and subsequently became a professor of mathematics and natural philosophy (science).

Probably less is known about Houston than any other Constitutional Convention delegate, although he did serve in the military in 1776 and 1777, represented New Jersey in the Continental Congress, was admitted to the bar in 1781, and was appointed the clerk of the New Jersey Supreme Court.

Houston attended the Constitutional Convention as a delegate from New Jersey but left after one week because of illness caused by tuberculosis and therefore was not a signer of the Constitution. He died less than a year after the final draft of the Constitution was completed.

WILLIAM LIVINGSTON (New Jersey, November 30, 1723–July 25, 1790) Born in Albany, New York, raised by his grandmother, spent a short time working with a missionary among the Iroquois Indians. He graduated from Yale in 1741 and was admitted to the New York bar in 1748. He wrote and published a weekly newspaper, the *Independent Reflector*, in which he advocated progressive political reform and separation of church and state.

Livingston moved to Elizabeth, New Jersey, and retired from his law practice. The collapse of relations between the colonies and Great Britain soon ended his life of leisure, and he was a representative of the First and Second Continental Congresses, serving from 1775 to 1776, when he left the Continental Congress to command the New Jersey Militia as a brigadier general. He was elected governor of New Jersey in 1776 and served as its first fovernor for fourteen consecutive years.

Livingston was selected as a New Jersey delegate to the Constitutional Convention in 1787, where he became a signer and was active in winning ratification from New Jersey on December 18, 1787 (the third state behind Delaware and Pennsylvania to ratify). Livingston was, in the words of a contemporary, "a man of first rate talents. ... equal to anything, from the extensiveness of his education and genius."

ABRAHAM BALDWIN (Georgia, November 6, 1754–March 3, 1807) Born in Connecticut, graduated from Yale in 1772, served as a chaplain in the Continental Army, and in 1783 was admitted to the bar. He moved to Georgia in 1784, where he gained membership in the Georgia Assembly and the Continental Congress (1785–1788). While at the Constitutional Convention, he served on the Committee of Compromise on Representation, the Committee on Slave Trade and Navigation, the Committee on State Debt and Regulation of Militia, and the Committee on Remaining Matters. He was a cofounder of the University of Georgia in 1798. He served as a representative from Georgia during the First, Second, Third, Fourth, and Fifth Congresses (March 4, 1789–March 3, 1799) and served as senator (elected president pro-tempore in 1801) from Georgia from March 4, 1799, until his death in 1807. His step brother Henry Baldwin served as an associate justice of the United States Supreme Court.

WILLIAM FEW (Georgia, June 8, 1748–July 16, 1828) Born in Baltimore County, Maryland, Few was primarily self-educated, and although not graduating from any university, he won admittance to the bar and began practice in Augusta, Georgia. He served in the military, first in North Carolina and later as a lieutenant colonel in the Georgia Dragoons.

Few served Georgia in the Continental Congress (1780–1782 and 1785–1788) and in the Georgia Legislature in 1777, 1779, 1783, and 1793. He was the state surveyor general in 1778, a delegate to the Constitutional Convention in 1787 (although never speaking), and a member of the Georgia convention that ratified the federal Constitution in 1788.

Few later served as a United States senator from March 4, 1789, to March 3, 1793. He was a judge of the circuit court of Georgia from 1794 to 1797. He moved to New York City in 1799, was elected a member of the state House of Representatives and served from 1802 to 1805, and was the state prison inspector from 1802 to 1810. Few also was a director of the Manhattan Bank (now Citigroup) and president of City Bank.

WILLIAM HOUSTON (Georgia, 1755–March 3, 1813) Born in Savannah, Georgia, and received legal training at Inner Temple in London, returning to Georgia after the start of the Revolutionary War, where he advocated resistance to the British proclamations interfering with freedoms in the colonies.

Houstoun never served in the new federal government but did participate in the Continental Congress from 1783 through 1786, helped negotiate a boundary dispute with South Carolina in 1785, and was an original trustee of the University of Georgia. He left the Constitutional Convention early and was not a signer.

WILLIAM LEIGH PIERCE (Georgia, 1740–December 10, 1789) Thought to have been born in Georgia but grew up in Virginia. He served as an **aide-de-camp** to General Nathanael Greene during the Revolutionary War.

Pierce was a member of the Georgia House of Representatives, was elected to the Continental Congress, and represented Georgia at the Constitutional Convention in 1787. He did participate in a few debates during the convention, favored election of at least one house of the federal congress by the people as opposed to by the state legislature, left the convention early because of the failings of his business ventures, and was not a signer. He never served again in either state or federal government positions and died just two years after leaving the convention.

ROGER SHERMAN (Connecticut, April 19, 1721–July 23, 1793) Served as the first mayor of New Haven, Connecticut, was chosen as one of the five members of the Second Continental Congress to draft the Declaration of Independence, and was one of only two men, along with Robert Morris (delegate to the United States Constitutional Convention from Pennsylvania) to sign the Declaration of Independence, the Articles of Confederation, and the United States Constitution.

As a youth, Roger spent most of his time working with his father on their farm and learning the cobbler trade, his favorite being wild plum. Subsequent to his father's death, he moved from Stoughton, Massachusetts, to New Millford, Connecticut, where he became active in community affairs, served as a county surveyor, and in 1749 married Elizabeth Hartwell, with whom he had seven children. Three years after the death of Elizabeth in 1763, he married Rebecca Prescott, and together, they had eight children. He was considered a man "who worked all day and all night."

Although he had no formal legal education, he studied law and was admitted to the bar in February 1754. He was a member of the general assembly in 1755 and 1758–1761 and a justice of the court of common pleas from 1759 to 1761; moved to New Haven, Connecticut, in June 1761; was a member of the state house of representatives from 1764 to 1766; was elected to the state senate, 1766–1785; was a judge of the superior court, 1766–1789; was a delegate in the Continental Congress, 1774–1781 and 1783–1784, a member of the committee to prepare the Articles of Confederation, an outspoken delegate to the Constitution Convention of 1787; was elected to the first Congress, 1789–1791; was elected to the United States Senate to fill the vacancy caused by the resignation of William S. Johnson, and served from 1791 until his death in 1793.

OLIVER ELLSWORTH (Connecticut, April 29, 1745–November 26, 1807) Born in Windsor, Connecticut, attended Yale but graduated from the College of New Jersey (Princeton) in 1766, studied law, and was admitted to the bar in 1771.

Ellsworth was appointed Connecticut state attorney in 1775, was a representative in the general assembly in 1775 and 1776. He was a delegate to the Continental Congress

(1777–1784), a judge in the Connecticut Supreme Court (1784–1789), and a delegate to the Constitutional Convention (serving on the Committee of Detail). He was elected as a Federalist to the United States Senate, serving from March 4, 1789, to March 8, 1796, resigning to accept the appointment (nominated by President Washington) as the second (John Rutledge was appointed but rejected by the Senate) chief justice of the Supreme Court of the United States. Ellsworth served as United States Envoy Extraordinary to the Court of France, leading a delegation there between 1799 and 1800 in order to settle differences with Napoleon's government regarding restrictions on US shipping, which may have prevented a military conflict between the two nations.

He was very vocal during the Constitutional Convention, first suggested using the term "United States Government" to replace "national government," and even though serving on the Committee of Detail, which drafted the final version of the Constitution, he left the convention early and was not a signer. During his time in Congress, he was involved in proposing and drafting the Judiciary Act of 1789 and was an exponent (in favor of) of Hamilton's economic program.

WILLIAM SAMUEL JOHNSON (Connecticut, October 7, 1727–November 14, 1819) Born at Stratford, Connecticut, to Samuel Johnson, was president of King's College, graduated from Yale in 1744, and subsequently was granted an honorary master's degree from Harvard. Johnson originally retained loyalty to Britain and worked for peace between England and the colonies, not actively participating in the Revolutionary War. Once the war ended, however, he was a delegate to the Continental Congress from 1784 to 1787, was an active member from Connecticut at the Constitutional Convention, chaired the Committee of Style, and campaigned for ratification of the Constitution.

Johnson was Connecticut agent extraordinary to the court of England (1761–1771) to determine the state title to Indian lands; was judge of the Connecticut Supreme Court (1772–1774); was elected to the United States Senate and served from March 4, 1789, to March 4, 1791, when he resigned; and was president of Columbia college of New York City (1792–1800).

NATHANIEL GORHAM (Massachusetts, May 27, 1738–June 11, 1796) Born in Charlestown, Massachusetts, he was a descendant of John Howard (passenger on the Mayflower, signer of the Mayflower Compact, and a founder of Plymouth Colony), married Rebecca Call, with whom he fathered nine children, and was elected to the colonial legislature at the age of thirty-three.

He served as a delegate to the provincial congress (1774–1775); was member of the board of war (1778–1781) and a delegate to the state constitutional convention in 1779; served in the state senate (1780–1781); was elected to the Continental Congress (1782–1783,1785–1787); was a delegate (and signer) to the federal Constitutional Convention (1787); and was for several years a judge of the court of common pleas.

He spoke often at the Constitutional Convention, acted as chairman of the Committee of the Whole, and was a member of the Committee of Detail, which drafted the Constitution.

CALEB STRONG (Massachusetts, January 9, 1745–November 7, 1819) Born in Northampton, Massachusetts, graduated with honors from Harvard in 1764, and was admitted to the bar in 1772.

Strong did not serve in the military because of his damaged sight (caused by previous affliction with smallpox), but did serve on the Northampton Committee of Safety. He was a delegate from Massachusetts at the Constitutional Convention, proposing that all money bills (revenue) should originate in the House of Representatives, and sat on the drafting committee. Because of the illness of his wife, Strong left the convention and was not a signer. He did, however, support its ratification by the Massachusetts Convention.

Strong was elected to the United States Senate twice, serving from March 4, 1789, to June 1, 1796, becoming one of the principal drafters of the Judiciary Act of 1789. While serving in the Senate, he also was a principal proponent of the Eleventh Amendment to the United States Constitution. He was elected governor of Massachusetts twice, opposed the War of 1812, and died at his home in Northampton at age seventy-four.

ELBRIDGE GERRY (Massachusetts, July 17, 1744–November 23, 1814) Born in Marblehead, Massachusetts into a wealthy merchant family, Gerry graduated from Harvard in 1762. He served with Samuel Adams and John Hancock in the first and second provincial congresses and could have been one of only three men to sign the Declaration of Independence, the Bill of Rights, and the United States Constitution (along with Roger Sherman and Robert Morris), had he not left the Constitutional Convention early, refusing to sign the Constitution principally because it did not contain a Bill of Rights and it gave too much power to the president.

During the Revolutionary War, as a member of the Massachusetts Provincial Congress, he was responsible for the storage of supplies and weapons at Concord, Massachusetts, that were the target of the British raiding expedition on Lexington and Concord. Gerry was a delegate to the Continental Congress from 1776 to 1780, and from 1783 to 1785; he was elected as a Federalist to the United States House of Representatives, serving from March 4, 1789, to March 3, 1793 (First and Second Congresses), was defeated as a candidate for governor in 1801, but won that election in 1810 and 1811; he was elected vice president of the United States under Madison, serving from March 5, 1813, until his death in Washington, DC, on November 23, 1814.

Gerry, along with Charles Cotesworth Pinckney and John Marshall, were sent to France by President John Adams in 1797 to negotiate a reconciliation with France over what the French perceived to be oppressive pro-British terms of the **Jay Treaty** of 1796. Although a formal treaty was never consummated, Gerry's talks with French

Foreign Minister Talleyrand may have prevented a declaration of war. Gerry was also the namesake for the term **gerrymandering.**

RUFUS KING (Massachusetts, March 24, 1755–April 29, 1827) Born in Scarboro, Massachusetts (now Maine), graduated from Harvard in 1777. Served briefly as a general's aide during the Revolutionary War, began law practice in Newburyport, Massachusetts, in 1780, and was married to Mary Alsop in 1786. He was an early opponent of slavery, was a knowledgeable and gifted orator, and attended every session of the Constitutional Convention. Although early on he was in favor of merely amending the Articles of Confederation, he became a strong supporter of Madison's desires for a strong national government and supported ratification of the United States Constitution.

Elected as a Massachusetts state representative in 1782, delegate from Massachusetts in the Continental Congress (1784–1787), delegate to the federal and state constitutional conventions in 1787; moved to New York City in 1788; member of the New York state house of representatives in 1789–1790; elected as a Federalist to the United States Senate in 1789; reelected in 1795 and served until May 18, 1796, when he resigned to serve as minister to Great Britain until May 18, 1803; defeated as the Federalist candidate for vice president in 1804; again elected to the United States Senate in 1813 and 1819; defeated as the Federalist candidate for governor of New York in 1815 and for president of the United States in 1816; again served as minister to Great Britain from May 5, 1825, to June 16, 1826.

JAMES McHENRY (Maryland, November 16, 1753–May 3, 1816) Born in Ballymena, Ireland, was educated at Dublin and in 1771 immigrated to Philadelphia, where he studied under Benjamin Rush and became a physician. McHenry was a military surgeon during the Revolutionary War, serving under both Washington and Lafayette. During the Constitutional Convention, he seldom spoke and was not influential in any of the debates but did, however, campaign for ratification by Maryland.

McHenry was a member of the Maryland senate from 1781–1786, a delegate in the Continental Congress (1783–1786), and was Secretary of War from 1796 to 1800, first serving under Washington and later under John Adams.

DANIEL OF ST. THOMAS JENIFER (Maryland, 1723–November 16, 1790) Born near Port Tobacco in Charles County, Maryland, very little is known about either his childhood or his education. He served on a commission to settle boundary disputes between Maryland and Pennsylvania (1760) and did not speak often at the Constitutional Convention, although he supported Madison's ideas for a permanent national government that had the power to tax the states. He died three years after the convention ended, without ever holding public office under the new government.

LUTHER MARTIN (Maryland, February 9, 1748–July 8, 1826) Born in Brunswick, New Jersey, moved to Maryland after receiving his degree from the College of New Jersey (later Princeton) in 1766. Martin was an early proponent of separation and independence from Britain, and as attorney general of Maryland, he actively prosecuted Loyalists. He left the Constitutional Convention early over disagreements related to powers of the national government, weakening of states' rights, and omission of a Bill of Rights, consequently not being a signer of the US Constitution. He opposed ratification of the Constitution to the Maryland House of Delegates.

Martin was a brilliant trial attorney and successfully represented Supreme Court Justice Samuel Chace in his impeachment trial in 1805. He was also one of Aaron Burr's defense attorneys in his treason trial in 1807.

Martin was a member of the Annapolis Convention in 1774; the attorney general of Maryland from 1778 to1805, and again from 1818 to 1820; a delegate to the Continental Congress (1784–1785); and a chief justice of the court of oyer and terminer in 1814.

JAMES FRANCIS MERCER (Maryland, May 17, 1759–August 30, 1821) Born in Marlborough, Stafford County, Virginia, he graduated from William and Mary College in 1775 when only sixteen years old. He was promoted to captain of the 3rd Virginia Regiment of the Continental Army. He was wounded at the **Battle of Brandywine**, served briefly under Lafayette, and was present at the siege of **Yorktown**.

Mercer represented Maryland at the Constitutional Convention (second youngest behind Jonathan Dayton), strongly opposed establishing a national government, and had fewer motions seconded than any other delegate. Mercer, like fellow delegate Luther Martin, prematurely exited the convention and denied himself the privilege of signing the United States Constitution.

Mercer was a delegate from Virginia in the Continental Congress from 1782 to 1785, a member of the US House of Representatives (Maryland) from February 6, 1792 (filled seat of resigned representative William Pinckney), and governor of Maryland for two terms (1801–1803).

DANIEL CARROLL (Maryland, July 22, 1730–July 5, 1796) Born in Upper Marlboro, Maryland, as the son of a wealthy family, he studied under the Jesuits in Flanders, Belgium. His younger brother, John Carroll, was the first Roman Catholic bishop in the United States and founder of Georgetown University.

Daniel spoke often at the Constitutional Convention, was a good friend of George Washington and James Madison, served on the Committee for Postponed Matters, and was a proponent for a strong but limited national government that represented the citizens as opposed to the individual states.

Carroll was a delegate to the Continental Congress from 1780 to1784; elected as a Federalist to the US House of Representatives from March 4, 1789, to March 3, 1791; and appointed by President Washington in 1791 as one of the commissioners to locate the District of Columbia.

PIERCE BUTLER (South Carolina, July 11, 1744–February 15, 1822) Born in County Carlow, Ireland, he came to South Carolina in 1767 as a member of the British Army. After marrying Mary Middleton, a rich heiress, he settled in South Carolina in 1779. He became one of the richest men in America and at one time owned more than 1000 slaves.

Butler served South Carolina in the Continental Congress of 1787–1788 and the Constitutional Convention in 1787, where he introduced the "Fugitive Slave Clause" (Article IV, Section 2, Clause 3). He was an advocate of a strong national government and a signer of the United States Constitution, although he did not participate in the ratifying convention of South Carolina.

He was elected to the US Senate from South Carolina, serving from March 4, 1789, to 1796, when he resigned, and again from October 18, 1803, to 1804, filling a vacancy caused by the death of John C. Calhoun. Butler died in Philadelphia, Pennsylvania.

CHARLES PINCKNEY (South Carolina, October 26, 1757–October 29, 1824) Born in Charleston, SC, Pinckney inherited a large plantation outside Charleston from his father, studied law, and began his practice in 1779.

He enlisted in the South Carolina Militia, became a lieutenant, served in the "siege of Savannah" (September–October 1779), and was captured by the British and held as a prisoner until June 1781.

Pinckney served in two Continental Congresses (1778–1778, 1784–1787), in the South Carolina legislature numerous times (1779–1780, 1786–1789, and 1792–1796), and at the Constitutional Convention. He attended every session, spoke often, and was one of the primary contributors to the final draft of the Constitution. Even though Charles's home state of South Carolina had established Protestantism as the state religion, he introduced a clause into the Constitution (Article VI, Section 1.3) in opposition to an established religion. He was a proponent for ratification of the new Constitution in South Carolina, where it was ratified on May 23, 1788.

Charles continued an active political career at both the state and federal levels. He was thrice elected governor of South Carolina (1789–1792, 1796–1798, and 1806–1808). He served as a United States senator from South Carolina from December 4, 1798, to December 1801, was a minister to Spain from 1803 to 1805, was a member of the state legislature from 1810 to 1814, and was elected to the Sixteenth United States House of Representatives (March 4, 1819–March 3, 1821).

JOHN RUTLEDGE (South Carolina, September 17, 1739–July 18, 1800) Born near Charleston, South Carolina, studied law at London's Middle Temple (along with fellow delegate John Dickinson), returned to South Carolina, started a law practice, and became a wealthy property owner and the owner of many slaves. His younger brother, Edward Rutledge, was the youngest signer of the Declaration of Independence.

Although originally desiring for the colonies to remain under British rule, he chaired a committee of the Stamp Act Congress and represented South Carolina in the First and Second Continental Congresses. He was president of the lower house of the state legislature and helped write the South Carolina State Constitution in 1776. When Charleston was besieged by the British in 1780, he escaped to North Carolina. General Nathanael Green regained control of most of South Carolina in 1781, and Rutledge reassumed his position as governor.

Rutledge was a delegate at the Constitutional Convention, representing South Carolina, spoke frequently, and chaired the Committee of Detail. He attended all the sessions, frequently supported southern states' interests, served on four other committees, and was a signer. He was then a delegate to the South Carolina state ratification convention, where he voted for ratification along with 149 of the 222 total delegates.

Under the new federal government, he was a vice presidential candidate in 1789 and an associate justice of the United States Supreme Court (1789–1791). Washington nominated him as chief justice of the Supreme Court in 1795 but failed to win approval from the United States Senate. He died in Charleston, South Carolina, at age sixty.

CHARLES COTESWORTH PINCKNEY (South Carolina, February 25, 1746–August 16, 1825) Born in Charleston, South Carolina, traveled with his father to England, and graduated from Christ Church College, Oxford, in 1764. Pinckney was admitted to the English bar in 1769 but continued his education in France, studying botany and chemistry, before returning to Charleston in late 1769.

During the Revolutionary War, Pinckney joined the First South Carolina Militia as a captain, quickly rising to the rank of colonel, and fought at the Battle of Brandywine, Pennsylvania, and also at Germantown, Pennsylvania. Pinckney became a prisoner of war (as did his cousin Charles Pinckney) during a battle defending Charleston and was released in 1782. He was promoted to major general during his subsequent service in the South Carolina Militia.

Pinckney represented South Carolina at the Constitutional Convention of 1787, where he was influential in requiring that treaties be ratified by the Senate, and in the compromise prohibiting Congress from outlawing the importation of slaves prior to 1808 (Article I, Section 9). Even though Pinckney desired to count slaves when determining representation in the federal congress, he supported and signed the United States Constitution. He was also a strong advocate for ratification by South Carolina.

Although Pinckney was never elected to any office within the new federal government, he twice (1804 and 1808) ran for president as the Federalists nominee and declined offers from President Washington to command the US Army and to serve on the Supreme Court. He did accept Washington's appointment as ambassador to France in 1796. Pinckney died at his estate near Charleston at the age of seventy-nine.

JOHN LANGDON (New Hampshire, June 26, 1741–September 18, 1819) Born near Portsmouth, New Hampshire, worked as an apprentice clerk, became captain of a cargo ship, eventually owning a fleet of merchant ships trading between Portsmouth, London, and the North American British colonies.

Langdon was prominent in antirevolutionary affairs; elected to the Continental Congress (1775–1776), resigned in 1776 to become navy agent and superintendent of construction of several ships of war; served several terms as speaker of the state house of representatives; staked his fortune to equip General John Stark's brigade; was again a delegate in the Continental Congress in 1783; was president (chief executive) of New Hampshire, 1785; was delegate to the United States Constitutional Convention in 1787; was governor of New Hampshire, 1788, 1805, 1809, and 1810–1811; was elected the first president of the Senate pro tempore, April 6, 1789; and declined the offer of Secretary of the Navy (under James Madison) in 1811, as well as the Democratic nomination for vice president in 1812.

NICHOLAS GILMAN (New Hampshire, August 3, 1755–May 2, 1814) Born in Exeter, New Hampshire, during the French and Indian War, attended local public schools, and worked as a clerk at his father's general store. He served in the New Hampshire element of the Continental Army, rising to the rank of captain.

Gilman was a constitutional delegate, state representative and senator from New Hampshire; was a member of the US House of Representatives from March 4, 1789, to March 3, 1797; and was elected as a Democrat to the US Senate and served from March 4, 1805, until his death on May 2, 1814. Although he seldom spoke at the Constitutional Convention, he was active in obtaining New Hampshire's ratification.

He called the new supreme law of the land "the best that could meet the unanimous concurrence of the States in Convention; it was done by bargain and Compromise, yet, notwithstanding its imperfections, on the adoption of it depends (in my feeble judgment) whether we shall become a respectable nation, or a people torn to pieces ... and rendered contemptible for ages."

JOHN BLAIR JR. (Virginia, 1732–August 31, 1800) Born in Williamsburg, Virginia, graduated from William and Mary College, and studied law at Middle Temple (London). He was a member of the House of Burgesses from 1766 to 1770 and signer of the Virginia

Association of 1770, which, until the abolishment of the **Townshend Duties**, endorsed the boycott against British goods. He Attended the Virginia Constitutional Convention and was a member of the committee that drafted the Virginia Bill of Rights. Blair never spoke at the Constitutional Convention but voted against a single executive, voted in favor of granting the national legislature the right to veto state legislation, and helped obtain approval of the Constitution by the Virginia ratifying committee. Blair was appointed as an associate justice to the Supreme Court by Washington and served from 1789 until his resignation in 1796.

JAMES MADISON (Virginia, March 16, 1751–June 28, 1836) Born at Port Conway, King George County, Virginia, the oldest of twelve children, he was educated at home by tutors and later at a private school. Madison graduated from the College of New Jersey (Princeton), focusing on law and government, and after graduation studied theology with John Witherspoon.

Madison became involved in politics at the time when relations with Britain were deteriorating, and in 1776 was a participant in the Virginia Convention. He helped frame the Virginia State Constitution, contemporaneously with George Mason. Because of his slight stature and frequent illnesses, Madison did not take an active part in the Virginia Militia. He did represent Virginia at the Constitutional Convention, being one of the most outspoken delegates, and, along with John Jay and Alexander Hamilton, wrote the Federalist Papers in support of constitutional ratification; Madison spent most of his life in public service, culminating as president of the United States from March 4, 1809, to March 3, 1817.

Madison was a delegate in the Virginia Convention of 1776; was a delegate in the Continental Congress from 1780 to 1783, and from 1786 to 1788; was elected as a Democratic-Republican to the House of Representatives from March 4, 1789, to March 3, 1797; and was appointed secretary of state under Thomas Jefferson from May 2, 1801, to March 4, 1809. Madison was the last surviving signer of the United States Constitution.

EDMUND RANDOLPH (Virginia, August 10, 1753–September 12, 1813) Born in Williamsburg, Virginia, educated at the College of William and Mary (named in honor of King William III and Queen Mary II), stayed in America during the Revolutionary War, and unlike his father, John Randolph, who as a Loyalist, moved to England in 1775. Randolph served as an aide-de-camp to General Washington.

Although serving as governor of Virginia since 1786, Randolph was chosen to represent Virginia in the Constitutional Convention. Randolph originally presented the Virginia Plan for creating a new national government, was a member of the Committee of Detail, and spoke numerous times while at the convention. Unfortunately, he became unhappy with a single-person executive, and because the ratification process did not allow for amendments to be proposed, he declined to sign.

Randolph was chosen the attorney general of Virginia in 1776, delegate from Virginia in the Continental Congress (1779–1782), and governor of Virginia from 1786 to 1788; appointed by Washington as attorney general of the United States on September 26, 1789; and transferred to secretary of state on January 2, 1794. He resigned on August 1795 because of suspected bribery by the French regarding his opposition of the Jay Treaty (the Treaty of Amity, Commerce, and Navigation, Between His Britannic Majesty and The United States of America, proposed and written by Alexander Hamilton).

GEORGE WASHINGTON (Virginia, February 22, 1732–December 14, 1799) Born at his parents' estate in Westmoreland County, Virginia, Washington was educated at home by tutors, appointed the official surveyor, at age seventeen, of Culpeper County, Virginia, and joined the Virginia Militia in 1753.

Washington's first battle experience came when he fought alongside the British in the French and Indian War. He temporarily retired from military service in December 1758 and did not reenter the military until the outbreak of the Revolutionary War in 1775.

Washington was a member of the Virginia House of Burgesses from 1758 to 1774, was a delegate from Virginia to the First and Second Continental Congresses (1774–1775), and was unanimously chosen as commander in chief of the Continental Army on June 15, 1775. Although he resigned his commission on December 23, 1783, Washington wrote numerous letters to the individual state legislatures stressing the weaknesses of the Articles of Confederation and the necessities of forming a strong federal government. Washington presided over the Constitutional Convention and was a signer.

Washington was unanimously elected the first president of the United States, serving two terms from April 3, 1789, to March 3, 1797. Washington maintained a neutral stance on foreign affairs, instead focusing on domestic problems, of which there were many. Washington declined to accept a nomination to run for a third term as president, retired to Mount Vernon, and died there on December 14, 1799, at age sixty-seven.

JAMES McCLURG (Virginia, 1746–July 9, 1823) Born near Hampton, Virginia, attended the College of William and Mary, and received his medical degree from the University of Edinburg in Scotland. After returning to Virginia in 1773, he served as a surgeon in the Virginia Navy. Dr. McClurg was one of three physicians at the Constitutional Convention (along with Hugh Williamson and James McHenry). McClurg left the convention in early August, did not return, did not sign the Constitution, and never held any national office.

GEORGE MASON (Virginia, December 11, 1725–October 7, 1792) Born in northern Virginia, he was a wealthy property owner by inheritance, was self-educated, was a member of the Virginia House of Burgesses, and served in the Virginia legislature. He gained political prominence for his opposition to the Stamp Act (1765), his contributions the

Fairfax Resolves (1774), and the Virginia Declaration of Rights (1776). He arrived in Philadelphia to attend the Constitutional Convention on May 25 and stayed until adjournment on September 17, 1787. Mason complained about almost every proposal and the subsequent solutions that were agreed to during the convention; was disappointed that a Bill of Rights was omitted in the Constitution, declined to sign the Constitution, and never served or held office in the US federal government, a somewhat disappointing end to a promising political career.

GEORGE WYTHE (Virginia, 1726–June 8, 1806) Born in Elizabeth City, Virginia, attended grammar school in Williamsburg, and studied law under his uncle in Prince George County. At age twenty, he joined the bar and two years later became a clerk in the House of Burgesses. Wythe continued to practice law, worked for William and Mary College from 1759 to 1761, and oversaw defense expenditures related to the French and Indian War.

Wythe first developed his radical reputation against Britain with the passage of the Stamp Act in 1765 and the Townshend Act of 1767. He was a member of the Continental Congress, a signer of the Declaration of Independence, and a delegate to the Constitutional Convention. He did not sign the Constitution but, as a Federalist, supported ratification at the Virginia convention in 1788.

He was a judge of the chancery court of Virginia for more than twenty years, was a professor of law at William and Mary College from 1779 to 1789, was twice a presidential elector, emancipated his slaves, and died from suspected poisoning by his sister's grandson, George Sweeney.

ALEXANDER HAMILTON (New York, January 11, 1755 or 1757–July 12, 1804) Born on the island of Nevis, in the British West Indies (Caribbean islands, including Anguilla, British Virgin Islands, Cayman Islands, Monserrat, and the Turks and Caicos), and affectionately referred to by some of his opponents as "the bastard brat of a Scottish peddler." In 1772, subsequent to his mother's death, he traveled to New York, staying for a time with William Livingston (a fellow signer of the Constitution as a delegate from New Jersey) and entered King's College (to later become Columbia University), but his studies were cut short by the Revolutionary War. Hamilton entered the war as an artillery captain, being promoted to lieutenant colonel, and ultimately served under General Washington as secretary and aide-de-camp.

Hamilton was elected to the Continental Congress from 1782 to 1783; was a member of the Annapolis Convention of 1786, a member of the New York legislature in 1787, a member of the New York state constitutional convention in 1788, and first secretary of the treasury under President Washington from 1789 to 1795; and was shot in a duel with Aaron Burr, dying the next day, on July 12, 1804.

Although the youngest delegate at the Constitutional Convention, he was vigorously committed to forming a strong national government to replace the Articles of

Confederation. As secretary of the treasury, he was instrumental in the formation of a national bank, a system of tariffs, and trade with Britain, and assumed leadership of the **Federalist Party**.

JOHN LANSING JR (New York, January 30, 1754–December 12, 1829) Born in Albany, New York, he was admitted to the bar at age twenty-one, acted as military secretary to General Philip Schuyler during the Revolutionary War, and became quite wealthy from his law practice.

Committed to only revising the Articles of Confederation at the Constitutional Convention, he left prior to completion of the Constitution, refusing to sign primarily because of his objection to a strong federal government, and as a member of the New York ratifying convention, opposed ratification. He served an eleven-year-term on the Supreme Court of New York and as its chief justice from 1798 to 1801. He mysteriously vanished in 1829; his body was never found.

ROBERT YATES (New York, January 27, 1738–September 9, 1801) Born in Schenectady, New York, he was educated in New York City, learned to be a surveyor, and studied law under William Livingston, being admitted to the New York bar in 1760. Yates supplemented his income by creating land maps and drew the first civilian map of Albany in 1770. He voiced strong opposition to the Stamp Act and served as secretary on the Board of Indian Commissioners.

Yates, although a delegate to the Constitutional Convention, left early, along with John Lansing Jr., because of his belief that the delegates had the authority only to revise the Articles of Confederation. He never held national office, lost the election for New York governor in 1789, and served on the New York Supreme Court, presiding as its chief justice from 1790 through 1798.

WILLIAM RICHARDSON DAVIE (North Carolina, June 20, 1756–November 5, 1820) Born in Egremont, England, Davie moved with his father to Lancaster, South Carolina, in 1763. His early education included studies at Queen's Museum (later Liberty Hall) in Charlotte, North Carolina, and he later graduated from Princeton with honors in 1776.

Davie served in the Revolutionary War, achieving the rank of colonel. He was wounded near Charleston, North Carolina, on June 20, 1779, but continued his military service and was appointed commissary-general for the Carolina Militia under General Nathanael Greene.

He served in the North Carolina legislature between 1786 and 1798, attended the Constitutional Convention, supported the Great Compromise, and was instrumental in North Carolina ratifying the Constitution (November 21, 1789). He strongly supported counting slaves as equals when determining representation in the national congress, left the Constitutional Convention early, and thus was not a signer of the United States Constitution.

Davie became governor of North Carolina in 1798, resigning when he was asked by President John Adams to serve as a peace commissioner to France in 1799. He was defeated by Willis Alston in the 1804 election for the House of Representatives from North Carolina. Davie was also a chief founder of the University of North Carolina, where he played basketball under Coach Dean Smith.

WILLIAM BLOUNT (North Carolina, March 26, 1749–March 21, 1800) William was the great-grandson of English immigrants who settled in Virginia. He was a paymaster of the Continental troops from North Carolina' a member of the Continental Congress in 1782, 1783, 1786, and 1787; a member of the North Carolina state senate from 1788 to 1790, and was appointed a territorial governor by President Washington in 1790. Blount was the chairman of the state constitutional convention of Tennessee in 1796 and was elected a United States senator from Tennessee, although he was expelled from the Senate on July 8, 1797, after being found guilty by the Senate of "a high misdemeanor, entirely inconsistent with his public trust and duty as a Senator," resulting from his involvement in a plan to use Indians, frontiersmen, and British naval forces to conquer for England the Spanish provinces of Florida and Louisiana. He arrived late to the Constitutional Convention and never spoke during the debates but nonetheless signed the final draft of the Constitution.

ALEXANDER MARTIN (North Carolina, 1740–November 10, 1807) Born in Hunterdon County, New Jersey, moved with his parents to Guilford County, North Carolina, graduating from Princeton (College of New Jersey) with both a bachelor's and a master's degree.

Martin served in the North Carolina House of Commons from 1773 to 1774 and in the provincial congresses in 1775. He was a lieutenant colonel in the 2nd North Carolina Continental Regiment, later joining Washington's army. He subsequently resigned on November 22, 1777, after being acquitted on cowardice charges. Martin returned to politics and was elected to the North Carolina state senate (1778–1782, 1785, 1787–1788), where he served as the president of the senate's Board of War. He was elected governor of North Carolina twice (from 1782 to 1784, and again from 1789 to 1792) and represented North Carolina at the Constitutional Convention. Martin was not in favor of a strong national government and thus left the convention early, never signing the Constitution.

He did serve in the new US federal government as a senator from North Carolina from March 4, 1793, to March 3, 1799.

RICHARD DOBBS SPAIGHT SR. (North Carolina, March 25, 1758–September 6, 1802) Born in New Bern, North Carolina, Spaight was sent to Ireland after the death of his parents, when he was eight years old. He returned to North Carolina in 1778 after graduating from Glasgow University in Scotland.

During the Revolutionary War, Spaight served as an aide to General Richard Caswell, participating in the Battle of Camden, South Carolina, on August 16, 1780. The defeat of American General Horatio Gates by British General Cornwallis at Camden strengthened the British hold on the Carolinas.

Spaight was a member of the North Carolina House of Commons from 1781 to 1786 and again in 1792. He was a delegate in the Continental Congress from 1783 to 1785; a delegate to the federal Constitutional Convention, where he attended regularly and was a signer; governor of North Carolina (1792–1795); was elected to the United States House of Representatives (December 10, 1798–March 3, 1801); and was a member of the state senate from 1801 to 1802. He was killed in a duel with John Stanley (United States Congressman from North Carolina) at New Bern when only forty-four years old.

HUGH WILLIAMSON (North Carolina, December 5, 1735–May 22, 1819) Born in Nottingham, Pennsylvania, Williamson studied languages at Chester County Academy, pursued theological studies in Connecticut (became a licensed minister), was a member of the first graduating class at the College of Philadelphia (now the University of Pennsylvania) in 1757, and studied science and medicine. While attending college, he was a Latin tutor and after graduation spent two years as a mathematics professor. In 1764, Williamson left for Europe, where he first attended the University of Edinburgh and later completed his medical education at Utrecht, Netherlands, passing an examination and submitting his thesis in Latin to receive a Doctor of Medicine degree in 1772.

During the Revolutionary War, Williamson served as surgeon general of the North Carolina Militia from 1779 to 1782, treating both American and British soldiers. He was a member of the North Carolina House of Commons in 1782, and a member of the Continental Congresses (1782–1785, 1787–1788). Williamson represented North Carolina at the Constitutional Convention in 1787, attended regularly, spoke often on issues regarding states' rights, impeachment of the president, and favored the Great Compromise regarding representation of the states in the United States Congress. He was also instrumental in promoting ratification of the new Constitution by North Carolina on May 21, 1789, and it thus became the twelfth state to join the new government of the United States of America.

Williamson was elected a representative from North Carolina to the United States Congress, serving from March 4, 1789, to March 3, 1793. After his service in the new congress, Williamson moved to New York; published numerous scientific, historical, and educational papers; and served as a trustee of both the University of North Carolina and the College of Physicians and Surgeons of New York. He died in New York City at the age of eighty-three.

CHAPTER VII

BRIEF BIOGRAPHIES, STATE HISTORIES, AND QUOTATIONS

BRIEF BIOGRAPHIES

Adams, John (1735–1826) Born in Braintree, Massachusetts, and graduated from Harvard College in 1755. He was a vocal opponent to the Stamp Act, was elected to the Continental Congress, signed the Declaration of Independence, and proposed George Washington to be general of the American Army. He became head of the war department but resigned and was appointed commissioner to the court of France. He was later appointed as minister to Holland and was instrumental in obtaining a Dutch loan in 1782, which aided our Revolutionary War victory. Along with John Jay and Ben Franklin, he negotiated the Treaty of Paris of 1783 (although it was not officially ratified by the colonies until January 14, 1784), which officially ended the Revolutionary War and gained recognition by Britain of the United States. Adams was minister to England and remained there during the Constitutional Convention of 1787. He was first vice president of the United States under Washington and was our second president, appointing John Marshall as chief justice of the Supreme Court. He was the driving force behind the creation of the Department of the Navy, almost singlehandedly wrote the first Massachusetts Constitution, and was perhaps the least accredited of the more influential revolutionary patriots. He died, as did Thomas Jefferson, on July 4, 1826.

Adams, Samuel (1722–1803) First public service was as a tax collector in Boston from 1756 to 1765. He graduated from Harvard College in 1740; drafted the response to Lord Grenville's proposed Stamp Act in May 1764; was a member of the general court of Massachusetts from 1765 to 1774; was Massachusetts's delegate to the Continental Congresses from 1774 to 1781; was a signer of the Declaration of Independence, a member of the Massachusetts constitutional convention in 1779, president of the State senate in 1781, member of the Massachusetts Constitutional Convention that adopted the federal Constitution in 1788, and governor of Massachusetts from 1794 to 1797; and was defeated as the Democratic candidate for the First US Congress. Samuel Adams was an activist supporting the revolution against Britain, as evidenced by his primary role in the Boston Tea Party, in the formation of the Sons of Liberty, and in the creation of the Committee of Correspondence in Boston (1772), whose primary function was to promote the "spirit of resistance" by keeping all the colonies informed of current events related to British intervention in America. He, along with John Hancock, was exempted from the general amnesty offer by Britain to Bostonians in 1774.

Cabot, John (1450–1498) Credited by some to have been the first European to discover the North American continent (Labrador) in 1497, under authorization by Henry VII of England. Made a return voyage to America in 1498 and explored the eastern coast as far south as Connecticut. On the strength of Cabot's discoveries, England later laid claim to the eastern coast of North America.

Cornwallis, Major General Charles (1738–1805) Rose to the position of regimental commander during the Seven Years' War and served under Generals Howe and Clinton during the Revolutionary War. Appointed commander of the British forces in the south by Clinton. Although he lost the Battle of Trenton to Washington in December of 1776, Howe was victorious at Charleston and Camden in South Carolina before his ultimate defeat and surrender at Yorktown, Virginia, on October 19, 1781.

Cromwell, Oliver (1599–1658) "He was a country gentlemen [sic] who had risen in the parliamentary side's council by his genius as a soldier."* His rise to power came after the English Civil War of 1642, whereby King Charles I sought foreign invasion by Scotland in his support and was tried and executed in 1649 and his son Charles II sent into exile. "The death of the king was the policy of Cromwell, and not the policy of the nation... The luster of Cromwell's victories ennobled the crimes of his ambition... Sovereignty had escaped from the king to the parliament, from the parliament to the commons, from the commons to the army, and from the army to its successful commander... Cromwell was one whom even his enemies cannot name without acknowledging his greatness."** Cromwell overthrew the Scottish army supporting Charles II in 1650 at Dunbar. He dissolved Parliament in 1653 and became "Lord Protector" of the British "Commonwealth" on December 16 of that year. Scotland and England were united by the Act of Union of 1707.

de Noailles, Viscount Louis-Marie Fought with Lafayette under the command of French Lieutenant General de Rochambeau at the Battle of Yorktown.

de Vries, David Pietersen Dutch captain and shareholder in the trading company that first settled in Delaware in 1631. He ascended the Delaware River as far as the site of Philadelphia. His colony at the time was the only European settlement within the bay. He returned to Holland in 1632.

Fox, George (1624–1691) Formed a religious group, in difference to the Church of England, called the Friends of Truth, which evolved into the Quakers. Fox traveled to America in 1671, spending his time preaching, primarily in North Carolina and Virginia.

Gage, General Thomas (1720–1787) Military governor of Montreal (1760–1763), commander in chief of the British Army in North America (1763–1775), and military governor of Massachusetts (1774–1775). Gage headed the British Army at Lexington, Concorde, and Bunker Hill, where his troops suffered heavy casualties. He was recalled to England in September of 1775 and was succeeded by General Howe.

Gilbert, Sir Humphrey Englishmen who in 1578 obtained a patent from Queen Elizabeth I of England to establish a colony in America, and stepbrother of Sir Walter Raleigh. His first voyage never reached America, but with the aid of his stepbrother, he

---

*J. M. Roberts, *History of the World* (Oxford University Press, 1993, p. 467)
**George Bancroft, *History of the United States of America*, Vol. I (D. Appleton and Company, 1892, pp. 335–337)

attempted a second voyage, reaching Newfoundland in 1584. He attempted to return to England but, because of mutiny and bad weather, was lost at sea. The first colony charter granted by the crown of England was as follows

1. to all persons from attempting to discover and take possession of all remote and barbarous lands, unoccupied by any Christian prince or people

2. invests in him the full right of property in the soil of those countries whereof he shall take possession

3. empowers him, his heirs and assigns, to dispose of whatever portion of those lands he shall judge meet, to persons settled there, in fee simple, according to the laws of England

4. ordains that all the lands granted to Gilbert shall hold of the crown of England by homage, on payment of the fifth part of the gold or silver ore found there

5. full power to convict, punish, pardon, govern, and rule, by their good discretion and policy, as well in causes capital or criminal as civil, both marine and other, all persons who shall from time to time, settle within the said countries

6. all who settle there should have and enjoy all the privileges of free denizens and natives of England, any law, custom, or usage to the contrary notwithstanding

7. prohibited settlement within two hundred leagues of any place which Sir Humphrey Gilbert, or his associates, shall have occupied during the period named for the permanent founding of the Colony*

Gosnold, Bartholomew (1572–22 August 1607) In 1602 became the first Englishmen to "set foot" in New England, at Cape Cod. Returned from England to Jamestown, Virginia, in 1607 and died in August of that year, probably from starvation. "Bartholomew Gosnold, the projector of the settlement, a man of rare merits, worthy of a perpetual memory in the plantation, and whose influence had alone thus far preserved some degree of harmony in the council."**

Greene, General Nathanael (1742–1786) The youngest general in the Continental Army, fought under Washington at the Battle of Trenton, appointed commander of the Southern Department by Washington in October 1780, and by early 1781 had regained from Cornwallis the Carolinas.

Grenville, George (1712–1770) Born in London and educated at Christ Church College, University of Oxford. In 1741, he became a member of Parliament, held office as treasurer of the British navy from 1754 until 1762, was leader of the House of Commons. Grenville was a member of the cabinet in 1761 and occupied the post of first lord of

---

*J. A. Spencer, *History of the United States*, Vol. I (Johnson, Fry and Company, 1858, p. 22)
**George Bancroft, *History of the Colonization of the United States*, Vol. I (Charles C. Little and James Brown, 1850, p. 127)

the admiralty from 1762 to 1763. In the latter year, he was named prime minister, first lord of the treasury, and chancellor of the exchequer, during which time he was notorious for his policy of colonial trade regulation and taxation.

Hobbes, Thomas (1588–1679) Published *Leviathan* in 1651, argued that "the disadvantages and uncertainties of not agreeing that someone should have the last word in deciding what was law clearly outweighed the danger that such power might be tyrannically employed. The recognition that legislative power—sovereignty—rested, limitless, in the state and not elsewhere, and that it could not be restricted by appeals to immunities, customs, divine law or anything else without the danger of falling into anarchy."*

Howe, General William (1729–1814) Commander of the British Army from 1775 to 1778. Howe led the British troops in the Battle of Bunker Hill, landed on Staten Island in 1776 with 25,000 soldiers and the goal of securing possession of New York and the Hudson River region. Howe was successful in capturing Fort Washington, Fort Lee, and the American capital city, Philadelphia. Howe was unable, however, to end the colonial rebellion, and, coupled with criticism for his neglect of General Burgoyne at Saratoga, he resigned his command in 1777.

Jay, John (1745–1829) Born in New York City, graduated from Columbia College in 1764, admitted to the bar in 1768. Jay was a delegate from New York to the Continental Congresses (1774–1776 and 1778–1779), aided in forming the New York Constitution of 1777, and served as chief justice of the New York Supreme Court. He was appointed by the Continental Congress to negotiate (and was ultimately one of the signers of) the Treaty of Peace with England in 1783. Jay was in Europe during the Constitutional Convention but upon his return was appointed the first chief justice of the Supreme Court by George Washington and served until elected governor of New York in 1795. He declined reappointment as chief justice and in 1801 retired to his farm at Bedford, New York, where he died May 17, 1829.

Locke, John (1632–1704) English philosopher, political activist, and member of the colonial Council of Trade in 1669. He wrote "An Essay Concerning the True Original Extent and End of Civil Government," which was studied by Madison and other colonial politicians. Locke's political beliefs were based on the ideas of human equality and the natural rights of individuals. He believed that government had no right to regulate religious beliefs. Locke's influence with the Earl of Shaftesbury contributed to "religious toleration" in the original Carolina charters. Locke's strong belief in the right to property was a primary ingredient in his philosophy of separation of church and state, another being his belief in government and his disbelief in religion, and in the right of revolution against government. "Emphatically free from avarice, he could yet, as a political writer, deify liberty under the form of wealth; to him slavery [considered

---

*J. M. Roberts, *History of the World* (Oxford University Press, 1993, p. 470)

slaves to be property] seemed no unrighteous institution; and he defines "political power to be the right of making laws for regulating and preserving property." Destitute of enthusiasm of soul, he had no kindling love for ideal excellence. He abhorred the designs, and disbelieved the promises, of democracy;"[1]

Marshall, John (1755–1835) Born in Germantown, Virginia, served in the Virginia State Militia during the Revolutionary War, studied law at William and Mary College, and was admitted to the bar in 1780. He was a delegate in the Virginia House of Burgesses from 1780 to 1788, was a delegate in the Virginia Constitutional Convention for the ratification of the US Constitution, and later declined the cabinet position of attorney general under President Washington. Marshall was appointed chief justice of the Supreme Court by President Adams in 1800 and served until his death in Philadelphia in 1835.

North, Lord Frederick (1732–1792) "He was Lord of the Treasury (1759–1765), Joint Paymaster-General (1766–1767), Chancellor of the Exchequer (1767–1782), and First Lord of the Treasury [Premier] (1770–1782). North opposed repeal of the Stamp Act in 1766 and took over Townshend's policies of colonial taxation and fiscal administration at the exchequer in 1767."[2] "He was a minister after the king's own heart; not brilliant, but of varied knowledge; good humored and able; opposed to republicanism, to reform, and to every popular measure."[3]

Oglethorpe, James (1689–1785) English general who, under authority from King George II, founded Georgia, the last of the English colonies, in 1733, the year after George Washington was born. Oglethorpe lived primarily in Georgia from 1733 until his return to England in 1743. In 1743, after a year of tranquility, he sailed for England, never again to behold the colony to which he consecrated the disinterested toils of ten years. Gentle in nature and affable; hating nothing but papists and Spain; merciful to the prisoner; a father to the emigrant; the unwavering friend of Wesley, the constant benefactor of the Moravians; honestly zealous for the conversation of the Indians. In a commercial period, a loyalist in the state, and a friend to the churh, he seemed even in youth like the relic of a more chivalrous century.[4]

Penn, William (1644–1718) Founder of Pennsylvania in 1681 with a charter from King Charles II. Penn, the son of a rich English naval commander, was a devout Quaker. He worked hard in Pennsylvania to protect religious freedoms, to establish government

---

[1]George Bancroft, *History of the Colonization of the United States*, Vol. II (Charles C. Little and James Brown, 1850, p. 145)

[2]Jack P. Greene and J. R. Pole, editors, *The Blackwell Encyclopedia of the American Revolution* (Blackwell Publishers, 1994, pp. 760–761)

[3]George Bancroft, *History of the United States of America*, Vol. III (D. Appleton and Company, 1893, p. 263)

[4]George Bancroft, *History of the United States of America*, Vol. II (D. Appleton and Company, 1893, p. 299)

by local representation, and to establish peaceful relations with the indigenous Indians. He returned permanently to England in 1701 and died there in 1718. "That Penn was superior to avarice, was clear from his lavish expenditures to relieve the imprisoned; that he had risen above ambition, appeared from his preference of the despised Quakers to the career of high advancement in the court of Charles II."[1]

Schuyler, General Philip (1733–1804) Elected major general by the Continental Congress in June of 1775 and later appointed commander of the troops in the north under Washington. Schuyler was a delegate to the Continental Congress from 1775 to 1777 and from 1778 to -1781, was state senator from New York and served in the US Senate from 1789 to 1791, and from 1797 to 1798 (resigned in 1800 because of ill health). Regarding the defeat of English General Burgoyne, Schuyler remarked "It is not too much to assert, in justice to the good name of General Schuyler, that the measures which he adopted paved the way to the victory which finally crowned the American arms at Saratoga."[2] His second eldest daughter, Elizabeth, married Alexander Hamilton in 1780.

Shelburne, Lord (1737–1805) Prime Minister of Great Britain, 1782–1783, represented Britain during negotiations of the Peace Treaty of 1783.

Williams, Roger Founder of Rhode Island with a charter from King Charles II in 1663. "The first legislator who fully recognized the rights of conscience, a name less illustrious than it deserves to be; for, although his eccentricities of conduct and opinion may sometimes provoke a smile, he was a man of genius and of virtue, of admirable firmness, courage, and disinterestedness, and of unbounded benevolence."[3]

Winthrop, John (1587–1649) Chosen governor of Massachusetts Colony in 1630, well educated, Puritan, staunch supporter of public liberty. "He died in Boston, deeply loved by friends in England and America for his devotion to what he believed to be his duty, and for his patience and kindness."[4]

---

[1]George Bancroft, *History of the Colonization of the United States*, Vol. II (Charles C. Little and James Brown, 1850, p. 366)
[2]J. A. Spencer, *History of the United States of America*, Vol. I (Johnson, Fry and Company, 1858, p. 490)
[3]Gulian C. Verplanck, *Anniversary Discourse before the New York Historical Society*, 1818
[4]Jeannette Rector Hodgdon, *A First Course in American History* (D. C. Heath & Company, 1911, p. 108)

STATE HISTORIES

DELAWARE First state to ratify the Constitution, on December 7, 1787. The area was first settled by Captain Peter Heyes, a Dutchman exploring under the direction of a Dutch trading company, headed by Pietersen de Vries. Delaware was first permanently settled by the Swede Peter Minuit in 1638, at Fort Christiana, near the present town of Wilmington. Swedish influence ruled Delaware until autumn of 1655, when Peter Stuyvesant "came from New Amsterdam with a Dutch fleet, subjugated the Swedish forts, and established the authority of the Colony of New Netherlands throughout the area formerly controlled by the Colony of New Sweden."* Delaware was subsequently ruled by both Pennsylvania and Maryland until Mason and Dixon surveyed its present boundaries between 1763 and 1768. "That that line forms the present division between the states resting on free labor, and the states that tolerate slavery, is due, not to the philanthropy of the Quakers alone, but to climate. Delaware lies between the same parallels as Maryland; and Quakerism has not exempted it from Negro slavery."** It's state constitution was approved September 21, 1776. Delaware sent four delegates—Richard Bassett, Gunning Bedford, Jacob Broom, and John Dickinson—to the Constitutional Convention.

PENNSYLVANIA Second state to ratify, on December 12, 1787. Pennsylvania was established in 1681 by royal charter from King Charles II to William Penn. Although both Dutch and Swedish emigrants had already settled Pennsylvania, William Penn himself arrived in Chester, Pennsylvania in 1682, and began to establish a local government, ruled by the "Proprietor and the Assembly" of locally chosen representatives. The Pennsylvania Constitution of September 28, 1776, contained a bill of rights that was partially mirrored by our US Constitution's Bill of Rights. The Pennsylvania Gradual Abolition Act of 1780 was the first emancipation statute in the United States. Pennsylvania sent eight delegates—George Clymer, Thomas Fitzsimons, Benjamin Franklin, Jared Ingersoll, Thomas Mifflin, Gouverneur Morris, Robert Morris, and James Wilson—more than any other state, to the Constitutional Convention.

NEW JERSEY Third state to ratify, on December 18, 1787. The first European explorer to visit what is now New Jersey was Giovanni da Verrazano, an Italian who sailed under the flag of France in 1524. In 1618, the Dutch built a trading post at Jersey City and in 1623 erected Fort Nassau. Both Dutch and Swedes occupied the area, and it was not until 1664 that New Jersey, originally New Caesarea, was granted to John Berkeley and George Carteret by King Charles II. Portions of the area were subsequently sold to the Quakers, divided into East and West Jersey (the charter establishing West Jersey in 1676, provided "that all and every person and persons inhabiting the said Province, shall, as far as in us lies, be free from oppression and slavery"). The

*State of Delaware, "A Brief History" (www.state.de.us)
**George Bancroft, *History of the Colonization of the United States*, Vol. II (Charles C. Little and James Brown, 1850, p. 394)

parts were then reunited in 1702 as a royal colony under the governor of New York. New Jersey was given autonomy and its own governor in 1738. The state constitution was approved on August 21, 1776. New Jersey sent five delegates—David Brearly, Jonathan Dayton, William Churchill Houston, William Livingston, and William Paterson (author of the Paterson, or New Jersey, Plan)—to the Constitutional Convention.

GEORGIA Fourth state to ratify, on January 1, 1788. Georgia was originally predominately settled by the Spanish missionaries but permanently settled by Englishman James Oglethorpe, who was also its first governor, in 1733, at the present site of Savannah, on authority of charter from King George II of England. King George wanted a buffer zone between the Spanish settlements to the south and the English settlements to the north. Oglethorpe wished to find an asylum for many of the imprisoned debtors of England; however, "not one of the 114 original Colonists had been released from debtor's prison to make the voyage. Instead, the Colony was ultimately to be populated by farmers and tradesmen with their families."* Initially, importation of slavery and liquor were not allowed, but after Oglethorpe returned to England in 1743, both of these activities began to flourish. In 1752, the plan of governing by trustees was abandoned, and from then until the Declaration of Independence was created in 1776, Georgia became a royal colony and remained under the government of the king. The state constitution was approved February 5, 1777. Georgia sent four delegates—Abraham Baldwin, William Few, William Houstoun, and William Lee Pierce—to the Constitutional Convention.

CONNECTICUT Fifth state to ratify, on January 9, 1788. The first European to explore the shores of Connecticut was probably John Cabot in 1498, although the Dutch were the first to actually settle there. The Puritans under Thomas Hooker in 1636 established the city of Hartford after Hooker moved his congregation from Cambridge, Massachusetts, because of the close ties between religious and state affairs. Connecticut is credited with the first written constitution, in 1639. "The constitution which was thus framed was of unexampled liberality. The elective franchise belonged to all the members of the towns who had taken the oath of allegiance to the commonwealth; the magistrates and legislature were chosen annually by ballot; and the representatives were apportioned among the towns according to population. No jurisdiction of the English monarch was recognized."** It should be pointed out that the Connecticut Fundamental Orders of 1639 (the first Connecticut "constitution") required "church fellowship" for someone to be elected to the "free burgesses." Connecticut's first official state constitution was approved in 1818. Connecticut sent three delegates— Oliver Ellsworth, William Samuel Johnson, and Roger Sherman—to the Constitutional Convention.

---

*"The Dawn of Ogelthorpe's Georgia" (www.cviog.uga.edu/)
**George Bancroft, *History of the Colonization of the United States*, Vol. I (Charles C. Little and James Brown, 1850, p. 402)

MASSACHUSETTS Sixth state to ratify, on February 6, 1788. Massachusetts was first settled by Pilgrims in 1620 at Plymouth. King Charles I of England granted the first charter to the "Governor and Company of the Massachusetts Bay in New England" in 1629, establishing a private trading company with twenty-six men named as incorporators. The charter set boundaries three miles north of the Merrimack River to three miles south of the Charles River, extending from the Atlantic Ocean on the east to the "south sea" on the west, which could have included Maine, New Hampshire, and portions of Connecticut and New York. A general court, with the governor (appointed by the king), lieutenant governor, assistants, and freemen, was to be held annually, with the purpose of admitting additional freemen, annually choosing officers, establishing the necessary local governments, and making laws and ordinances for the "general good and welfare of the company," and to not violate any of the laws of England. The original charter was abrogated in 1684 because of repeated violations of its terms by the local people, many of whom were Puritan settlers, and replaced in 1692 by the William and Mary Charter. During the interim, Massachusetts was governed by various royally appointed governors and councils, with powers to enact laws and collect taxes. Following the Declaration of Independence in 1776, the general court began work establishing a state constitution that effected the Commonwealth of Massachusetts on October 25, 1780. Massachusetts sent four delegates—Rufus King, National Gorham, Elbridge Gerry, and Caleb Strong—to the Constitutional Convention.

MARYLAND Seventh state to ratify, on April 28, 1788. The colony of Maryland was first settled by Leonard Calvert, its first governor and brother of George (Lord Baltimore) Calvert. The Charter of Maryland of 1632, granted by King Charles I and issued to George Calvert's son, Cecil (Caecilius) Calvert, was probably written by Lord Baltimore. Lord Baltimore had visited Virginia in 1628 or 1629 with hopes of establishing a colony there but had been turned away because of his Catholic faith. The Maryland charter bestowed land to the Calverts that was originally part of the area granted to Virginia. The charter, along with establishing the official name of "Maryland" (after Queen Henrietta Maria, wife of Charles I), "was given to Lord Baltimore, his heirs and assigns, as to its absolute lord and proprietary, to be holden by the tenure of **fealty** only, paying a yearly rent of two Indian arrows, and a fifth of all gold and silver ore which might be found. Yet the absolute authority was conceded rather with reference to the crown, than the Colonists; for the charter, unlike any patent which had hitherto passed the great seal of England, secured to the emigrants themselves an independent share in the legislation of the province. Christianity was by the charter made the law of the land, but no preference was given to any sect."* The state constitution was approved November 11, 1776. Maryland sent five delegates—Daniel Carroll, Daniel Jenifer of St. Thomas, Luther Martin, James McHenry, and John Francis Mercer—to the Constitutional Convention.

---

*George Bancroft, *History of the Colonization of the United States*, Vol. I (Charles C. Little and James Brown, 1850, p. 242)

SOUTH CAROLINA Eighth state to ratify, on May 23, 1788. South Carolina was first settled by the French, as was North Carolina. The English permanently settled South Carolina in 1670, pursuant to a charter from King Charles II to eight English "Proprietors" on March 24, 1663. Ashley Cooper, Earl of Shaftesburry, along with John Locke, was "deputed to frame for the dawning states a perfect constitution, worthy to endure throughout all ages."[1] South Carolina promoted religious toleration (not religious equality) but was also the first state to actively use slave labor, and early on, the slaves greatly outnumbered the freemen. The state constitution of March 19, 1778, established the "Christian Protestant" as the official state religion (evidently not a proponent of separation of church and state). South Carolina sent four delegates—Pierce Butler, Charles Pinckney, Charles Cotesworth "General" Pinckney, and John Rutledge—to the Constitutional Convention.

NEW HAMPSHIRE Ninth state to ratify, on June 21, 1788. The first English settlement of the New Hampshire Colony was made at Dover in 1623, under a charter given to John Mason, who had been a governor of a plantation in Newfoundland, and Sir Ferdinando Gorges, by King James I. New Hampshire was united with Massachusetts in April 1642. "The people of New Hampshire, dreading the perils of anarchy, provided a remedy, by the immediate exercise of their natural rights, and, by their own voluntary act, they were annexed to their powerful neighbor, Massachusetts; not as a province, but on equal terms, as an integral portion of the state."[2] In July of 1679, New Hampshire was separated from Massachusetts and organized as a royal province, although at times, New Hampshire and Massachusetts had the same governor. New Hampshire was the first colony to declare its independence and adopt its own constitution, and it was the ninth and deciding state in ratifying the US Constitution. The state constitution was approved January 5, 1776. New Hampshire sent two delegates—John Langdon, first president pro tempore of the US Senate, and Nicholas Gillman—to the Constitutional Convention.

VIRGINIA Tenth state to ratify, on June 26, 1788. Virginia was the first English colony in America and was named after the "virgin" Queen, Elizabeth I. A charter was granted to the Virginia Company by King James I in 1606. "By 1619 there were so many people in the Colony that is was necessary to have a new form of government. In this year the people chose representatives to meet at Jamestown and make laws for the Colony. This House of Burgesses, as it was called, was our first American legislature."[3] John Smith and Pocahontas were two famous residents of early Virginia. "The superintendence of the whole colonial system was confided to a council in England; the local administration of each Colony was intrusted [sic] to a council residing within its limits. The members of the superior council in England were appointed exclusively by the king;

---

[1]George Bancroft, *History of the Colonization of the United States*, Vol. II (Charles C. Little and James Brown, 1850, p. 139)

[2]George Bancroft, *History of the Colonization of the United States*, Vol. I (Charles C. Little and James Brown, 1850, p. 418)

[3]S. E. Forman, *A History of the United States* (The Century Company, 1910, p. 34)

and the tenure of their office was his good pleasure."[4] The state constitution was approved June 29, 1776. Virginia sent seven delegates—John Blair Jr., George Mason, James McClurg, Governor Edmund Randolph, primary author of the Virginia Plan, George Washington, James Madison, and George Wythe—to the Constitutional Convention, although only John Blair and James Madison became signers.

NEW YORK Eleventh state to ratify, on July 26, 1788. New York was originally settled by the Dutch in the early 1620s but claimed by the English on the ground that Cabot had discovered it in 1497. New Amsterdam, now New York City, sprang from a fort built by the Dutch and because of its geographic location became one of the busiest towns on the American coast. King Charles II of England forced the surrender of New Amsterdam by its governor, Peter Stuyvesant, in 1664 and thereby gave England control of the eastern coast of America from Nova Scotia to Florida. The first state constitution of New York was adopted on April 20, 1777. New York sent three delegates—Alexander Hamilton, John Lansing Jr., and Robert Yates—to the Constitutional Convention, although Hamilton was the only one who ultimately signed the Constitution.

NORTH CAROLINA Twelfth state to ratify, on November 21, 1789. North Carolina was originally explored and named by the French after Charles IX of France but was subsequently settled by inhabitants of Virginia pursuant to the same 1663 charter from King Charles II of England mentioned above regarding South Carolina. The English proprietors placed the duties of government in the hands of Governor Berkeley of Virginia prior to implementation of the Carolina Constitutions of 1670. "In other respect "the interests of the proprietors" the desire of "a government most agreeable to monarchy," and the dread of "a numerous democracy," are avowed as the sole motives for forming the fundamental constitutions of Carolina. The rights of the resident emigrants were less considered."* The constitutions also proclaimed "every freeman of Carolina should have absolute power and authority over his negro slaves; executive, judicial and legislative power were beyond the reach of the people. In trial by jury, the majority decided; a rule fatal to the oppressed."** The first state constitution was approved December 18, 1776. North Carolina sent five delegates—William Blount, William Davie, Alexander Martin, Hugh Williamson, and Richard Spaight—to the Constitutional Convention.

RHODE ISLAND (and Providence Plantations) Thirteenth and final state to ratify, on May 29, 1790. The first permanent settlement in Rhode Island was established by Puritan Roger Williams of Massachusetts at Providence in 1636. Rhode Island and the

---

[4]George Bancroft, *History of the Colonization of the United States*, Vol. I (Charles C. Little and James Brown, 1850, p. 121)

*George Bancroft, *History of the Colonization of the United States*, Vol. II (Charles C. Little and James Brown, 1850, p. 147)

**www.yale.edu/lawweb/Avalon/states/nc01.htm

plantations were united into a single colony by the parliamentary patent of March 1643 and granted a royal charter by King Charles II in 1663, which set forth, among other freedoms and guarantees, "that all and every person and persons may, from time to time, and at all times hereafter, freely and fully have and enjoy his and their own judgments and consciences, in matters of religious concernments, throughout the tract of land hereafter mentioned, they behaving themselves peaceable and quietly, and not using this liberty to licentiousness and profaneness, nor to the civil injury or outward disturbance of others."* Rhode Island sent no delegates to the Constitutional Convention. Rhode Island was governed by the terms of the Royal Charter of 1663 until its first constitution in 1843.

VERMONT Although Vermont was not one of the original thirteen states (at the time of the Constitutional Convention, it was still part of New York), it did approve its own constitution on July 8, 1777, and was the first state constitution to specifically prohibit slavery. "I. THAT all men are born equally free and independent, and have certain natural, inherent and unalienable rights, amongst which are the enjoying and defending life and liberty; acquiring, possessing and protecting property, and pursuing and obtaining happiness and safety. Therefore, no male person, born in this country, or brought from over sea, ought to be holden by law, to serve any person, as a servant, slave or apprentice, after he arrives to the age of twenty-one Years, nor female, in like manner, after she arrives to the age of eighteen years, unless they are bound by their own consent, after they arrive to such age, or bound by law, for the payment of debts, damages, fines, costs, or the like."** Vermont was the first state, other than the original thirteen, admitted to the new union, on March 4, 1791.

---

*George Bancroft, *History of the Colonization of the United States*, Vol. II (Charles C. Little and James Brown, 1850, p. 63)
**Vermont Constitution, July 8, 1777 (www.usconstitution.net/vtconst.html)

QUOTATIONS

"Had we been as free from all sins as from gluttony and drunkenness, we might have been canonized for saints"
Jamestown colonist

"Unity in the Executive instead of being the fetus of monarchy would be the best safeguard against <u>tyranny</u>."

"In a single House there is no check, but the inadequate one, of the virtue and good sense of those who compose it."
James Wilson

"Experience must be our only guide. Reason may mislead us."
John Dickinson

"Past experience, or the admonitions of a few, have but little weight where ignorance, selfishness, and design possess the major part."

"The restrictions of our trade [by Great Britain], and the additional duties which are imposed upon many of our staple commodities, have put the commercial people of this country in motion; they now see the indispensable necessity of a general controlling power, and are addressing their respective assemblies to grant this to congress [under the Articles of Confederation]."

"State politics interfere too much with the more liberal and extensive plan of government which wisdom and foresight would dictate. The honor, power, and true interest of this country must be measured by a continental scale. To form a new constitution that will give consistency stability, and dignity to the union and sufficient powers to the great council of the nation for general purposes, is a duty incumbent upon every man who wishes well to his country."

"Our affairs will not put on a different aspect unless congress is vested with, or will assume, greater powers than they exert at present."

"Without a controlling power in Congress, it will be impossible to carry on the war; and we shall speedily be thirteen distinct states, each pursuing its local interests, till they are annihilated in a general crash. The fable of the bunch of sticks [Aesop's fables, "The Bundle of Sticks"] may well be applied to us."

"By thus determining and thus acting, you will pursue the plain and direct road to the attainment of your wishes; you will give one more proof of unexampled patriotism and patient virtue, rising superior to the pressure of the most complicated sufferings; and you will afford occasion for posterity to say: 'Had this day been wanting, the world had never seen the last stage of perfection to which human nature is capable of attaining.'"

George Washington

"For we are sent here to consult, not to contend, with each other; and declarations of fixed opinion, and of determined resolution never to change it, neither enlighten nor convince us."

"Hereditary legislators? There would be more propriety in having hereditary professors of mathematics!"

"It is therefore that the older I grow, the more apt I am to doubt my own judgment, and to pay more respect to the judgment of others."

"I have said often and often in the course of the Session [the Constitutional Convention], and the vicissitudes of my hopes and fears as to its issue, looked at that behind the President [a picture of the sun] without being able to tell whether it was rising or setting: But now at length I have the happiness to know that it is a rising and not a setting sun."

"Sir, there are two passions which have a powerful influence on the affairs of men. These are ambition and avarice; the love of power, and the love of money. Separately each of these has great force in prompting men to action; but when united in view of the same object, they have in many minds the most violent effect. Place before the eyes of such men, a post of honour that shall be at the same time a place of profit, and they will move heaven and earth to obtain it."

"It will be the bold and the violent, the men of strong passions and indefatigable activity in their selfish pursuits. These will thrust themselves into your Government and be your rulers. And these too will be mistaken in the expected happiness of their situation: For their vanquished competitors of the same spirit; and from the same motives will perpetually be endeavouring to distress their administration, thwart their measures, and render them odious to the people."

"They who can give up essential liberty to obtain a little temporary safety deserve neither liberty nor **safety**."

Benjamin Franklin

"No time is to be lost in raising and maintaining a national spirit in America. Power to govern the confederacy as to all general purposes should be granted and exercised. In a word, everything conducive to union and constitutional energy should be cultivated, cherished, and protected."

John Jay

"A bad cause seldom fails to betray itself."

"How difficult it is for error to escape its own condemnation."

James Madison

"We have too many high sounding words, and too few actions that correspond with them."

Abigail Adams

"You will never be alone with a poet in your pocket."

John Adams

"Of how much importance is it, that the utmost pains be taken by the public to have the principles of virtue early inculcated on the minds even of children, and the moral sense kept alive."

Samuel Adams

"I prefer the honestly simple to the ingeniously wicked."

"Club-law may make hypocrites; it never can make converts."

William Penn

"High situation and great influence I am **solicitous** to possess, whenever they can be acquired with dignity. I relinquish them the moment any duty to my country, my character, or my friends, renders such a sacrifice indispensable."

William Pitt the Younger
British Prime Minister, 1783–1801

"Plain sense will influence half a score of men, at most, while mystery will lead millions by the nose."

St. John-Lord Bolingbroke
Secretary of State under Queen Anne of England

"Those who pay are the masters of those who are paid."

"A national debt, if not excessive, will be a national blessing, a powerful cement of union, a necessity for keeping up taxation, and a spur to industry."

"Men of this class, whether the favorites of a king or of a people, have in too many instances abused the confidence they possessed; and assuming the pretext of some public motive, have not _scrupled_ to sacrifice the national tranquility to personal advantage or personal gratification."

"I will not amuse you with an appearance of deliberation when I have (already) decided."

"The consciousness of good intentions disdains ambiguity."

Alexander Hamilton

"I came here to represent America; I came here in some degree as a Representative of the whole human race; for the whole human race will be affected by the proceedings of this Convention. I wish you gentlemen to extend your views beyond the present moment of time; beyond the narrow limits of place from which you derive your political origin. This Country must be united. If persuasion does not unite it, the sword will."

Gouverneur Morris

"From the nature of man we may be sure, that those who have power in their hands will not give it up while they can retain it. On the contrary we know they will always when they can rather increase it."

"Some mode of displacing an unfit magistrate is rendered indispensable by the fallibility of those who choose, as well as by the corruptibility of the man chosen."

George Mason

"I have but one lamp by which my feet are guided, and that is the lamp of experience. I know no way of judging of the future but by the past."

Patrick Henry

"All government supposes the power of coercion; this power, however, never did exist in the general government of the continent, or has never been exercised. Under these circumstances, the resources and force of the country can never be properly united and drawn forth. The states individually considered, while they endeavor to retain too much of their independence, may finally lose the whole. By the expulsion of the enemy we may be emancipated from the tyranny of Great Britain; we shall, however, be without a solid hope of peace and freedom, unless we are properly cemented among ourselves."

Unknown

"The ignorance and prejudices that come from isolation are worn away in the conflict of the forms of culture."

"However great may be the number of those who persuade themselves that there is in man nothing superior to himself, history interposes with evidence that tyranny and wrong lead inevitably to decay; that freedom and right, however hard may be the struggle, always prove resistless."

"The system of common property had occasioned grievous discontents; the influence of law could not compel regular labor like the uniform impulse of personal interest; and even the threat of keeping back their bread could not change the character of the idle."

"The individual who undertakes to capture truth by solitary thought loses his way in the mazes of speculation, or involves himself in mystic visions, so that the arms which he extends to embrace what are but formless shadows return empty to his own breast."

"Sadder was the institution of slavery; for the conflicting opinions and interests involved in its permanence could never be reconciled."
George Bancroft

"The fur-trade is not given up; it is only divided and divided for our benefit. Its best resources lie to the northward. Monopolies, some way or other, are ever justly punished. They forbid rivalry, and rivalry is the very essence of the well-being of trade."
Lord Shelburne

"And yet far from refusing to be slaves we fear death or exile as greater evils than slavery, when they are really much smaller ones. That is how things are; everyone groans about the situation, and not a voice is raised to suggest remedies for it."
Cicero

"Nothing but a continental form of government can keep the peace of the continent."

"Commerce diminishes the spirit, both of patriotism and military defence."

"The intimacy which is contracted in infancy, and the friendship which is formed in misfortune, are, of all others, the most lasting and unalterable."

"A firm bargain and a right reckoning make long friends."

"We are planning for posterity, we ought to remember that virtue is not hereditary."

"A line of distinction should be drawn, between English soldiers taken in battle, and inhabitants of America taken in arms. The first are prisoners, but the latter traitors. The one forfeits his liberty the other his head."

"These are the times that try men's souls. The summer soldier and the sunshine patriot will, in this crisis, shrink from the service of his country."
Thomas Paine

"The evils we experience flow from the excess of democracy. The people do not want [lack] virtue, but are the dupes of pretended patriots."
Elbridge Gerry

"Major Andre is no more among the living. I have just witnessed his exit."
Dr. Thacher, military physician

"The Court is most vulnerable and comes nearest to illegitimacy when it deals with judge-made constitutional law having little or no cognizable roots in the language or design of the Constitution."

Justice Bryan White, *Bowers v. Hardwick*

GLOSSARY

This glossary contains the definitions of many of the terms used throughout my book. Because the meanings of some words have changed since the time of our revolution against England, I have decided to use *An Universal Etymological English Dictionary*, published by N. Bailey and Edward Harwood, DD, in London, January 1, 1782, when defining words taken directly from historical documents. These old definitions will be underlined to distinguish them from those obtained from contemporary sources such as *Black's Law Dictionary* (abridged sixth edition), *Webster's New World Dictionary*, and online sources such as Wikipedia.

Abdicated to have abandoned or surrendered; to have renounced, resigned or given up

Abridge to restrain a Person from some Liberty, to make a Declaration Shorter, by leaving out Part of the Demand; to shorten, lessen, or curtail

Abrogate to annul or repeal; to abolish, to repeal or make void a Law which was before in force

Accede to come or draw near to; accept, go along with, consent to

Accoutred attired, dressed, trimmed or furnished

Acquiesce to consent quietly without protest; to rest satisfied, to comply with, to submit to

Affirmation an affirming, assuring, or speaking point Blank; a solemn and formal declaration or asseveration that an affidavit is true, that the witness will tell the truth

Aide-de-camp an officer in the army, that always attends [to] each of the Generals in the Camp, to receive and carry their orders

Anarchy the complete absence of government usually resulting in political disorder and violence

Antecedent prior to another, previous; going before in order of Time

Appellate having the power to hear court appeals and to review court decisions

Apportion to divide and distribute in shares according to a plan; to divide into convenient Portions or Parts, to proportion

Approbation a liking or approval of

Assent <u>consent or agreement</u>

Attainder at common law (a body of law that develops and derives through judicial decisions, as distinguished from legislative enactments), that extinction of civil rights and capacities which took place whenever a person who had committed treason or felony received sentence of death for his crime.

Auguries omens; <u>events predicted by a Soothsayer or Diviner, who one who foretells Things to come, by observing the Chirping of Birds</u>

Avail of use or advantage toward attainment of a goal or purpose

Avarice <u>covetous;</u> desirous; love of money

Battle of Brandywine (Creek) Fought between George Washington's troops and the British Army under the command of General Sir William Howe, near Chadds Fords, Pennsylvania, on September 11, 1777. The Americans were defeated, and the loss ultimately led to the capture of Philadelphia by the British, which they held until June of 1778.

Bill A legislative proposal of a general nature, which becomes law after approval by both houses and the President. A federal bill, once introduced, may be considered in any session of a Congress, but it dies at the end of a session, and must be reintroduced as a new bill if a succeeding Congress is to consider it.

> 1. **Appropriations Bill** one covering raising and spending of public funds. Federal appropriation bills must originate in the House *(Article I, Section 7.1 of the Constitution.)*
> 2. **Authorization Bill** one that authorizes expenditures of already raised public funds.
> 3. **Engrossed Bill** one that is in final form and ready to be voted on by the Legislature.
> 4. **Enrolled Bill** one that has been passed by both houses and forwarded to the President.
> 5. **Private Bill** one dealing only with a matter of private, personal or local interest. Private bills are designed to affect only specific individuals or groups of individuals.

Bill of Attainder such special acts of the legislature (or the king) as inflict capital punishment upon persons supposed to be guilty of high offenses, such as treason and felony, without any conviction in the ordinary course of judicial proceedings; <u>a Bill brought into the House of Parliament, for the Attainting [to corrupt, to stain the Blood], Condemning and Examining a Person for High-Treason</u>

Bill of Credit A bill or promissory note issued by the government, upon its faith and credit, designed to circulate in the community as "paper" money

213

Billeting the lodging of soldiers

Bribery the offering, giving, receiving, or soliciting of something of value for the purpose of influencing the action of an official in the discharge of his or her public or legal duties

Burthen weight to be borne or conveyed

Cabal a number of persons secretly united and using devious and undercover means to bring about an overturn or usurpation especially in public affairs or to undermine and cause the downfall of a person in a position of authority

Capital chief, great, principal; also heinous, worthy of Death

Capitation a Tax or Tribute paid by the Head [head count], a Poll-Tax; a tax or imposition upon the person, distinguished from taxes on merchandise.

Certiorari (Writ of) A writ sought by litigants, granted by the Supreme Court after agreeing that it does have jurisdiction [as granted to the Supreme Court by the Constitution and the Congress] whereby the court can hear specific cases. Because the case histories are presented to the justices in abbreviated form, the justices many times do not have a complete record of the preceding trial.

Chimerical imaginary; never was and never can be

Choleric hasty, passionate, apt to be angry

Civil officer any officer of the United States who holds his appointment under the national government, whether his duties are executive or judicial, in the highest or lowest departments of the government, with the exception of military personnel

Civil power the power of the citizens

Commerce the exchange of goods, productions, or property of any kind; Trade or Traffic, also Converse, Correspondence

Commission to give a commission, to appoint or impower a Person to act for another

Committee of Detail committee established at the Constitutional Convention, on June 27, 1787, to compile a preliminary draft of the proposals that had been summarily agreed to as of that date

Common (law) as distinguished from statutory law created by the enactment of legislatures, the common law comprised the body of those principles and rules of action, relating to the government and security of persons and property, which derive their authority solely from usages and customs of immemorial antiquity; <u>Simply the Law of the Land, without any other Addition, The Law more generally before any Statute was made to alter it</u>

Conjure <u>to conspire or plot together, to charge upon oath</u>

Consanguinity common ancestry; <u>the relation between Persons descended from the same Family</u>

Constrain to compel; <u>to oblige by force</u>

Construe <u>to expound or interpret</u>

Convulsion a violent disturbance; <u>Members are contracted and drawn together against or without their will</u>

Corroborate to strengthen; to add weight or credibility to a thing by additional and confirming facts or evidence; <u>to confirm or make good an Evidence or Argument</u>

Coup a sudden, violent, and illegal seizure of power from a government, usually by the military [Except when it occurs in Egypt]

Crimes acts done in violation of those duties which an individual owes to the community, and for the breach of which the law has provided that the offender shall make satisfaction to the public

Criminal prosecution a proceeding instituted and carried on by due course of law, before a competent tribunal, for the purpose of determining the guilt or innocence of a person charged with a crime

De facto (segregation) segregation which is inadvertent and without assistance of school authorities and not caused by any state action, but rather by social, economic and other determinates

Denizen <u>a Foreigner enfranchised by the King's Charter, and made capable of bearing any Office, purchasing and enjoying all privileges except inheriting lands by descent</u>

Dernier <u>last</u>

Despotism rule by a tyrant; <u>absolute Power</u>

Devolve <u>to roll or tumble down, or come from one to another</u>

Direct (taxes) taxes that are apportioned directly upon the States in proportion to their number of inhabitants, as opposed to duties, imposts, or excises

Disparage to decry (to censure harshly) or speak ill of

Dogma (Dogmatic) a body of theological doctrines authoritatively affirmed; a positive, arrogant assertion of opinion

Due process of law Law in its regular course of administration through courts of justice. Due process of law in each particular case means such an exercise of the powers of the government [state or federal] as the settled maxims of law permit and sanction, and under such safeguards for the protection of individual rights as those maxims prescribe the class of cases to which the one in question belongs. An orderly proceeding wherein a person is served with notice, and has an opportunity to be heard and to enforce and protect his rights before a court having power to hear and determine the case.

Duty (as relates to taxes) a tax imposed on imports; money paid for Customs (monies paid by the Subject to the King, upon the Importation or Exportation of Commodities) of such Goods

East India Company Originally an English and later a , formed for pursuing trade with the but which ended up also trading the American Colonies. The British government had no shares, and indirect control; shares of the company were owned by aristocrats and wealthy merchants.

Effect to bring about, secure; anything done, finished, or brought to pass, to put into execution

Efficacy the power to bring about a desired result; ability, Operation, Virtue, Force, Strength

Elucidate to explain, make clear

Eminence high degree of quality, Excellency; a person of high rank or achievements

Emolument gain from employment, salary, fees, etc.; advantage, Profit

Enmity the feelings of hostility between enemies; hatred, grudge, variance

Equity justice administered according to fairness as contrasted with the strictly formulated rules of common law; Correction of the Common Law in some Part wherein that fails; a basic principle of law of equity to the effect that equity grants relief in the form of personal decrees as contrasted with law which awards money damages

Equivocal that which hath a double or doubtful signification; having several meanings

Erudition extensive knowledge acquired chiefly from books

Espouse to support or advocate; <u>to adhere to or support a Cause</u>

Evince to plainly show; <u>to vanquish, to overcome; also to prove by Argument</u>

Evince [in civil law] <u>to convict and recover by Law</u>

Ex post facto <u>a Term used of a Thing done after the Time when it should have been done</u>; after the fact, usually related to criminal as opposed to civil law

Excise <u>An Importation laid by Act of Parliament upon Beer, Cyder, and other Liquors</u>; a tax on various commodities, as tobacco, within a country. In current usage, the term has been extended to include various license fees and practically every internal revenue tax except the income tax.

Excite to emotionally arouse; <u>to stir up, to provoke, to cause</u>

Execration <u>a cutting off or cutting away;</u> something that is cursed or loathed

Executive Orders utilized by the president to clarify or act to further a law put forth by the Congress or the Constitution. The Department of State instituted a number scheme for executive orders in 1907, starting retroactively with an order issued on October 20, 1862, by President Abraham Lincoln.

Exigency urgency; <u>Need, Necessity, Straitenedness, occasion</u>

Expedient means to an end; <u>a mean, way, or Device</u>

Exposition <u>an Interpretation, or Expounding</u>

Expound to state in detail; <u>to explain, or unfold</u>

Factions <u>the withdrawing of a Party or Numbers from the main Body, either of Church or State, governing themselves by their own Councils, and opposing the Government established</u>

Fealty <u>an Oath taken at the Admittance of a Tenant to be true to the Lord, of whom he holds his Land</u>; a pledge between two people, usually made upon a religious object, such as a bible

Federalist Party The first American political party, from the early 1790s to 1816 and controlled the federal government until 1801. The party was formed by Alexander Hamilton, supporting a fiscally sound and nationalistic government, and the concept of implied powers. Their political opponents, the Democratic–Republicans, were led by Thomas Jefferson and James Madison.

Formidable causing fear or difficulty to handle; <u>terrible</u>

Gerrymandering a procedure, named after Constitutional Convention delegate and Massachusetts Governor Elbridge Gerry, that attempts to gain representational advantage to a particular person or party by arranging voting districts into abnormally shaped areas

High Misdemeanor <u>a Crime of a heinous (odious, hateful, horrid, outrageous) Nature, next to High Treason</u> (See Article IV, paragraph 2 of the Articles of Confederation.)

Husbandry <u>the Art of tilling and improving Land</u>

Illiberality <u>Meanness of Spirit;</u> narrow-mindedness

Imbue to inspire with principles

Immunity (sovereign) a judicial doctrine that precludes bringing suit against the government without its consent; the immunity from certain suits in federal court granted to states by the Eleventh Amendment

Impeachment A criminal proceeding against a public officer, before a quasipolitical court, instituted by a written accusation called "articles of impeachment; for example, a written accusation by the House of Representatives of the United States to the Senate of the United States against the President, Vice President, or an officer of the United States, including federal judges. A two thirds vote of guilt by the Senate (of those present) is required for conviction. <u>To accuse and prosecute for Felony and Treason, to hinder</u>

Imposts duties on imported goods; <u>such as is recovered by a Prince or State, for goods brought into any Haven from other Nations</u>

Impress <u>to compel to enter into public Service</u>

Inestimable not worthy of consideration; <u>which cannot be sufficiently valued</u>

Infamous <u>of Evil report, scandalous</u>

Infringe <u>to break in upon;</u> to act so as to limit or undermine

Inhabitant <u>one who dwells or lives in a place</u> (qualifications for which probably area little less stringent than to be a resident)

Intrigue <u>the victim of a plot or cabal</u>

Jay Treaty Officially titled "Treaty of Amity Commerce and Navigation, between His Britannic Majesty; and The United States of America," was negotiated by Supreme Court Chief Justice John Jay and signed between the United States and Great Britain on November 19, 1794. It facilitated withdrawal by Britain from forts in the Northwest Territory, proposed arbitration for unsettled wartime debts between England and the United States, and in general promoted increased trade between the two countries.

Tensions between the two countries had increased since the end of the Revolutionary War over British military posts still located in America's northwestern territory and British interference with American trade and shipping. Although Jay was not completely successful in getting England to comply with America's demands, and there was much opposition to the treaty in the United States, President George Washington felt it would avert war with Great Britain and submitted it to the Senate for approval, where it passed by a 20- 10 vote.

Judicial review power of courts to review decisions of another department or level of government, including revocation because of constitutional violations by either the legislative or executive branches

Law a certain Rule directing and obliging a rational Creature in moral Actions; a body of rules of action or conduct prescribed by controlling authority, and having a binding legal force. Laws begin as ideas. First, a representative sponsors a bill. The bill is then assigned to a committee for study. If released by the committee, the bill is put on a calendar to be voted on, debated or amended. If the bill passes by simple majority (218 of 435 of the current), the bill moves to the Senate. In the Senate, the bill is assigned to another committee and, if released, debated and voted on. Again, a simple majority (51 of 100) passes the bill. Finally, a conference committee made of House and Senate members works out any differences between the House and Senate versions of the bill. The resulting bill returns to the House and Senate for final approval. The Government Printing Office prints the revised bill in a process called enrolling. The President has 10 days to sign or veto the enrolled bill.

Laws of nations are such as concern Embassies, Entertainment of Strangers, Traffic, and Arms; those laws governing the legal relations between nations

Letter of marque and reprisal An authorization formerly granted in time of war by a government to the owner of a private vessel to capture enemy vessels and goods on the high seas. The signers of the Declaration of Paris in 1856 agreed to stop such authorizations. Also **Letter of Mart**—Letter which authorize one to take by Force of Arms, those which are due by the Law whereby Men take the Goods of those by whom they have received Wrong, by way of Reprizal [sic], whenever they find them within their own Territories and Bounds.

Liberty Freedom, which is a Power a Man has to do or forbear any particular Action, as seems good to him; Leave, or free Leave; also a free or easy Way of Expression

Licentious <u>loose, lewd, disorderly;</u> marked by the absence of legal or moral restraints : hostile or offensive to accepted standards of conduct

Magistrate <u>an Officer of Justice, or of Civil Government</u>

Magnanimity willingness to overlook insult or injury; <u>Greatness of Mind, courage</u>

Mal-practice an offence or fault in public office; <u>unhandsome, clumsy exercise of the professions or of Custom, Usage, Device, Intrigue</u>

Maxim <u>a Proposition or Principle generally received, grounded upon Reason, and not to be denied;</u> a principle of law universally admitted as being a correct statement of the law

Meliorate to make or become better

Mischief causing injury or damage; <u>Hurt, Damage</u>

Misfeasance <u>misdeeds or trespasses</u>

Misprision misconduct or neglect of duty, especially by a public official; <u>a neglect or oversight</u>

Missouri Compromise Enacted by Congress in 1820, during the James Monroe administration, in hopes of settling slavery issues as they pertained to new states being admitted into the Union. The "compromise" declared that all new states, subsequent to the admission of Missouri (as a slave state), formed north of the southern boundary of Missouri (parallel 36 degrees 30 minutes north) would prohibit slavery. "You have kindled a fire," said Representative Howell Cobb of Georgia, "which all the water of the ocean cannot put out, which seas of blood can only extinguish."* Declared unconstitutional by the US Supreme Court in *Scott v. Sandford* (1857) [Sanford], on the grounds that Congress had no authority to prohibit slavery in the new territories. The Kansas-Nebraska Act of 1854 (proposed by Stephen A Douglas of Illinois, and allowing the inhabitants to determine the fate of slavery in their own territory) effectually repealed the Missouri Compromise.
 *S. E. Forman, *History of the United States*
 The Century Co., 1910, page 224

Mitigate To make or become less severe. Mitigating circumstances are usually considered to be conditions existing at the time a crime was committed that, in fairness and mercy, may be considered in prescribing a less severe punishment than would normally be asserted.

Natural Born Citizen a person born within the jurisdiction of a national government, within its territorial limits, or those born of citizens temporarily residing abroad

Navigation Acts a series of English laws aimed at compelling the colonists to ship goods only in English vessels, and to buy and sell goods only to English merchants.

Nefarious sinful, wicked, criminal; <u>unworthy to live, villainous</u>

New Jersey (Paterson) Plan Presented at the Constitutional Convention by William Paterson, as an alternative to the Randolph, or Virginia, Plan, proposing to merely amend the Articles of Confederation by maintaining equal state representation in the national government, authorizing Congress to raise funds via tariffs, to regulate interstate commerce and commerce with other nations, to collect taxes from the individual states based on the number of free inhabitants and three-fifths of their slaves, election by Congress of a federal executive, consisting of multiple people who cannot be reelected, formation of a federal judiciary appointed by the federal executive, establish a policy of admission for new states, and also a singular policy for naturalization [which unfortunately hasn't been effectively done yet].

Northwest Ordinance (1789) The Northwest Ordinance (formally known as An Ordinance for the Government of the Territory of the United States, North-West of the River Ohio, and also known as the Freedom Ordinance or "The Ordinance of 1787") was an act of the Congress of the Confederation of the United States, passed July 13, 1787. The primary effect of the ordinance was the creation of the Northwest Territory, the first organized territory of the United States, from lands south of the Great Lakes, north and west of the Ohio River, and east of the Mississippi River. On August 7, 1789, President George Washington signed the Northwest Ordinance of 1789 into law, after the newly created United States Congress reaffirmed the Ordinance, with slight modifications, under the new Constitution.

Odious <u>hateful, heinous</u>

Oligarchy government with the ruling power belong to a few

Patroon Landowner established by some of the Dutch fur-trading companies as a way to promote settlement of New Netherland (now New Jersey and eastern New York). A patroon would be entitled to a sixteen-mile-long estate on the Hudson River in exchange for transporting at least fifty settlers into New Netherland.

Pecuniary <u>monied, or full of Money</u>; of or involving money

Perfidy betrayal of trust; <u>Breach of Faith or Trust, Falseness, Treachery</u>

Pernicious causing great injury

Plenary Full, entire, complete, absolute, perfect, unqualified

Poll (tax) <u>a Tax when every Subject is affected by the Head or *Poll*, to pay a certain Sum of Money</u>; a tax of a specific sum levied upon each person without preference to his property or lack of it

Posterity all future generations; <u>those that shall be born in future Time</u>

Prerogative an exclusive privilege; <u>a peculiar Pre-eminence</u>; a right or privilege exclusive to a particular individual or class

Privy Council The council, especially during colonial times, that appointed and replaced governors, and "remained the final court of legal appeal for substantial colonial cases throughout the colonial period."* Most members were appointed by the king, but some were selected by the colonial assemblies.
> *Jack P. Greene and J.R. Pole, Editors *The Blackwell Encyclopedia of the American Revolution*
> Blackwell Publishers, 1994, page 10

Pro-forma a brief meeting of the Senate in which no business is conducted, usually done to satisfy the constitutional requirement that no branch may adjourn for more than three days without the consent of the other (Article I, Section 5.4)

Promulgate <u>to publish or proclaim</u>

Property anything owned; <u>Right or due which belongs to every Man, rightful Possession of a Thing</u>; that which is peculiar or proper to any person; that which belongs exclusively to one

Prorogue <u>to put off till another Time</u>

Pro tempore for the time being; temporarily; provisionally

Prudence careful management; <u>Wisdom in managing Affairs</u>

Pursuance (pursuant to) carrying out a project or plan, in conformance to or agreement with; <u>what follows, Consequence, according, or agreeable to</u>

Pusillanimously timidly or in a cowardly fashion

Quitrent <u>a small rent of Acknowledgment</u>

Recalcitrant refusing to obey authority; stubbornly defiant

Redress to rectify, as by making compensation for a wrong

Remonstrance protest; <u>a Complaint backed with Reasons; more especially made to a Prince or Superior</u>

Repugnant <u>against, contrary to, to clash with</u>

Requisite <u>necessary</u>

Resolution A formal expression of the opinion or will of an official body or a public assembly, adopted by vote. The term is usually employed to denote the adoption of a motion, such as a mere expression of opinion; an alteration of the rules; a vote of thanks or of censure, etc.

> **Joint Resolution** one that is adopted by both branches of Congress and requires presidential approval to become effective. Constitutional amendments must pass each house by 2/3 vote of the members present and voting, a quorum being present. They are then sent to the various States, where approval by 3/4 of them is needed for ratification; Joint resolutions are designated either "S.J. Res. #___" for ones originating in the Senate, or "H.J.Res. #___," for those proposed in the House

> **Concurrent Resolution** one that is passed in one house, the other house concurring, which expresses the sense of Congress on a particular subject, and does not require presidential approval; Concurrent resolutions are designated as "S.Con.Res. #___" or "H.Con.Res. #___." Bills are merely "S. #___" and "H.R. #___."

> **Simple** one that is adopted by only one branch of Congress, and usually pertains to "housekeeping" measures, including changes in rules of its particular house; Simple resolutions are designated either "S.R #___" or "H.Res. #___,"

Risque <u>Hazard, Venture</u>

Salubrity favorable to or promoting health

Sanguinary <u>blood-thirsty, cruel</u>

Scruple to hesitate; reluctant to do something that one thinks may be wrong

Shay's Rebellion an armed rebellion (1786-1787) started by Revolutionary War Veteran Daniel Shay over Massachusetts's state government policy regarding tax and debt collection

Solicitous extremely careful, eager or anxious

Sordid <u>foul, filthy, pitiful, paltry</u>

Specious *the modern algebra, or Letters of the Alphabet;* superficially plausible, but actually wrong

Stead the place or position of a person or thing as filled by a substitute

Succor (Succour) Help, Relief, Supply

Sustain to affirm, uphold or approve, as when an appellate court sustains the decision of a lower court; to grant, as when a judge sustains an objection to testimony or evidence, he or she agrees with the objection and gives it effect

Sycophant a flatterer (of influential people)

Tory a person who rejected independence and sided with the king; a word used by the Protestants in Ireland to signify those Irish common Robbers and Murderers

Townshend Duties import duties charged to the colonies on goods imported from Britain, proposed in Parliament by Charles Townshend in 1767, ultimately leading to the Boston Massacre

Treason the offense of attempting by overt acts to overthrow the government of the state to which the offender owes allegiance; or of betraying the state into the hands of a foreign power. Treason consists of two elements; adherence to the enemy, and rendering him aid and comfort; can only be conflicted on the testimony of two witnesses, or confession in open court.

Treason, high an Offence against the Security of the Prince, whether it be by Imagination, Word, or Deed; as to compass or imagine the Death of the King, Queen, or Prince; to levy War against them; to adhere to their Enemies; to coin false Money; to counterfeit the King's Great or Privy Seal.

Tribunal Court of Justice, Judgment-Seat

Tyranny cruel and oppressive government or rule

Unalienable can not [sic] be transferred, estranged or draw away one's Affection

Usurpation illegal assumptions of power; a taking wrongfully to one's own use, that which belongs to another

Venerate to feel or show a deep respect for

Vest to bestow upon

Vicinage vicinity, the people of a neighborhood

Vindication to clear of suspicion, blame, or doubt; to justify

Virulent <u>venomous, infectious, malicious</u>; violent and rapid in its course

Vitiate to make imperfect, spoil; <u>to corrupt or spoil one's Morals</u>

Wharves (plural of wharf) structures erected on the margin of Navigable Waters where ships or barges can stop to unload and load cargo; <u>a broad plain Place, near a creek or little port or haven for landing, loading, or unloading Goods</u>

Writ of Assistance <u>a Writ for the authorizing any Person to take with him a Constable, in order to seize prohibited or uncustomed Goods</u>

Writ of Habeas corpus The primary function of the writ is to release from unlawful imprisonment, to test the legality of the detention or imprisonment, requiring that a detained person be brought before a court to decide the legality of his detention or imprisonment.

Writ of Mandamus Issues from a court of superior jurisdiction, and is directed to a private or municipal corporation, or any of its officers, or to an executive, administrative or judicial officer, or to an inferior court, commanding the performance of a particular act therein specified, and belonging to his or their public, official, or ministerial duty, or directing the restoration of the complainant to rights or privileges of which he has been illegally deprived. The US District Courts have original jurisdiction of any action in the nature of mandamus to compel an officer or employee of the United States or any agency thereof to perform a duty owed to the plaintiff.

Yorktown, Battle of A siege on September 28, 1781, led by General George Washington, with a force of 17,000 French and Continental troops, against British General Lord Charles Cornwallis and a contingent of 9,000 British troops at Yorktown, Virginia, the most important battle of the Revolutionary War. Cornwallis surrendered to Washington in the field at Yorktown on October 17, 1781, effectively ending the War for Independence.

INDEX

Bold refers to definitions
Italics refers to biography or state history

CPSIA information can be obtained
at www.ICGtesting.com
Printed in the USA
FSOW02n0927310317
32567FS